FIGHTING WORDS

James McEnteer

FIGHTING WORDS

Independent Journalists in Texas

UNIVERSITY OF TEXAS PRESS   AUSTIN

First Edition, 1992

Requests for permission to reproduce material from this work should
be sent to Permissions, University of Texas Press, Box 7819, Austin,
Texas 78713-7819.

∞ The paper used in this publication meets the minimum
requirements of American National Standard for Information
Sciences—Permanence of Paper for Printed Library Materials,
ANSI Z39.48-1984.

Library of Congress Cataloging-in-Publication Data
McEnteer, James, 1945–
    Fighting words : independent journalists in Texas / by James
  McEnteer. — 1st ed.
      p.   cm.
    Includes bibliographical references and index.
    ISBN 0-292-72474-8 (cloth)
    1. Journalists—Texas—Biography. 2. Journalism—Texas—
History. I. Title.
PN4871.M28 1992   91-32797
070′.922764—dc20   CIP

for *Andrea*
my favorite independent journalist

Contents

Illustrations

Acknowledgments

For generous and timely financial support I am grateful to Rolf Kaltenborn of the Kaltenborn Foundation.

For helpful research assistance, my thanks to Ralph Elder and the staff of the Barker Texas History Center, University of Texas at Austin; Cathy Henderson of the Harry Ransom Humanities Research Center, University of Texas at Austin; Michael Toon and his staff at the Texas Collection, Baylor University, Waco; Cyndy Martin and Troy Solís of the Southwest Collection, Texas Tech University, Lubbock; Robert Schaadt and Melinda Barton at the Sam Houston Regional Library in Liberty; and Joan Dobson of the Dallas Public Library.

A special thanks to Stoney Burns for his generous interview and hospitality. Thanks also to Ray Reece, Daryl Slusher, Sammy and Diana Jackson, Billy Porterfield, Vicki Hartin, Zeal Stefanoff, Webb Branen, and Joe Gaddy for lengthy interviews.

For varying degrees of strategic advice and critical evaluation of earlier manuscript versions, I wish to thank Marvin Olasky, Norman Brown, Shelley Fishkin, Gene Burd, and Tom Fensch, of the University of Texas at Austin. I am particularly indebted to James Tankard, whose clear head and wise counsel helped me from early to late stages of this project.

For other sorts of assistance not easily categorized but nonetheless crucial, I am grateful to Robin Cravey, Alicia Garces, Andrea Greene, Jack Hart, Bill McCann, Jack McNamara, Joe Nick Patoski, and J. Patrick Wiseman.

Introduction

Independent journalism has always been a risky business. To write the truth without equivocation and damn the consequences requires a courage surpassing common sense. Yet in every generation, since before shots were fired at Lexington and Concord, the American urge for independence has found expression in the fighting words of rebellious journalists and pamphleteers.

From Thomas Paine to Ralph Nader, obsessive truth-sayers have thrust their lances at this country's icons. William Lloyd Garrison crusaded against slavery. Mark Twain satirized the arbiters of taste and truth in the Gilded Age. Ida Tarbell, Upton Sinclair, Lincoln Steffens, and other muckrakers exposed corporate and governmental abuses. George Seldes and I. F. Stone uncovered realities missing from mainstream media. And these are but a few of the better-known American iconoclasts.

Texas, with its own fierce tradition of independence, has produced iconoclastic journalists at least as fervent and colorful as their peers in other parts of the country. This book looks at five Texas writers whose lives and work span more than one hundred years, from the late nineteenth century to the present. These journalistic mavericks challenged social and political institutions, sometimes at great personal cost. Each of them was threatened many times, legally and physically. William Brann was shot down in the street. Stoney Burns was hounded into prison.

Journalism is an ephemeral art. Yesterday's news largely eludes historical memory. Most of what these journalists wrote has been forgotten. But some of their words deserve to survive the moments that inspired them. Part of my purpose here is to recall those words, because the language of these writers reveals their strength. Working outside the press establishment, the Texas iconoclasts developed very personal voices. Their prose styles proclaimed their independence.

Their voices—angry, humorous, ironic, despairing—served as dramatic counterpoints to the strictures of so-called objective journalism. Relentlessly, with a vehemence reserved for traitors, the Texas independents attacked the mainstream media for their unstated biases, their connections to vested interests, and their failure to cover certain important stories. By investigating events and issues other journalists neglected, the independents helped widen the scope of public discourse.

Radical individualists without orthodox platforms, these journalists chose sides on particular issues on their merits. Unhappy with labels such as liberal or conservative, they based their opinions on a stubborn conviction that they knew right from wrong. The iconoclasts viewed most organized causes and programs with suspicion. They believed all of us should think for ourselves, never a popular stance.

Taylor Branch, chronicler of the civil rights movement, describes history as "a struggle between the insiders and the outsiders." In that sense, the work of the independent Texas journalists, all quintessential outsiders, is a history written by participants. Though they lived in different eras, these writers all dealt with issues we continue to face: racism, religious freedom, educational reform, official corruption, political extremism of the left and right, the clash of urban and rural values, and the fear of change that often drives social and political upheavals.

Antiestablishment sentiment has always been a motivating force in Texas journalism. The first paper printed in Texas—*La Gaceta*, in 1813—came into existence to protest Spanish rule. Indeed, the first several presses in Texas existed primarily to rally support for radical change. After the Mexicans threw out the Spanish, Texas fought a war with Mexico and declared itself a republic. Texas gained statehood, then joined the Confederacy partly to avoid "foreign" (i.e., unionist) interference.

In strong reaction to post–Civil War Reconstruction policies, the land, cattle, and cotton kings who ran the Texas economy determined never again to lose control to outsiders. The commodities of the oligarchs evolved to include oil leases, urban development, high-tech industries, and instruments of mass media. Most newspapers and, later, radio and television stations, even when not directly owned by establishment figures, served as their boosters and beneficiaries.

In its zeal to maintain its own prosperous status quo, the mostly white, mostly male, mostly conservative Texas establishment tended to ignore, repress, or attack individuals and groups with different values. Any sign of deviation from the approved norm—religious, moral, racial, or economic—was perceived as a threat and quickly punished. This uncompromising stance on behalf of the Texas power structure may have created its own antithesis—a strong, colorful tradition of iconoclastic journalism. By stifling a reasonable range of dissent, the Texas establishment may have forced individualist writers to more radical stands and more flamboyant rhetoric.

Some readers may regard Texas as an exotic special case with its own culture and its own values, having little to do with the rest of America. That may have been true once but is no longer. Moving through the chronology of Texas independent journalists, we can witness the convergence of Texan and mainstream American values. The power of the state establishment has been superseded in large measure by a consolidation of governmental and corporate authority at the national level. In that sense, Texas provides a model and a forerunner of the current American power structure.

I want to emphasize that the five writers in this book are only a few of many courageous journalists throughout Texas history who have dared to dissent from the prevailing ethic. Writing in German, Spanish, and English, men and women, black, white, and brown, have joined the ongoing struggle for democracy on which a free society depends, often in trying circumstances. Other books can and should be written about these individuals.

My intention was to focus on journalists who remained as free as possible from political platforms, organized social movements, and orthodox ideologies. I excluded a number of colorful writers from consideration because their identification with a particular cause or group—whether socialism, the Anti-Saloon League, the Ku Klux Klan, or denominational religion—mitigated their independence in my view.

Nor did I include any of the public figures who practiced journalism primarily to promote themselves or their cronies. At least four governors of Texas—James Hogg, Oscar Colquitt, Will Hobby, and Ross Sterling—launched political careers from the newspaper business. Another governor, James Ferguson, turned journalist to rescue his political life after his impeachment from office. I wanted writers for whom journalism was a vocation, not a stepping-stone.

Flawed, self-indulgent, limited by their gifts and their educations, the writers in this book were neither perfect journalists nor perfect human beings. Some of their values were less than admirable, some of their causes less than inspired. But they all believed in their right to speak freely about whatever they chose.

The Texas iconoclasts challenge us, as they challenged the mainstream media of their own times, to define the function of journalism and to examine the mandate of the First Amendment. We may doubt the wisdom of some of their convictions, but not the courage these writers possessed to express them in the face of ridicule, hostility, intimidation, and death. More than any specific causes they fought for, it is their passion for truth that constitutes their greatest legacy to us and to the profession.

FIGHTING WORDS

1. The Apostle
of the Devil

Don't imagine for one moment that this paper
is published expressly to please you.

—*William C. Brann*

On April 1, 1898, William Brann was walking along Fourth
Street in Waco, Texas, when someone stepped from a
doorway and shot him in the back. Brann whirled, draw-
ing his Colt pistol. He and his assailant fired at each other at close
range until their guns were empty. Both men died within eighteen
hours. Brann was forty-three.

The gunfight that ended Brann's life set the seal on his legend.
Brann had cultivated controversy as an editorial writer for newspapers in Houston, Austin, Galveston, and San Antonio. When his
opinions proved too volatile for such mainstream publications, he
started his own monthly journal, the *Iconoclast*. Here he attacked
the social, political, and religious hypocrisy he saw all around him.

His cutting satire, his surprising erudition, and his blunt, colorful
prose attracted a large readership. Brann shrewdly aimed his *Iconoclast* at a national audience, a market largely unexploited at the
time. By offering his witty, outrageous opinions at a price less than
half that of his few rivals, Brann soon brought the paid circulation of
the *Iconoclast* to nearly one hundred thousand worldwide.

Brann addressed his sophisticated far-flung readership with opinions on everything from women's fashions to Tolstoy's latest novel.
He mocked the doings of high society and defended religious minorities from persecution. He wrote long, outraged essays on the stupidity of the public press and the "problem of the negro." He dis-
trusted all politicians and parties, but as he saw little hope for
political reform, he spent most of his venom elsewhere, as a social
critic.

He defended Jews as he defended Mormons and Roman Catholics—vehemently, directing a vengeful passion at the persecutors of
these unpopular sects. Brann's real enemy was the illiberal mind,
though he himself was an unregenerate racist, had his own quack
remedy for the economy, and was burdened with a Victorian ambiva-

William C. Brann, The Iconoclast, at his desk in Waco, 1895.
(Courtesy of The Texas Collection, Baylor University.)

Brann's body after the Waco gunfight, April 1898.
"It is thus, alas! that Texas disposes of a literary style."
(Courtesy of The Texas Collection, Baylor University.)

lence about women complicated by the suicide of his daughter. Brann professed a desire to protect women from vulgarity and exploitation while hinting pruriently that he would like to see them wear more revealing clothes and offering five hundred dollars for a look at the "prettiest woman in the world."

Though Brann's work amused readers in New York, London, and Sydney, in Waco, where he lived, it caused an uproar. Unrelentingly he applied his wit and rhetoric against two community mainstays, Baylor University and the Baptist church. A believer in classical education and religious freedom, Brann thought by attacking the failings of these institutions he could spur reform. His writing provoked extreme reaction from the Baylor community and among Baptist loyalists in Waco. By the time of his death, Brann had already survived a public beating on one occasion and abduction and abuse by a mob of Baylor students on another. He had received numerous threats. A friend of his had killed two men in a fight over Brann's writing.

Debate about the meaning of Brann's life and work began at his death and continues today. His partisans saw Brann as a champion of free speech and his assassination as a martyrdom. According to this view, Brann "laid down his life for the protection of a principle; he died in the defense of truth and honor." Brann's critics, including several who suffered his verbal abuse, characterized his death as the inevitable result of his intemperate prose. He had reaped the whirlwind he himself had sown.

"The deplorable tragedy at Waco, Friday, is another demonstration of the evils growing out of the peculiar kind of journalism pursued by one of the victims," according to Brann's former employer, the *Houston Post*. By way of a eulogy for its onetime editor, the *San Antonio Express* said Brann had "a giant intellect and a sarcastic pen," and "set himself up ostensibly as an iconoclast and incidentally as judge, jury and executioner of the reputations of men."

Most of the papers Brann had worked for made no comment at all. He had quit or been fired from each of them and heaped scorn on their editorial and publishing policies in the pages of his *Iconoclast*. The *Austin Statesman* was silent at the time of Brann's killing. Nearly thirty years later the paper declared that "William Cowper Brann was the most extraordinary writing genius that Texas has ever known," with an "astounding captivating" writing style even though "he did not have a well-balanced mind."

But editors of smaller Texas papers and others around the country found Brann a versatile writer, a strong thinker, and a profound historian. Some went further, seeing Brann as a hero and his death as a "crucifixion." His friend William Marion Reedy, editor of the *St. Louis Mirror*, called him "the most gorgeous intellect west of the Mississippi. There have not been four men since Shakespeare's time who could equal him as a writer." Walter Hurt started his own monthly paper in the *Iconoclast* mold in Cleveland, Ohio, a few months after Brann was killed, the first issue a "Brann Memorial Number." Hurt characterized Brann as "brave as Bayard, guileless as Galahad, chivalrous as Quixote . . . the champion of every weak and worthy cause, the defender of the downtrodden . . ."

The strongest tributes to Brann seemed to come from the farthest points away. As one writer said at the time, "Brann was idolized from a salubrious distance by a vast clientage . . ." Brann was feared for his pen, not his person. Those who knew him best described a slight, bookish, gentle man, dedicated to his family, whose quiet life betrayed no hint of his passionate beliefs or his extravagant expression of them.

In the nine decades since his death, Brann's reputation has endured adulation and insult. In 1929, Brann's continuing notoriety was sufficient to attract movie cowboy Tom Mix for what we would call a photo opportunity. Mix, attired "in all his gaiety of riding trousers, red jacket and wide hat, laid a great wreath of flowers on the grave of 'The Iconoclast.'" Told that feelings still ran high in Waco over the dispute that caused Brann's death, Mix said, "I take no sides in the controversy . . . but I am a great admirer of the man and his writings."

The greatest homage to Brann has been that paid by journalists. The other writers whose lives we look at in this book owed much to Brann's example. Most of them acknowledged that debt specifically. But at least one Houston newspaperman found Brann harmful in this regard. "Too many men have sought to imitate or emulate Brann. They have been willing to defame the best and dent the worst for financial gain. The path of iconoclasm leads but to the grave, for life and for ideals . . ."

At least two plays based on Brann's life have been written and performed. The more recent script, by *Fort Worth Star-Telegram* reporter Jerry Flemmons, features an actor as Brann in a one-man show and consists of excerpts from Brann's writing. Cheap and portable to stage, the production enables the funny, flowery language of the long-dead Waco editor to continue entertaining Texas audiences.

At the height of his popularity, Brann told his friend Reedy, "I am only a fad. I'll pass away when my vogue is done . . ." Brann refuses to pass entirely away, though some who profess admiration for the man—even some who have modeled their own careers on his legend—have little idea what he wrote. Although the violent manner of his death ensured his remembrance, it has also obscured his words. Certainly it is easier to idealize Brann if we maintain a "salubrious distance" from his writing. His sentiments, and the language he used to express them, were the necessary weapons Brann created to engage the world of his time, where he was always an outsider.

The Making of an Iconoclast

William Cowper Brann was born January 4, 1855, in Humboldt Township, Illinois. His mother died when he was two. His father, Noble Brann, a Presbyterian minister, placed the child with a farm couple, William and Mary Hawkins. Early on the boy helped work the farm. As Brann recalled, he spent little time in school. "Instead of being fed on the transcendental philosophy of Plato, I was stuffed with mealy Irish spuds and home-grown 'punkin' pie . . . I was following one of McCormick's patents around a forty-acre field or arguing a point of ethics with a contumacious mule."

Brann would later recall his boyhood infatuation with locomotives and describe how he stole a freight train at age ten. When he was thirteen, Brann left his adoptive home to make his own way in the world. He had completed only three years of school. Beginning as a hotel bellboy, Brann held a variety of jobs, as painter, grainer, salesman for a printing company, printer, and later reporter. One biographer adds the occupations of railroad brakeman, opera company manager, and semiprofessional baseball pitcher to Brann's résumé. The last job seems especially improbable considering Brann's later attitude toward the sport: "The base-ball season is again here, and for six months the 'great dailies' will fairly reek with the esoteric lingo of 'the diamond.' It is deeply interesting—to small boys and smaller men."

Brann never wrote about one of his greatest achievements, his self-education. Somehow, as he knocked about from job to job through adolescence and young manhood, Brann managed to read widely and discriminately enough to acquaint himself with the major, and many minor, classics. Blessed with an excellent memory and a perceptive intelligence, Brann absorbed and retained a prodigious amount of information from philosophy, history, the sciences, and the literatures of several countries.

His exposure to the great minds of his own and previous ages produced his idiosyncratic writing style, a strange mixture of the colloquial and the overripe, mock-heroic, larded with literary allusion and a monstrous vocabulary. His ideas, acquired independently of academic interpreters, formed a unique philosophy. Brann's writing was fresh, free of conventional thinking if sometimes of coherence as well. Though his genuine erudition and quick wit made Brann formidable in debate, he suffered the pride of the autodidact. Once he made up his mind he never changed it, defending his insights and his prejudices with equal vigor.

His unconventional education convinced Brann that most people did not know how to think for themselves. Too many followed religious and political leaders without question, even when the pronouncements of these leaders contradicted common sense. As he lashed out at the frauds and fakers he saw declaiming from pulpits, political platforms, and the editorial columns of newspapers, Brann berated their followers as complaisant sheep, spellbound by outworn truisms and transparent clichés. And he assigned responsibility for this dismal situation to the public school system, "the greatest evil of the present age, the assassin of genius, the mother of mediocrity." Brann modestly offered Lincoln as a model nongraduate instead of himself: "Our great men were 'self-made'—those whom some blessing in disguise kept out of the clutches of the gerund-grinders; or who were strong enough to burst thro' the terrapin crust of dead formalities miscalled education. Lincoln is the only really great man America has yet produced . . . and Lincoln was his own *alma mater*."

On March 3, 1877, William Brann married Carrie Martin at Rochelle, Illinois. Their daughter Inez was born December 19. Exactly where or when Brann began to write for newspapers is not now clear, but in 1883 he was hired as a reporter for the *St. Louis Globe-Democrat*. Brann continued his self-education at the St. Louis Public Library while learning the journalism trade from his editor, Joseph McCullagh.

In 1886 Brann left St. Louis to write for the *Galveston Evening Tribune*. One of his biographers claims Brann lost his position at the *Globe-Democrat* because of "protests to the paper" concerning his "indiscreet revelations and slashes at St. Louis society." Certainly Brann derived lifelong pleasure from mocking the pretensions of the wealthy and well-connected. Years later he would label a highly publicized marriage between the elite Marlborough and Vanderbilt families an "Alliance of Plebians and Pimps." The American upper class was undeserving of the servile respect accorded it by press and public alike. "We know full well that no man ever honestly earned a million dollars," he wrote. "If he possess that sum it is plain that, in some way, he has managed to put his fingers in his neighbors' pockets . . ." Brann was no socialist. His grudge against the rich was not political. It was personal, passionate, and permanent.

Brann's earliest years in Texas were not uneventful. "While editing the *Galveston Evening Tribune* I was arraigned for libeling a bull whose harem adjoined a public school." In May 1889 he went to work for the *Galveston News* as an editorial writer at twenty-five dollars a week. In September he was fired from the *News* "for the usual reason: his restless and rebellious nature flared up in print once too often and too flamboyantly to please the editor."

That same year, the prolific Brann registered three plays with the Library of Congress. All three center on a noble and virtuous woman and feature an innocent, working-class hero. Only one, *Retribution*, was ever produced. In 1890 Brann started as an editorial writer for the *Houston Post*. On July 25, his twelve-year-old daughter, Inez, committed suicide.

In an essay devoid of his usual rhetorical pyrotechnics and unpublished until after his death, Brann explained what happened. Boys had begun to pay Inez attention, especially "one of her own age, who seemed to haunt the street." Brann forbade her to see or speak to him. Inez denied knowing the boy, but Brann caught the children together and accused the girl of deception.

The next day, Inez swallowed all the morphine tablets in the medicine cabinet. She left an apologetic note: "I don't want to live. I could never be as good as you want me to." And Brann "knew that he had killed her. And ever in his heart there is a cry, 'I killed her!' And night and day that cold, sweet face doth haunt him." Brann paid dearly for his Victorian view that women could only be virtuous ladies or wanton whores. His obsession with female purity, which motivated his playwriting and destroyed his daughter, would later be the main ingredient in the feud with Baylor that led to four murders, including his own.

Carrie Brann said her husband never fully recovered from his daughter's suicide. But his was a secret sorrow. He never spoke of Inez, nor did he share the plaintive essay that revealed his remorse. He threw his energies into his work as a *Post* editorial writer, but the bitter zeal of his attacks soon brought him into conflict with *Post* management. Whether or not Brann left voluntarily, the parting was unfriendly. In an editorial several months afterward, the *Post* implied that Brann had been fired. Brann had his own version: "In the year of our Lord, 1891, I became pregnant with an idea. Being at that time chief editorial writer on the *Houston Post*, I felt dreadfully mortified, as nothing of the kind had ever before occurred in that moral establishment. Feeling that I was forever disqualified for the place by this untoward incident, I resigned and took sanctuary in the village of Austin."

Brann started work at the *Austin Statesman* in July but immediately issued a prospectus for a new monthly magazine, the *Austin Iconoclast*. Not surprisingly, Brann had trouble finding financial backing for his new venture. It would have been difficult to convince potential sponsors they would ever realize a return on their investment. Brann could promise witty commentary, but a humorous monthly, *Texas Siftings*, had recently had to leave Austin for New York in search of a larger audience.

Laughter was a by-product for Brann, not a primary purpose. As his friend J. D. Shaw said, "Mr. Brann has been classed as a humorist . . . but he was not content with merely having amused . . . He made of his humor a whip with which to scourge from the temple of social purity every intruder there . . ." Brann would have found it as hard to sell the idea of a reform journal as a humor sheet.

In 1891 Texas had more than forty daily papers and about five hundred weeklies, many dedicated to reforms of various sorts, with more papers starting and failing all the time. Brann did not even represent a particular platform or party. In fact, his freedom from partisan politics was a point of pride. Brann called his publication "simply an independent American journal, exercising its constitutional prerogative to say what seemeth unto it best, without asking any man's permission." But amid the din of Texas voices clamoring for justice and power in a turbulent economy, why would anyone listen to William Brann grinding his own ax?

The Smasher of Shams

The decades following post–Civil War Reconstruction brought great prosperity to many Americans but deprivation to many more. The majority of Texans lived in rural communities and worked small farms. Most Texas farmers raised cotton as a cash crop. But the price of cotton had declined steadily since the end of the war, driving many into debt. Banking laws forced the indebted farmers to borrow from loan companies and certain private banks at high rates. The railroads, operating without regulation or restraint, "controlled freight rates and often discriminated against the farmer."

Discontented farmers formed the Farmers' Alliance to press their case for relief through legislative reform. As the Alliance gained momentum, the Democratic party ran James Hogg as a reform candidate for governor in 1890. Elected to office, Hogg promptly appointed a Railroad Commission. But he failed to include an Alliance member, contributing to the disillusion of farm leaders with Hogg's program. In 1891, as Brann looked for money to publish his own paper, these leaders formed the Populist party, which would prove a potent force in Texas politics in the coming years.

Prohibition of alcohol became a major issue in the last quarter of the century. Temperance organizations joined with Baptist ministers and others to form a Prohibition party. They succeeded in having an amendment barring the production, sale, or exchange of liquor in Texas put to a vote in 1887. The amendment was defeated, leaving local option laws in place, but Prohibitionists continued vocally in the cause. The Knights of Labor, a national organization, fought actively in Texas for the rights of industrial employees. The Knights led several successful strikes, including one against Jay Gould's railroad system.

A constitutional amendment had, technically, enfranchised the black voter. But white Texans who opposed black participation in the electoral process found ways to keep blacks from voting or holding public office. Their methods included intimidation, the use of white men's associations to nominate candidates, and primary elections in which only whites could vote. Similar tactics disenfranchised Mexican voters in the Rio Grande Valley. Women's groups began to press for suffrage in the 1860s. They nearly succeeded in getting a suffrage plank included in the Prohibition party platform of 1890.

Texans also joined the national debate about fiscal policy. Populists and many Democrats favored the free coinage of silver to increase the amount of money in circulation. The conflict between these "silver Democrats" and others who thought the United States should remain committed to a gold standard simmered throughout the 1890s.

Brann was one of many who proposed various schemes for managing the money supply to try to address the increasing inequities in American society. The idea he had been "pregnant with" at the *Houston Post* was something he called the "Inter-convertible Bond-currency plan." The plan called for the sale of government bonds to increase the money supply to a certain point. When that point was reached, bond sales would cease, to resume when the supply fell below the designated level. Brann's economic theories stirred little enthusiasm, but his new magazine provoked strong, immediate responses.

In the first issue of the *Austin Iconoclast*, published August 1, 1891, Brann came out slugging hard at some of his favorite targets.

Two articles about newspapers, "The American Press—Its Hypocrisy and Cowardice" and "Playing the Pimp—The 'Personal' Column in Newspapers," left little doubt about Brann's attitude toward his journalistic colleagues. The premiere issue also contained two articles about women ("Female Chastity—What Is It?" and "The Woman Thou Gavest Me—Is She Man's Intellectual Peer?"), an essay calling legislators and lawyers the "Criminals' Pards," and a denunciation of the newly formed People's party entitled "Another Political Monstrosity." Brann attacked Negro voting enfranchisement as part of the "crime of the century." He also took shots at organized religion, recommended nationalizing the railroads, and dismissed rival economic schemes.

The *Austin Statesman*, Brann's employer when he launched the *Iconoclast*, devoted considerable space to a review of the new periodical, which it called a "handsome monthly" whose apparent mission was to "make a good sized portion of the human race wish that they or it had never seen the light of day. It strikes at pretty much everything it sees and at quite a number of things that it don't see but imagines it does, and it strikes below the belt with both hands and does not scruple to use its teeth. . . . [Brann] is perhaps the most vigorous manipulator of the English language to be found in the entire South . . . unfortunately he is a misanthrope, a pessimist, and takes the worst possible view of everything . . . The *Iconoclast* should bear in mind . . . it does not possess all the wisdom in the world or a very great deal."

The *Statesman* kept track of other responses to Brann's writing, such as that of the *Dallas News*, which said, "The *Austin Iconoclast* appears to be suffering with fatty degeneration of the liver." The *Statesman* replied that the *News* appeared to be "suffering a fatty degeneration of the brain." Calling Brann's effort "about the sourest, crossest publication," which "does not appear to approve of anybody or anything on earth except W. C. Brann," the *Greenville Banner* thought the *Iconoclast* "likely to become a chronic nuisance."

Brann's old employer, the *Houston Post*, thought even negative reaction to the *Iconoclast* suited Brann's "dearest purpose . . . The success of a venture like his depends upon the amount of advertising given it by other papers, and it is immaterial what kind of advertising it is." Such advertising came pouring in from around Texas and beyond. Now, as later, Brann's distant readers seemed far more appreciative of his work than those closer to home. A Louisville newspaper predicted the *Iconoclast* would follow *Texas Siftings* out of the state. The *Waco Day* noted that "while a number of Texas dailies are sneering at the *Austin Iconoclast* . . . some of the greatest American and Canadian dailies are hailing its editor as an epoch maker in American literature . . . There are critics and critics."

Editors chose sides, for and against Brann. The *Houston Post* conveyed all the hostile responses it could find, including "The Negro, an Intelligent Member of the Race Presents Some Reflections," the statement of a black man who objected to Brann's racism. Judgments by small Texas papers like the *Crockett Economist*—that the *Iconoclast* was "putrid matter"—and the *Terrell Star*—that it "takes a cast-iron stomach to stand it"—found their way into the *Post* editorial pages.

The *Austin Statesman*, despite strong reservations concerning the *Iconoclast* and its editor, noted that "In nearly every state in the Union the leading dailies are reprinting articles from the *Austin Iconoclast*." Somehow the misanthropic Brann had "succeeded in securing more free advertising for the Lone Star State than any journals ever published within her borders." The *Iconoclast* was read in Canada, Europe, and "beyond the equator." To its awed, if slightly mystified, assessment of this improbable Texas booster, the *Statesman* added some chilling words of praise. "Many people disagree with the editor and would break away in the middle of a horse trade to attend his funeral, but he 'makes them talk about Texas.'"

Brann thought his widely quoted magazine would succeed financially. He quit his *Statesman* job in September just after the second issue appeared. Criticism did not intimidate Brann but seemed to goad him on. He struck back at his detractors in print. "A contemporary critic says that 'the editor of The *Iconoclast* is a crank and a fanatic.' Well, if that be true, let frauds beware, for cranks always turn things over and fanatics fight to the finish . . . It is much better to be a fanatic than a journalistic weather-vane." Brann took Texas newspaper editors to task for various sins: accepting ads for phony miracle cures, puffing high society, printing sensational scandals, and promoting themselves shamelessly.

Brann argued his unconventional religious beliefs. He allowed as how the Holy Bible was a book "worth reading," but that to take the whole of it as literal truth was "nothing short of blasphemy, an insult to the Creator." Besides, Christianity was not the only true path. He advised his readers to "seek light wherever it is to be found, whether in the Bible or the Vedas, ethic philosophy or science," because "all religions that have brought comfort to humanity were Divine." He wrote a long, impassioned defense of the Jews, "naturally the most sympathetic and generous" of people, and another of the

Mormons. In both cases Brann spent more energy attacking the persecutors of these unpopular religions than explaining or defending their beliefs.

"Instead of hounding the Mormons it would be infinitely better for us to look a little more closely to our own shortcomings. It is possible that religious intolerance may be as great a vice as polygamy . . ."

The *Iconoclast* did not concern itself overmuch with political issues, though Brann managed to put down the Populists and their critics in a single swipe. He thought the economic policies of the newly formed People's party "made up chiefly of long-exploded fallacies and the wildest empiricism, but as the platforms of both the so-called great parties are built on the same plan, they have no license to throw stones." Characteristically he neither identified the policies in question nor explained how they might be fallacious.

Brann called the jury system "another venerable nuisance" and suggested it be abolished, on the grounds that most jurors were largely unqualified for the task. He proposed the election of professional jurors, to be paid in the manner of magistrates. He thought such a system would raise the standard of legal justice.

Brann's lack of faith in the judgment of the average person, in or out of law courts, contradicted his own assertion that frauds and hypocrites would fall if individuals would only think for themselves. At his rhetorical best in discussions of social philosophy, Brann shocked his readers by attacking the icons of conventional wisdom such as "the equality of man." He called social equality "that unhappy state where the fool will be as potent as the philosopher."

In an essay titled "Is Civilization a Sham?" Brann claimed the progress of the previous century and a half was misguided. He indicted the popular concept of success. "Our boasted progress is but a mighty agitation of that great ocean of humanity which sends the lightest particles to the top as froth and foam, there to catch the prismatic colors of the sun, while the great mass surges sullen beneath, the only hope of each particular particle that it too may become foam and float to the sunny surface of that dark troubled sea."

And he sounded the lament of the Industrial Revolution that echoes in our own time, the alienation of human beings from their spiritual ground. "Our boasted progress is turning God's great world into a machine; making men but manikins, who dance, not of their own volition, but because the showman pulls the strings."

To help support the *Iconoclast* when he quit the *Statesman*, Brann took to the lecture circuit. Finding public speaking profitable and enjoyable, he would continue touring American lecture halls from time to time for the rest of his life. Another public speaker gave Brann an unintended boost. The Reverend Thomas DeWitt Talmage, a notorious "pulpit-pounder" in Brooklyn, denounced Brann for his religious views, calling him "the Apostle of the Devil." Because of Talmage's prominence—and the syndication of his sermons in more than 3,500 newspapers—Brann gained much more renown. Appreciating the value of the nickname, Brann adopted it as an occasional pseudonym, "frequently signing himself, 'Yours in Christ, the Apostle.'"

But neither Talmage's publicity assistance nor his own lecture fees could sustain the *Austin Iconoclast.* Brann's financial backer pulled out in November 1891. Brann brought out a December issue, then tried to regroup. The *Texas Iconoclast,* volume 2, number 1, came out March 24, 1892. Desperately Brann speeded up publication to a weekly schedule, reprinting articles from earlier issues to help fill the space. His bitterness led Brann to scold even those who wished him well.

"I get letters by the hundred, by the thousand . . . beginning—Mr. Editor—You are engaged in a holy crusade and I pray earnestly for your success, etc., but three out of five are devoid of the sinews of war—wouldn't feed a jaybird . . . The writers are humbugs who stand around the newsstands and read the *Iconoclast* without buying it, then borrow a stamp of a neighbor and soothe their conscience by sending me a useless slug of 'moral support.'"

But it was no use. He was broke.

Outcast Iconoclast

In the late spring of 1892, Brann turned over the *Iconoclast* to his business manager, Tom Bowers. To support his wife and two children, he accepted a job as a reporter back at the *St. Louis Globe-Democrat.* He did not last long. Later Brann described how he covered a St. Louis society ball that autumn. After a "brief survey of the assembled imbeciles," Brann turned in a "roast" of the affair "that would have created a riot had it not burned a hole in the wastebasket." That was the last time he was sent "to spill social slobber over full-dress functions. The city editor got the idea somehow that my slobber-tank had stood out in the Texas sunshine and soured." Brann was rescued from the slobber circuit by an offer to edit the *San Antonio Express.* In October 1892, Brann returned to Texas.

When Brann arrived in San Antonio, the *Express* was one of the largest, most influential dailies in the state, with a pronounced conservative outlook. It is surprising not that Brann ultimately left the *Express* but that he lasted there so long. Brann quickly alienated many in and beyond San Antonio with attacks on ministers, lawyers, newspaper editors, the court system, the State Board of Pardons, and Susan B. Anthony and other advocates of women's suffrage, among others. His old enemies—and some new ones—quickly cried "Foul."

The *Waco News*, a paper that would later hire him, said that "as editor of the *Express* . . . Brann is a greater curse to Texas, with his yankeeism and republicanism, than all the stirrers-up of litigation in the legal profession, as he is diseased mentally and morally." The *Austin Statesman* noted that Brann's *Express* was "battering away at the local preachers, and it is evident from the battle cry of the paper that the preachers are battering away at the paper . . . There are apostles and apostles . . ."

Brann recalled how "I was in the habit of writing a short sermon for the Sunday edition, for the benefit of those who could not go to church." He professed surprise that the ministers of the city did not appear grateful for his effort.

"I dropped into a swell church one Sunday morning to get a little grace—a building that cost up in the six figures while people were . . . subsisting on 50 cents a week within sound of its bells—and the minister was holding a copy of the *Express* aloft in one hand and a Bible in the other and demanding of his congregation: 'Which will you take—Brann or God?'" Whether or not Brann's church visit was apocryphal, he "kept hammering away," in his words, until "the Ministerial Association met, perorated, whereased, resoluted and wound up by practically demanding of the proprieter of the *Express* that I be either muzzled or fired."

It was not a minister who ended Brann's editorial tenure at the *San Antonio Express* but a lawyer named W. H. Brooker. On July 25, 1894, the *Houston Post* published a letter from Brooker accusing an *Express* reporter of misrepresenting a speech delivered by Governor Hogg. Brann wrote "A Word to Mr. Brooker," full of threats and insults, printed it on the *Express* editorial page, and signed his name. Brann said later, "I expected trouble, for he was a powerful (tho' one-armed) Hercules who had beaten up several larger men than myself on less provocation."

Brooker went not to Brann but to the owner of the paper, Frank Grice. Grice printed an apology in the *Express*. Brann promptly resigned in protest. He asked Grice to publish word that he "was no longer editor of the *Express* and not responsible for the apology." Grice refused, so Brann took his announcement to the rival *Light*, where he was "suddenly assaulted by the man I had criticized and got the worst of the fisticuff." Brooker told Brann to print a retraction or "he would blow my brains out."

Brann refused, and began to carry a gun. Brooker's friends intervened to end the quarrel. Brann decided Brooker's charges might have been true and that he "could scarce afford a shooting match on behalf of grown men who remained in the employ of a paper that had apologized for resenting the charge that they were a couple of lying curs." Brann remained in San Antonio for months after the fracas, perhaps to prove he had not been driven out of town. His refusal to yield a point of journalistic honor or retreat from the fight revealed a stubborn determination that would ultimately prove fatal.

In March, Brann sold the name and remaining stock of his moribund *Iconoclast* for $250 to an Austin bank teller. The young clerk, William Sydney Porter, later became famous as a short story writer under the pen name "O. Henry." Porter published two issues of the *Iconoclast* before Brann regretted his decision and negotiated to regain the rights to the name *Iconoclast.* Porter agreed and changed the name of his humor magazine to the *Rolling Stone.*

Though he claimed that *Express* publisher Frank Grice offered him his job back with a raise, Brann refused. He gave lectures around San Antonio in preparation for a tour. The August 10 issue of the *Express* announced that "Apostle Brann will make his last talk in San Antonio at the Opera House. He is a hot talker and somebody will squirm." Brann chose to depart San Antonio by "Speaking of Gall," a favorite lecture he would deliver in many cities, reprint in the *Iconoclast,* and issue as a separate pamphlet.

Gall was the perfect Brann topic, an acerbic catchall that gave him license to roam through various subjects in a manner approximating free association. He could offer witty, sardonic condemnations of individuals or institutions without lingering on any to the point of boredom or complexity. He roasted all his favorites: greedy politicians, political preachers, uppity women, designing women, foolish plutocrats, pandering journalists, and secretly tipsy Prohibitionists. In fact, he indicted everyone, heaping the most scorn on the most pretentious.

In the world according to Brann, three aristocracies existed: "The aristocracy of the intellect, founded by the Almighty; the aristocracy of money, founded by Mammon, and the aristocracy of family, founded by fools. The aristocracy of brains differs from those of birth and boodle as a star differs from a jack-o'-lantern, as the music of the spheres differs from the bray of a burro, as a woman's first love differs from the stale affection hashed up for a fourth husband."

Truly intelligent individuals were modest, knowing human accomplishments to count for little in the immensity of God's universe. Those who struggled for wealth and power in the transience of time mistook the point of existence. The "grandest success of the century," one of Brann's few heroes, was Father Damien, the priest who administered to the lepers of Molokai and finally succumbed to the disease himself.

The audience who came to hear Brann's farewell speech on gall was "the largest . . . ever to attend a lecture in San Antonio." Then the Apostle took his act on the road.

After several months of touring and speaking publicly on a number of subjects, Brann came to Waco. The *Waco News*, which had called him "diseased mentally and morally," now offered Brann a job as an editorial writer. He started work in November and began to plan the resurrection of the *Iconoclast*. For Brann, with his eye for humbugs and his taste for satire, Waco was just too tempting.

Geyser City Gall

At a Brazos River crossing about midway between Dallas and Austin, Waco had grown from an Indian village to a fort to a trading post. By 1894 it was the sixth largest city in Texas. Waco's workers earned low wages in the town mills, processing cotton, wool, flour, and cottonseed oil, and lived in Edgefield, a Waco slum. Waco's saloon-keepers and prostitutes entertained cattle drovers from the nearby Chisholm Trail. The exuberance of the gun-toting cowboys on their days off gave the town a reputation for violence and gunplay.

The Baptists who ran the Waco City Council tried to maintain order without alienating the lucrative transient trade. The council passed curfew and Sunday closing laws and restricted prostitution to a small shabby zone known as "the reservation," where brothels were subject to medical inspections but immune from prosecution. Brann enjoyed the situation: "Waco, we would have you know, is the religious storm-center of the Universe, and one of the few places that licenses prostitutes—a fact for the consideration of students of cause and effect."

Baptists dominated Waco. Besides the fourteen Baptist churches in town, three Baptist periodicals published in Waco, including the powerful *Baptist Standard*. J. B. Cranfill, the *Standard*'s editor, was a Prohibition activist who took himself and his beliefs very seriously, precisely the sort of person Brann despised. Cranfill and his *Baptist Standard* quickly became staples of ridicule in the revived *Iconoclast*. Baylor University was the jewel in Waco's Baptist crown.

Founded in 1845 at Independence, Texas, Baylor moved to Waco in the 1860s. By the mid 1890s Baylor enrolled about seven hundred students, male and female.

Another factor in the Waco equation was the discovery of hot artesian water under the city in 1889. Tourists came to drink and bathe in the waters the city liked to advertise as a cure for various ailments. Brann's mock promotion of Waco's virtues made city fathers nervous and infuriated some residents. "Well supplied with pure artesian water, a saloon in every block, a church around every corner and a fire or failure every day, Waco is indeed a land flowing with milk and honey—a place 'Where every prospect pleases and only man is vile.' Her streets are so smooth that a mountain goat can traverse them with comparative ease, and so clean that it is seldom a mule gets lost in the mud. The tax rate is so low that if your property be well located you can usually persuade the collector to accept it as partial payment."

Brann's Iconoclast made its debut February 1, 1895. On the back page of this first issue, readers learned that "the *Iconoclast* is not revived with the expectation that it will reform the world. . . . If it does but succeed in exposing a few Frauds and peeling the cuticle from an occasional Fake—if it can but recover a few square acres of Mother Earth from the domain of Falsehood and Folly, from the Dominion of Darkness and the Devil, it will not have lived and labored in vain."

Brann immediately announced his preoccupations and his point of view, leading with "Woman's Wickedness—Chastity Going Out of Fashion," a titillating if uninformative essay featuring suggestive rhetorical questions. "What is it that is railroading so large a portion of young women to hell? What mad phantasy is it that leads so many wives to sacrifice the honor of their husbands and shame their children?"

Brann renewed his campaign of defamation against blacks with "The Buck Negro," a racist rant blaming the Negro for the backwardness of the South. He said the Negro would remain "until he is faded out by fornications,—until he is absorbed by the stronger race, as it has absorbed many a foul thing heretofore." Brann's bigotry offended many readers outside the South as it offends us today. His staunchest admirers found his racial views shocking, even criminal. But no criticism kept Brann from berating the Negro with a kind of blind rage that seemed at least partly related to his obsession about female purity. In a later essay, "The Rape Fiend Remedy," Brann opined that black men were primarily motivated by a desire to rape white women. The only way to prevent such crimes was either to

send the blacks back to Africa or to kill them all. He said it "were
better that a thousand 'good negroes'—if so many there be—should
suffer death or banishment than that one good white woman should
be debauched."

In his study of the antilynching movement, Donald Grant cites
Brann as one of "a corps of editors" who helped spread the "myth of
racial inferiority . . . with its implications of bestiality . . . [and] su-
pervirility." The myth of the oversexed black rape fiend helped racists explain the increase in lynchings in the 1880s and 1890s. Rape
was merely the excuse. In fact, "lynching was used to maintain the
new patterns of economic, psychological and sexual exploitation of
blacks that were initiated following the Civil War." Though racist
mythology "was propagated in most of the white press," including
Brann's Iconoclast, by the mid 1890s "the larger metropolitan white
newspapers" began to condemn lynching as a threat to civilized society. Between 1882 and 1927, Texas ranked third behind Mississippi
and Georgia, with 534 lynchings, including 370 of blacks.

In other articles Brann argued for the abolition of prayer in the
Texas Legislature, the use of the gold reserve to run the U.S. government, and against the annexation of Mexico. He took issue with
Robert Ingersoll's atheism while praising him for making believers
examine their faith. He blasted the public education system for sub-
jecting a genius and a blockhead to the same curriculum and urged
his readers to spend less time reading and more time reflecting. "We
make of our heads cold-storage warehouses for other people's ideas,
instead of standing up in our own God-like individuality." He excoriated preachers who "imagine that a criticism of them is an insult to the Almighty."

Brann ridiculed his former *Houston Post* editor, and did not neglect the minister who had bestowed his nickname:

The Tyler *Telegraph* humbly apologizes for having called that
wide-lipped blatherskite, T. DeWitt Talmadge, "a religious
faker." Next thing we know our Tyler contemporary will apolo-
gize for having inadvertently hazarded the statement that water
is wet. When a daily newspaper tells the truth, even by accident,
it should stick to it instead of crawling on its belly in the dust to
humbly ask pardon of the Devil. The *Iconoclast* will pay any
man $10 who will demonstrate that T. DeWitt Talmadge ever
originated an idea, good, bad or indifferent. He is simply a monstrous bag of fetid wind. The man who can find intellectual food
in Talmadge's sermons could acquire a case of delirium tremens
by drinking the froth out of a pop bottle.

A measure of the response to this new *Iconoclast* appeared in the second issue. In "The Apostle's Biography," Brann replied to critics who said he was "an ex-convict, who tramped into Texas carrying a false trade-mark; that I have been driven out of several cities, and fired by various managers of morning newspapers; that I have been thrashed by aged cripples . . ." His sarcastic boast that his detractors missed even more damning evidence against him cleverly implied that the charges were false, though several were generally accurate.

He also brought criticism of religious and journalistic hypocrisy home to Waco. Chiding religious publications for accepting ads with dubious health claims and impious sentiments, Brann singled out Cranfill's *Baptist Standard* for "A Brotherly Rebuke."

> . . . what lies heaviest on my heart is the fact that most, if not
> all the religious contemporaries of the *Iconoclast* are in the habit
> of ladling out saving grace with one hand while raking in the
> shekels with the other for flaming advertisements of syphilitic
> nostrums, "lost manhood" restorers and kindred quack remedies
> for diseases with which the faithful are supposed to be unfa-
> miliar. . . . like the Texas *Baptist Standard* flaunting in the
> middle of a page of jejune prattle anent the Holy Spirit a big dis-
> play ad. for the "French Nerve Pill"—guaranteed to re-stallionize
> old roues—. . . it does grate . . . to see a really good sermon in
> the Texas *Baptist Standard* and *Herald* flanked by an advertise-
> ment of "Pennyroyal Pills"—especially designed to produce·
> abortions!

In the April *Iconoclast*, Brann claimed his attack had succeeded, "that one blast upon its bugle-horn was sufficient to banish un-savory advertisements from the columns of its religious contempo-raries." In the same issue he gave notice that his own periodical would now accept paid advertising. "Jim Crow establishments and quack doctors need not apply for space."

Though reluctant to rely on ads for income, Brann was determined his new *Iconoclast* would not go the way of its predecessor. To this end he worked to secure national distribution. We may assume he followed the standard practice of successful monthlies such as *Scribner's*, *McClure's*, *Cosmopolitan*, and others of sending free subscriptions to newspaper editors around the country in exchange for a notice in their pages. But Brann did not offer premiums to sub-scribers, denouncing the practice in banner lines in his magazine.

At ten cents a copy, or one dollar for a year's subscription, *Brann's Iconoclast* quickly built from an initial printing run of three thousand copies to twenty thousand copies a month within its first year. Before the second year of publication ended, the *Iconoclast* claimed eighty thousand readers. Brann augmented his newfound prosperity with lectures and pamphlets of his selected essays, some in a "Best of Brann" format.

As his audience grew, he campaigned relentlessly against Prohibition "not because I am the friend of liquor but because I am the friend of liberty. I would rather see a few boozers than a race of bondmen." Brann accounted the Prohibitionists as naive for not realizing that as long as "whiskey is made it will be drank—that Prohibition means simply a poorer brand of booze."

When Cranfill and his friends brought Prohibition to a vote at the local level, Brann called them "two-by-four fanatics, as intolerant as Cotton Mather," who were "trying to alter the physical constitution of the human race by means of a county election." He quoted studies showing the average life span of drinkers to be twelve years longer than that of alcohol abstainers and wondered why Prohibitionists had never produced any great men but "multiply chronic meddlers as a dead dog does maggots." In "The Apostle in Perdition," Brann paid an ironic visit to Hell, where he found lots of Baptists and the persecutors of Socrates (but not Socrates himself), and learned it was the only place where Prohibition actually prohibited anything.

It was the overbearing nature of many so-called reforms that got under Brann's skin, especially the sort practiced by the editor of the *Baptist Standard*. "Waco has entirely too much of the Cranfillian brand of pseudo-piety which manifests itself in chronic meddling with the rights of other people." At various times Cranfill proposed a boycott by Baptists of non-Baptist businesses, a boycott of newspapers quoting the atheist Ingersoll, and stricter Sunday closing laws. Brann abused each of these campaigns in their turn, along with their author.

He called the *Baptist Standard* a "sectarian sewer," "Waco's great repository of intellectual tommy-rot," and "a mental miscarriage" run by "Dr. Jehovah Boanerges Cranfill, professional Christian and candidate for President on the pink-lemonade ticket," who, "finding piety a paying investment, began to preach; that the more money you made the harder you loved Jesus." Brann suggested the strict enforcement of the Sunday laws until the people "seize a dog-whip and drive Cranfillism howling into its hole . . . I move that we substitute Cranfill's shirt-tail for Old Glory until we have demonstrated our right to float our fathers' flag by regaining our lost liberties."

Brann had not been publishing long when Cranfill's magazine advertised the arrival in Waco of Joseph Slattery, a former Catholic priest who lectured on the evils of the Roman Catholic church. Slattery belonged to the American Protective Association, or APA, an anti-Catholic, anti-Semitic secret society. Brann referred to the APA as the "Aggregation of Pusillanimous Asses" and denounced Slattery before his visit. Alerted to Brann's attack, Slattery accused the *Iconoclast* of "pope-loving" subversion. At Slattery's second lecture, for men only, concerning the tyrannical and salacious practices in Catholic nunneries, Brann showed up to confront Slattery and the men insulted each other in front of the capacity crowd at the Opera House. Brann got the last word in "Brann vs. Slattery" in the June issue, an attack on religious bigotry that implied the Christian shortcomings of the Baptists as well as the APA.

Cranfill made no public response to Brann's taunts. Brann's name never appeared in the pages of the *Baptist Standard.* Nor did Cranfill mention Brann in either of his two autobiographies. But he could not make Brann disappear or hide all traces of his feelings. Nearly forty years after Brann's death, Cranfill wrote: "Brann was a meteoric polemic, who feared not God, neither regarded man. He reveled in personalities and was not choice concerning his facts." To a Brann biographer Cranfill labeled Brann "a power for evil." But while Brann was still alive, Cranfill's anger was less genteel. According to B. G. McKie, editor of the *Waco Morning Times* who rode a train with Cranfill after Brann had been beaten on a Waco street, "Dr. Cranfill said Brann was a buzzard spewing foully on every thing pure and decent, that he was a jewist priest in disguise, and Judge Scarborough should have beat him to death and rid the world of such a man."

Despite Cranfill's murderous rage, Brann might have survived taunting the Waco Baptists had he not included Baylor University among his targets. The pretext for his frontal assault was irresistible to Brann's chauvinistic sense of chivalry—a damsel in distress.

Stalking the Deadly Inevitable

On June 16, 1895, the *Waco Morning News* reported that Antonia Teixeira, a fifteen-year-old Brazilian girl attending Baylor, had charged one Steen Morris with sexual assault. Morris, a printer, was the brother of the Reverend Silas Morris, editor of the *Baptist Guardian* and son-in-law of Baylor's president, Rufus C. Burleson. Teixeira boarded with the Burleson family, helping with household chores in exchange for her educational expenses. She was training to return to Brazil as a Baptist missionary.

Teixeira accused Morris, who took his meals at the Burleson residence and lived nearby, of repeated sexual assaults. She said she had reported his conduct to Mrs. Burleson after the first two assaults but that nothing was done. Morris denied the charge. He was arrested and released on bail. Asked for comment, President Burleson said "with exceeding great reluctance" that though he had treated the Brazilian girl "as my granddaughter," she was "utterly untrustworthy" and that "in addition to the other faults, the girl was crazy after the boys." Friends of Morris started a rumor that Teixeira had been raped by a Negro. But on June 17 she gave birth to a white female baby.

Brann jumped on the Baylor scandal in the July *Iconoclast*. He accused President Burleson of exploiting Antonia Teixeira. "Instead of being prepared for missionary work, this 'ward of the Baptist church' was learning the duties of the scullion—and Dr. Burleson has informed the world through the public prints that she was not worth her board and clothes." Brann scolded Burleson for his attack on Teixeira's character and dismissed Burleson's charges. "No matter how 'crazy after the boys' a girl in short dresses may be, she is not permitted to go headlong to the Devil—to be torn to pieces and impregnated by some lousy and lecherous male mastodon." Baylor and the Baptists had betrayed their trust, then tried to blame the victim.

President Burleson felt compelled to answer Brann's charges. After meeting with the Baylor trustees on August 20, he issued a typewritten statement to rebut the false charges of "the rabble and 'lewd' fellows of the baser sort." Burleson denounced as "black and damnable lies" Brann's charges that Baylor was responsible for Teixeira's plight, and that the Burlesons had "cast her off in the kitchen to be ruined and then thrust her into the streets to be picked up by Catholics and other 'publicans and sinners.'" Burleson said Waconians should not tolerate the slander of Baylor, an honorable institution "that has done so much for the moral and material development of Waco." He called upon the people to "rise up and vindicate Baylor University," and upon those who had attacked the school to "repent and confess openly their sins and receive forgiveness, before they are everlastingly lost."

Brann pursued the case month to month. The majority of his distant readership, with no access to the statements of President Burleson or other Waco periodicals, had only Brann's version of the soap opera to follow. The August installment, "Baylor in Bad Business," deplored the release of Morris on bail and declared that Teixeira's "ill-gotten babe" was "her diploma from Baylor." Nor could Brann resist quick jabs such as his remark in the September *Iconoclast* that "Baylor college is considering the advisability of establishing a medical department. Perhaps no better place could be found for the study of obstetrics."

In October Brann tore into President Burleson's public statement. Dr. Burleson should have acted the Christian and tried to save and protect the Brazilian girl "instead of denouncing her in public and turning her adrift to go headlong to the devil." Jesus forgave Mary Magdalene, a professional prostitute. "Cannot his professed disciples do as much for an ignorant child in short dresses?" Brann leavened these high-minded sentiments with a sophomoric quip elsewhere in the same issue: "Baylor University boasts a larger list of male students this year than last. The extraordinary inducements it offers gay young gentlemen are becoming more generally known." Brann rehashed the case again in the November issue, and in January 1896 opined that the Morris request for a continuance was the action of a guilty man. He also repeated his grotesquerie that Baylor was "offering illegitimate babies as certificates of graduation" and derogated Dr. Burleson as a man who "permits a child, entrusted to his care, to be debauched, then brands her as a public bawd."

"To Build a Monument" in the March *Iconoclast* was Brann's proposal to erect a memorial to Antonia Teixeira's baby, who had died the previous autumn. He thought a "rectangular pyramid of pure white marble, surmounted by a life-size bust of Dr. Burleson," should be erected at a prominent place on the Baylor campus. The monument would celebrate Baylor's accomplishment. "It received an ignorant little Catholic as raw material and sent forth two Baptists as the finished product. That important triumph of mind over matter should be preserved . . ." In June Brann noted it had been a year since H. Steen Morris, "a young man who parts his name on the side," had been charged in the Teixeira assault case. "The *Iconoclast* gave it a little attention at the time; but as a dozen or two people have subscribed since then," Brann thought it reasonable to summarize the case once more. That way his new readers would "know what to expect should they choose to commit their children to the care of the great Baptist sanctuary of the South."

In September, "The Teixeira Affidavit" took note that Antonia Teixeira had sworn an affidavit exonerating Steen Morris from the charge of assault. Brann also noted Teixeira's immediate departure from Texas to Brazil, and wondered who had paid for her ticket. He made no secret he was skeptical of the affidavit and ran through the facts of the case yet again.

Brann kept up his attack on Morris, Burleson, Baylor, and company with the same relentless pressure he applied to Cranfill, the Prohibitionists, political preachers, and others, local and foreign, he considered frauds and fakes. Though the remarkable success of the *Iconoclast* allowed Brann, for the first time in his life, to provide his wife and two children with a comfortable home, he did not slacken the pace he had pursued out of poverty. Until December 1896, the *Iconoclast* ran a banner saying "No Room for Contributed Articles." Brann wrote his twenty-page magazine all by himself. Advertising came in slowly, never filling more than a few pages. He reprinted much of the material from his original *Austin Iconoclast*, but after nearly two years of monthly publishing and frequent lecturing, Brann began to accept work from select contributors.

To the end Brann feuded with other editors, especially old enemies such as Rienzi M. Johnson of the *Houston Post*. As an odd joke that quickly turned tiresome, Brann wrote articles in the form of letters to "Rebecca" Johnson, addressing his former editor as a female suitor who had fallen out of love with him. Sometimes Brann was less subtle with "the editor of the Houston *Post*, who probably knows less about more things than any man alive . . ." Brann called another previous employer, the *Austin Statesman*, "a paper that has no valid excuse for existing, yet . . . lacks sufficient energy to get off the earth." "The editorial page of the Dallas *News* reminds me of the Desert of the Sahara after a simoon," said Brann. "It is such an awful waste of space . . ." He thought the staff of the *St. Louis Republic* a "delectable mob of free-lunch fiends, hack-writers and journalistic Charley-horses."

Besides the name-calling and the personal insults he leveled at particular publications, Brann had many more serious criticisms of contemporary journalism. "Having grown grizzly in the service of the day-breakers, I am qualified to speak 'from the bench;' and I repeat that, under current conditions, a daily newspaper that is at once prosperous and independent is an absolute impossibility." Since newspapers depended on their advertisers, they took care never to attack the morals of those patrons or to question their politics. That was why, "with three-fifths of the reading public supporting the Democratic ticket, four-fifths of our daily papers were in the Republican push." Modern press critics might argue that Brann's analysis remains pertinent.

Brann considered the American press generally "a brake on the wheels of progress," exerting little real influence except to "aggravate all social deformities." The conservative press was incapable of entertaining new ideas, content to attack any who dared question the status quo. But the "non-conservative press" offered up one simplistic notion after another to settle the world's problems—communism, prohibitionism, socialism, greenbackism—"such remedy as its narrow visual range can espy, such as its scant knowledge of social therapeutics can suggest." The American press persisted in be-

lieving the myth of its own power. But the only real power it possessed was keeping good men out of politics, since those men
dreaded the public insults of the partisan press. Brann thought the
"journalistic standard of intelligence" below the average, because
"the intelligence of the country is drawn to the gain-getting avoca-
tions and journalism is not one of them."

He accused the Associated Press of operating a "shameless and
rapacious" trust, of "flagrantly and persistently" violating its charter
to supply news to "all who pay the fixed tolls." Instead, the AP sold
or withheld its service, "building up or tearing down newspapers at
pleasure . . ." Nothing was done because "few politicians care to
engage in a struggle with a concern which has the power to black-
guard them seven days a week from one end of the country to the
other . . ." Brann thought the huge Sunday editions of the "would-be
great" New York and Chicago papers, "about the size of the census
report," to be "journalistic idiocy." Pulitzer's *New York World* led
the lot, spoiling "more white paper than any other publication on
earth—with the possible exception of the *Houston Post.*"

He attacked numerous newspapers for playing the pimp with their
"personals" columns, profiting from false or tasteless advertising,
and filling their pages with tragedy and depravity instead of provocative thought. He pronounced journalism schools superfluous institutions.

Journalism is no esoteric science; it is "easy as lying." Really it
were as fatuous to establish schools of journalism as to found
professorships for instructions in the art of making chile-con-
carne or bad smells. Any one can learn it without a preceptor.
Here is the recipe for making a "great daily;"

A scandal-in-high-life, first page, double-leaded, screamer head;
two or three columns of rocking-chair speculation on matters political, Washington date line; a few bogus or garbled interviews
with prominent politicians; a suicide; a scandal-in-low-life; a
thrilling account of an impossible accident in Timbuctoo; report
that a billion Chinese have been drowned by an overflow of the
Hwang-Ho; full . . . report of a sensational divorce trial . . . two-
column account of a prize fight; a hanging, with all the ghastly
details "worked up;" two columns of esoteric base-ball lingo in
which the doughty deeds of "Fatty," "Shorty," "Squatty," "Bow-
legged Bill," and "Short-stop Sam" are painted . . . account of the
elopement of a society belle with a negro coachman; heavy editorial on the "Power of the Press;" more editorial inanity and
offensive self-glorification; a pimping "personal" column; . . .

budget of foreign news—manufactured in New York; . . . advertisements of quack doctors, lost manhood restorers, syphilitic
nostrums . . . Jam to a mux and serve hot.

Readers of *Brann's Iconoclast* over the years became familiar with
Waco and Texas through the eyes of its trenchant adopted son. General Phil Sheridan once said that if he owned Texas and hell he
would "rent out Texas and live in hell." In 1880 Sheridan visited
Texas and apologized for his earlier remark, but Brann liked to refer
to it occasionally. He thought Sheridan "was probably cooped up in
a Prohibition precinct when he declared Hell to be preferable as
a place of permanent residence." Brann declared Texas a pleasant
enough place, "despite the fact about one half the inhabitants have
partisan politics on the brain, while the remainder are troubled with
religious pains in the abdominal region."

Brann thought the Lone Star State could "furnish forth more hidebound dogmatists, narrow-brained bigots and intolerant fanatics in
proportion to population than can any other section of these United
States. That's why the *Iconoclast* is in Texas." When a reader in-
quired as to why the *Iconoclast* "has so little to say about the town
from which it draws its support . . ." Brann's response showed his
sense of vulnerability but also his power.

That's a difficult problem. Perhaps it's because I cannot get my
life insured. Maybe it's because I'm a poor runner and a worse
shot. Perhaps it's because I only weigh 140 pounds with my
shoes on, and have but one door to my office, while the windows
are a long ways from the ground. Then, again, it may be because I
have property in the town and do not care to depreciate its value
by exposing the frauds of the people. But my correspondent
should take me into his confidence. To what town does he refer?
If he means Waco, the explanation is dead easy. I do not write it
up because I'm infatuated with the place. I can have more fun
here for my money than anywhere else on earth. Among its
30,000 inhabitants are at least a hundred whom I'd hate dreadfully to see hanged. But Waco is not "the town from which the
Iconoclast draws its support." Not much, Mary Ann. It's the
place from which it receives eleven-sevenths of the abuse that is
heaped upon it. But the *Iconoclast* is a consistent Christian and
invariably turns the other cheek to the smiter. It goes smiling on
its way, collecting money from every State in the Union and
pouring it into the yawning tills of Waco tradesmen . . . That's
why the *Iconoclast* is widely advertising Waco simply by carry-

ing her name on its masthead, while a gang of goody-goodies, who pray with their lips while plotting petit larceny in their hearts, are imploring people not to buy it. There are millions of people who, but for the *Iconoclast*, would not know that Waco's on the map of the world.

Brann's enemies realized that his hyperbolic boasting had a basis in fact. The size and geographical distribution of his burgeoning subscription list made Brann far more dangerous than any local critic. When Brann said, "The dreadful scandal at Baylor University suggests that we do not hold our Baptists under water long enough," readers around the country and the world had a laugh at local expense, but the targets of Brann's sarcasm had no similar outlet for their response.

Shortly after Brann started publishing the *Iconoclast* in Waco, he commented on the amount of critical, even threatening, mail he received. The longer he remained and the more he turned his pen against Cranfill, the Baptists, and especially Baylor, the more hate mail he got. In August 1897, Brann printed the letter of "An Indignant Citizen," inviting Brann to leave town. The writer called Brann the "chief of ingrates." "You exercise your wit at the expense of our best society and ridicule our leading citizens . . . If you don't like Waco, why don't you pack up your traps and leave?" Brann penned a lengthy, withering reply. "I trust that 'Indig. Cit.' will reconsider my sentence of expulsion and permit me to linger yet a little longer in this terrestrial paradise; for it would certainly break my tender heart and might fracture the mainstream of my poetic soul to be compelled to 'pack my traps' in a paper collar-box and bid a sad farewell to the Geyser City . . . I not only 'like Waco' but I love it . . . How could it be otherwise when 'Indig. Cit.' and various other cattle of his kidney have so exerted themselves to make my pathway pleasant . . ." Brann reiterated his financial contribution to Waco. Orders for the *Iconoclast* and his pamphlets paid printers and helped the local economy. He hinted he might be a prophet without honor in his own land, a city of meddlers whose idea of "heaven is an eternity of keyholes" to peep through. Brann entitled one of his musings on Waco "The Mouth of Hell."

Waco is so pious that the very policemen emit an odor of sanctity—and it is at the same time the rottenest political hole this side of Hades . . . Waco is the only town in Texas of any consequence where men are boycotted in business for questioning the Immaculate Conception; it is likewise the only one that licenses

bawdy houses and considers the buying and selling of votes as a
virtue rather than a vice . . . Some may suppose from the forego-
ing that the *Iconoclast* has soured on the Geyser City. Not so . . .
The *Iconoclast* is too good a friend to Waco not to tell her of her
faults; Waco loves the *Iconoclast* too well not to accept in a
grateful spirit this gentle courtesy.

But Brann's enemies had reached the limit of their frustration. Unable to battle him on his own terms, with wits or words, they re-
sorted to violence.

The Wages of Satire

As the 1897 academic year began, Baylor claimed a record high enrollment. At the same time, Dr. Rufus Burleson, now seventy-four,
indicated his wish to retire. A subsequent study shows more bravado
than truth in Baylor's enrollment claims for the year. Brann did not
dispute Baylor's claims, but his "support" was insupportable to Baylor loyalists.

> I note with unfeigned pleasure that, according to claims of
> Baylor University, it opens the present season with a larger con-
> tingent of students, male and female, than ever before. This
> proves that Texas Baptists are determined to support it at any
> sacrifice—that they believe it better that their daughters should
> be exposed to its historic dangers and their sons condemned to
> grow up in ignorance than that this manufactory of ministers
> and Magdalenes should be permitted to perish . . .
> The *Iconoclast* would like to see Baylor University, so called,
> become an honor to Texas instead of an educational eyesore,
> would like to hear it spoken of with reverence instead of sneer-
> ingly referred to by men about town as worse than a harem . . .
> There is no reason, however, why the institution should be in
> the future so intellectually and morally unprofitable as in the
> past. Change is the order of the universe, and as Baylor cannot
> very well become worse it must of necessity become better . . .

The issue of the *Iconoclast* bearing these sentiments appeared October 1, 1897. The next day, Brann was at the office of his printer
when three Baylor students burst in. One boy pointed a gun at him
while two others hustled him out the door and into a waiting carriage. They drove him quickly through town to the Baylor campus,
where a student mob was waiting. Charles Carver said the boys

wound a rope around Brann and were shouting, "Lynch him!" "Hang him!" One of the students involved, recalling events more than sixty years later, disputed Carver's description, saying it "slanders Baylor," though the former student added that the faculty saved Brann's life. "The Baylor boys might have harmed him that day. I know that he needed hanging." Other eyewitnesses said the students intended to tar and feather the editor, but someone, possibly a Baylor professor, hid the tar. Whether or not the students entered the armory, obtained rifles and ammunition, and held off the city police and Brann's friends, the fact is no one from off-campus interfered with the mob.

The Baylor students roughed Brann up, cutting and bruising him. They demanded he sign a statement admitting he was a malicious liar and promising to leave town. Amid the jostling, jeering crowd, Brann quickly signed. Faculty members pleaded for Brann's release. He was shoved into a carriage and sent, badly shaken, back to town. Brann told the *Dallas News* later that day he had signed the paper without reading it, "but as it was a matter of force, I am not bound by its terms."

Two days after this incident, the Baylor Board of Trustees held an emergency meeting. Far from condemning the students' actions, the group unanimously adopted a resolution endorsing Baylor and denouncing the *Iconoclast*. Several of Brann's friends urged him to file charges against the students involved in his abduction, but Brann refused. He tried to clarify his position with a statement in the *Waco Daily Telephone*. "It was not the students, but the management that I criticized . . . I would deserve to be shot if I defamed the humblest girl within its walls."

Judge John Scarborough, whose daughter had just graduated from Baylor and whose son, George, had been one of Brann's three abductors, decided the editor deserved more punishment. On October 6, Judge Scarborough, his son, George, and another student who had been in the Baylor mob met Brann in the hall of his office building. The men disarmed Brann and forced him into the street. They beat him with the butts of their pistols as he tried to run. When Brann fell, Judge Scarborough struck him repeatedly with a cane while the boys held off passersby with their guns.

Brann answered his assailants in "BRANN VS. BAYLOR. Revolvers, Ropes and Religion," the lead article in November's *Iconoclast*.

   I have just been enjoying the first holiday I have had in fifteen years. Owing to circumstances beyond my control, I devoted the major part of the past month to digesting a couple of installments of Saving Grace presented by my Baptist brethren, and carefully rubbed in with revolvers and ropes, loaded canes and miscellaneous cudgels—with almost any old thing calculated to make a sinner reflect upon the status of his soul . . .

My Baptist brethren desired to send me as a missionary to foreign lands, and their invitation was so urgent, their expressions of regard so fervent that I am now wearing my head in a sling and trying to write with my left hand.

Truth to tell, there's not one of the whole cowardly tribe who's worth a charge of buckshot . . . If Socrates was poisoned and Christ was crucified for telling unpalatable truths to the splenetic-hearted hypocrites of their time, it would ill become me to complain of a milder martyrdom for a like offense.

Brann continued on at great length to deny he had impeached the honor of female Baylor students. That was merely the excuse of the cowards who attacked him. He challenged them to face him one by one if they had the courage.

"I walk the streets of Waco and I walk them alone. Let these curristians shoot me in the back if they dare, then plead that damning lie as an excuse for their craven cowardice. If the decent people of this community fail to chase them to their holes and feed their viscera to the dogs, then I'd rather be dead and in hades forever than alive in Waco a single day . . ."

His appeal to community decency fell upon deaf ears. Brann had his supporters, but the majority believed he had earned his punishment. Brann's friend J. D. Shaw, a Methodist minister turned freethinker who edited the *Independent Pulpit*, scolded Cranfill for not speaking out against mob violence. Shaw said "the mobbing of Mr. Brann was only for some intemperate criticism of Baylor University, and however provoking that may have been, it was not worse than what the editor of the *Standard* has said of the Catholic convert." But Cranfill was hardly the one to speak in defense of Brann.

Shaw regarded the Brann-Baylor conflict as "a religious rumpus, all the way through," since "Mr. Brann is a defender of religion and deals my Agnosticism some hard, though harmless, blows." Shaw concluded that the whole episode "goes to show that religion, as a peace maker and a moral factor, is a humbug and a fraud." Brann was far too shaken, angry, and terrified to enjoy the irony of Shaw's observation.

Though Brann reiterated Baylor's shortcomings in his November *Iconoclast*, he also announced his intention, partly at the behest of friends, to "drop the subject until another attempt is made to run me out of town." But one of Brann's supporters refused to leave the matter alone.

G. B. Gerald, a former Confederate officer and later a county judge, wrote an indignant article about the violence against Brann and took it to J. W. Harris, editor of the *Waco Times-Herald*. Harris took the article but did not run it. Gerald, known for his hot temper, returned to reclaim his article. For some reason, Harris did not give it back. The men exchanged words, then blows. Gerald printed up a handbill telling his side of the story and attacking Harris in violent terms "as a liar, a coward, and a cur." Harris prudently stayed home from work for three weeks.

On November 19, Harris came to town and ran into Judge Gerald. As Gerald approached, Harris fired several shots, wounding him. But Gerald kept coming, drew his pistol, and dropped Harris with one shot. The editor's younger brother ran up behind Gerald and shot Gerald in the back. As a police officer grabbed the younger Harris, Gerald shot and killed him. The people of Waco considered the killing of the Harris brothers a part of the feud between Brann and Baylor.

Brann's supporters, appalled by the mounting violence in Waco, tried to get him to leave town. B. G. McKie, editor of the *Corsicana Light* and the *Waco Morning Times*, was typical of friends who tried to reason with Brann. "I . . . begged him to let up on the row with Baylor and go with me to Corsicana and let me publish his *Iconoclast* there. He said he would not leave under fire or threats. I told him no man could fight a community or a fanatic or a mob." The season of bloodshed made national headlines, boosting the circulation of the *Iconoclast* still higher but alarming some of its readers.

> To the kindly offers of other cities to afford the *Iconoclast* an asylum and protect its editor from outrage, I will simply say that I do not consider either my property or my person in the slightest danger . . . [The *Iconoclast*'s contributors] are a bouquet of pansy blossoms of whom any publisher might well be proud. Should the editor chance to swallow too much water the next time he is baptized, they can be depended upon to keep the flag of the *Iconoclast* afloat until the red-headed heir-apparent learns to write with one hand and shoot with the other. Let it go at that. BRANN.

But Brann could not quite let it go at that. In the same December issue where the above sentiments appeared, he expressed his doubts that Baylor might relocate in Dallas. "Dallas doesn't want Baylor even a little bit. There isn't a town in this world that wants it except Waco. It is simply another Frankenstein that has destroyed its architect . . . The institution is worth less than nothing to any town. It is . . . a storm-center of misinformation. It is the Alma Mater of mob violence. It is a chronic breeder of bigotry and bile. As a small Waco property owner, I will give it $1000 any time to move to Dallas, and double that amount if it will go to Honolulu or hell . . ."

In the *Iconoclast* of February 1898, Brann rebutted those who blamed his reputation for keeping a Masonic widows' and orphans' home from locating in Waco. He said it was the violent Baptists who had kept the home away. As for the *Iconoclast*, Brann said, "There are not Baptists enough in Texas to drive it out of this town. If they kill the editor, another and a better man will step into his shoes and continue the old fight against hypocrites and humbugs . . ."

Brann's friends persuaded him the time was right to make an extended lecture tour. He and his wife agreed to leave their two children at home and travel across the South. They planned to leave Waco on the train April 2. On April 1, Brann went downtown to pick up the tickets. He and his business manager, William Ward, were walking on Fourth Street about six o'clock when a man named Tom Davis stepped out from a doorway and shot Brann in the back. Brann turned quickly and fired his pistol at Davis, who fell to one knee. Ward tried to get Davis' gun away from him, but Davis shot Ward through the hand. Only about ten feet apart, Davis and Brann continued firing at each other.

Police marched Brann to city hall before they realized the extent of his injuries. He had been shot three times. Taken home on a cot in a delivery wagon, Brann died about two the next morning. His assailant, Tom Davis, died about twelve hours later. Why Davis shot Brann is not clear. Perhaps he meant to avenge the honor of his daughter, who attended Baylor. Brann's deathbed hypothesis concerned a political campaign Davis had managed and Brann had criticized. Fuller Williamson, a deputy sheriff, said later Davis was suspected in several cases of forgery. Williamson thought Davis probably killed Brann to win the favor of the Baptists, who he hoped would help him in the forgery case. Whatever motivated Davis to murder, Brann's violent death shocked many but surprised few.

The funerals of Brann and his assassin were held at the same hour on Sunday, April 3, in different parts of Waco. Both drew large crowds. In death as in life, Brann provoked extreme, disparate opinions. His admirers considered him a hero and a martyr. His detractors thought him a blasphemous troublemaker. Brann's friends helped his widow publish the *Iconoclast* for six months after his death. In July the magazine was sold and moved to Chicago. Editors attempted to carry on in the Brann tradition, but the Chicago circulation never reached the Waco level. In 1926 the name *Brann's Iconoclast* was dropped.

In the months following Brann's murder, Judge Gerald protested in the *Iconoclast* against "the pack of journalistic jackals who are raising their infamous howl over the body of Brann." He also accused several public speakers of plagiarizing Brann's material. In 1903 Michael Monahan called Brann "the most brilliant and daring guerilla-publicist of our time . . . As an antidote to this pen that dripped poison . . . the enemies of Brann could propose only the pistol of the assassin . . . It is thus, alas! that Texas disposes of a literary style."

Brann's style, honored in a twelve-volume set of his complete works in 1919, was never captured by his imitators. But his life and legend inspired other independent journalists to speak out for causes they believed in, however unpopular. Brann became an icon for Texas iconoclasts to follow.

2. The Lone Coyote

When a man comes along with some new ideas or advanced positions on important questions we call him a crank, a fanatic, an anarchist, a socialist, a plain damphool, or something of that sort. Some years later our children call him a great man and wonder why we didn't have any better sense.

—*Don Hampton Biggers*

Don Hampton Biggers was a restless spirit, an itinerant journalist who wandered West and Central Texas in search of stories no one else would touch. In the course of his long life he edited, printed, bought into, founded, folded, sold, or quit more newspapers and magazines than we can know. But the list that remains to us is longer than a dozen journalists together might reasonably assemble.

Born near the high plains in 1868, Biggers grew up in a period of dramatic changes on the frontier. The great roaming herds of buffalo gave way to a cattle boom, succeeded in turn by ranches and farms. Biggers developed a love for the land and for the settlers and ranchers who worked that wild territory. He sought out stories of the old-timers and dug into public records in order to chronicle the quickly passing scene. The title of one of his earliest books, *History That Will Never Be Repeated* (1901), conveys his sense of pathos and urgency about capturing the fading frontier in print.

Apprenticed at sixteen to a printer, Biggers mastered the trade. His printing skills provided him the freedom of speech and movement his brand of journalism required. He could write and produce his own work. It also gave Biggers a profession to fall back on in lean editorial times. His passion for independence, and his volatile temperament, made Biggers a difficult employee when occasional economic necessity forced him into journalistic collaboration. He became a vigorous critic of daily newspapers.

"There is no place on the daily newspaper for men of advanced thought and independent expression," Biggers wrote in 1908. "These kind of men can only commune with the public through the medium of magazines or individual publications. The story of . . . Brann and dozens of others amply verify and substantiate this statement."

Because newspapers served establishment policies and politics in order to make money, they were necessarily corrupt, in Biggers' view. His advantage as an independent was given added power by his transience. Beholden to no vested interests, Biggers could enter cleanly into a new location and cut to the truth of an issue as he saw it, no holds barred. He also possessed a stubborn, Brann-like courage in the face of life-threatening opposition.

He started the *Independent Oil News and Financial Reporter* in the Eastland County oil fields in 1921. Refusing all ads from oil stock promoters, Biggers exposed a number of frauds. He continued to publish in spite of threats made against him. Eventually material he collected resulted in the successful prosecution of many fraudulent promoters. He also worked with the Texas Attorney General's office to draft the state's Blue Sky Law, to prevent future promotion of stock fraud. Biggers exhibited a similar courage when the Ku Klux Klan reacted violently to his numerous attacks on their organization in several publications.

His love of the land and his outspoken independence led Biggers inevitably to the other great passion of his life—politics. He quickly saw that land issues in Texas—water rights, mineral rights, and transportation rights-of-way—were matters of big money and enormous political pressure. His avid interest in political matters at local, state, and national levels led him to run for office on several occasions. His earlier campaigns, lighthearted and even satirical, earned him two terms in the Texas Legislature at different times and, characteristically, from different districts. When he waged more earnest efforts later on, the voters failed to take him seriously.

But Biggers was more effective politically in the editorial campaigns he took up against corrupt or abusive politicians. He was instrumental in helping expose highway scandals in the administration of Governor Miriam Ferguson in 1925. He started the *Record*, an Austin weekly, in 1930 specifically to oppose the gubernatorial ambitions of Ross Sterling, a man Biggers considered hopelessly in thrall to the oil interests. He serialized his own muckraking history of corruption in the oil industry, emphasizing Texas, a bit of journalistic bravado no other newspaper emulated.

Besides his Progressive sense of outrage at injustice and hypocrisy, Biggers possessed a fierce sense of humor. He published his own pointed editorial cartoons in many newspapers and magazines. Biggers enjoyed homespun anecdotes as well as more sophisticated wordplay. He issued several satirical publications and broadsides at various times. But occasionally the sarcastic style he adopted in serious discussion became almost indistinguishable from his barbed satires.

Don H. Biggers "about 1916." Josher, Coyote, Bombardier.
(Courtesy of the Southwest Collection, Texas Tech University.)

"Same Old Tune, Same Old Artist." Biggers cartoon from
The Record (Austin), March 27, 1930.
(Courtesy of the Southwest Collection, Texas Tech University.)

Biggers' 1933 book about the career of Jim Ferguson, *Our Sacred Monkeys, or 20 Years of Jim and Other Jams (Mostly Jim),* suffers from a blurring of heavy-handed wit and studied political commentary. The clash of style and substance suggests that Biggers himself was not always clear about his attitude toward certain issues. The huge correspondence Biggers maintained, especially in the last two decades of his life, reveals a man alternately humorous and bitter, appalled at the abuses of public figures and the endless capacity of the people to be misled. Even his correspondents were clearly confused at times by the truths he wanted to express.

A colleague wrote of Biggers, "He is one of those rare characters whom even those who cuss him will trust." No one ever challenged the honesty of Don Biggers. But his was a painful honesty at times, asking more than many of his friendships could bear. Politicians who owed Biggers a great deal did not take it kindly when he turned critical, as he almost inevitably did.

Biggers played a small but important role in the rise of Tom Connally, refusing Connally's offers of patronage in return. As a United States senator, Connally kept up a wary epistolary friendship with Biggers, sending him small checks on his birthday, careful to humor him. But Connally avoided the man and his ideas. Nor did he mention Biggers in his memoirs.

The integrity Biggers refused to sell or compromise made him a tenacious crusader but an unpredictable ally. His mobility—physical and political—enabled him to speak freely and to change his mind publicly. But his independence ultimately turned to isolation. Of necessity a frugal man, Biggers spent his last years supported by his children.

In his seventies and eighties, he accompanied his wife, Nettie, who had followed him to so many newspaper towns, as Nettie sought out subjects for her art. They wandered many thousands of miles around the Southwest year after year, and when Nettie would stop to paint a plant or a landscape that caught her eye, Don would haul out his typewriter wherever they were and fire off his views in letters to editors, politicians, and old friends. He became, almost literally, a voice crying out in the wilderness.

Cattle Range and Cotton Patch and Editors and Kings

Don Hampton Biggers was born in Meridian, Texas, on September 27, 1868. As he wrote to a friend near the end of his life, "Town didn't amount to anything until I was born there. Hasn't amounted to anything since." His father, Samuel Washington Biggers, a Confederate veteran, turned from carpentry to ranching.

In 1876 the elder Biggers located his herd of about five hundred head of cattle on a ranch near Breckenridge, where Don and his three younger brothers grew up. Don's mother, Elizabeth Biggers, died in 1882. Don helped his father with the cattle and attended school in Cisco. "The school term was six months. When school was out I would head to Albany, and herd sheep for Bill and Wat Earhart, Radford, or someone else, and then head back to Cisco . . . and spin scary yarns about the wild west."

In the fall of 1877 Biggers accompanied a buffalo hunter, a friend of his father's, on a visit to the buffalo range. The experience impressed him sufficiently that he recounted it in two of his books. "It was 175 miles as well as I now remember, from Ft. Griffin to the head of Duck creek, and we made the trip in about five days. We met not a soul nor saw a sign of human habitation . . ." Biggers wrote in *History That Will Never Be Repeated.* "The mesquite grass was knee high everywhere . . . The country was full of turkeys, prairie chickens, antelope, plover, kerlew, cayotes, lobos, skunks, snakes and pure atmosphere . . . Mr. Daugherty showed me two or three big killing grounds, and I noticed a great many bones and buffalo heads . . . A few years later I saw these same bones selling for twelve dollars per ton, and being shipped east to fertilize the soil . . . The cayote wolves were a source of much trouble to us. They would come right into our camp at night and do all kinds of devilment . . ."

Biggers finished his formal schooling at sixteen. "I took my first academic degree in the public schools of Cisco, which accounts for the town's fame as an education center." In 1884 he went to work for a newspaper in Colorado City, the *Clipper.* "I was just a cub when I first worked on the Clipper. I could set type (straight matter), feed the presses and sweep out the office."

He later worked at a print shop in Cisco and possibly soon afterward at the *Baird Star.* At least, a 1920 *Star* editorial claimed that "Don Biggers, as a young man 31 years ago, worked on the Star, and is one of the best all round printers and newspaper men in Texas." In a reminiscence written in 1910, Biggers remembers his Baird experiences less fondly. "I used to work for Billy Gilliland, of the Baird Star, but he voluntarily gave me an indefinite leave of absence one day and I quit . . . While Baird is a healthy town it is by no means a health resort for Populist newspapers."

In 1889 Biggers wrote and printed his first book, of thirty pages, *A Handbook of Reference Containing Directory and Description and a Summary of the Various Advantages of Eastland County, Texas.*

The unwieldy title, the failure to note where the book was published, and the clumsy, tentative prose show a young author and printer learning his trade. Biggers would never again be so wordy or deferential.

"The most labored effort has been to make this work as brief as possible, and yet give a full and comprehensive description of the country and a correct presentation of its various advantages. While some minor errors have possibly found their way into these pages— for no man, it matters not how gifted, is infallible—the privilege is assumed to say that they are indeed trivial, and can in no way effect the purport of the work nor tint its assertions with discredit."

By 1890 Biggers had saved enough money to purchase his own weekly paper, the *Midland Gazette.* On October 5, he married Nettie Lee Cox, his intimate partner until her death in 1957. They moved to Midland, but a few months after their arrival disaster struck. As Biggers wrote much later, "Cut my eye teeth in Midland. Stayed too long, whole town, including my print shop, burned, left me flat broke." Don and Nettie left Midland and began the gypsy existence they would lead the rest of their lives.

The next several years were unsettled ones. Nettie moved in with her parents in Carbon for the birth of their first child, Earl, on October 25, 1891. Don got temporary work back at the *Colorado Clipper* that winter. "I worked mostly on the outside as a news gatherer and ad. and job work solicitor, making a hand on the inside when needed there." He established the *Ranger Atlas* in 1891, then sold out and went to work for the *Albany News* until 1893. He briefly edited the *Breckenridge Texian* and then found work in a print shop in Cleburne.

Nettie joined Don in Cleburne, where their second son, Dale, was born. During the family's three-year stay in Cleburne, their third son, Clele, arrived. By this time Don Biggers had already developed a strong interest in politics. His lifelong friend, John Lee Smith, who served as lieutenant governor of Texas in the 1940s, recalled an incident from this period that shows Biggers' political interest as well as his occasionally rambunctious high spirits. In 1894 Jerome Kearby was running for Congress on the Populist ticket. According to notes made by Seymour Connor at his interview with Smith:

> Biggers and a group of Democrats put on badges faking themselves as a reception committee of Populists and boarded Kearby's train . . . They gave him drink after drink and took him to every saloon in Cleburne, trying to get Kearby so intoxicated that he would be unable to debate that night. However, Biggers

himself became inebriated and in his exuberance declared, "It's not fair to give this damn Populist all this whiskey!" So Biggers took a bottle to the Democratic candidate who quickly got drunk with Biggers. That night, at the time of the debate, Kearby was still on his feet, but Biggers, and the Democratic candidate, were unable to be present.

In 1896 or early 1897, Biggers bought a small bilingual newspaper in Clayton, New Mexico, the *Union-Democrat*. His wife joined him there after the birth of their daughter, Eula. Within a year Biggers sold the paper and returned to Colorado City, where his son Homan was born in 1901. During the summer of 1900 Biggers took work as a livestock enumerator for the census. He "made an extended buggy trip through the western counties, visiting with old time ranchers, former buffalo hunters and Indian fighters." He made notes on the many stories he heard for articles and books.

In the fall of 1900 he bought the *Colorado Spokesman* and issued the first of many declarations of independence: "I propose to publish the Spokesman as an independent newspaper, fawn at the feet of no man or clans, hold principles above avarice and contend for what I believe to be right, regardless of the opinion of others, for I believe newspaper toadyism is the lowest depths of degradation to which a human being can descend."

Biggers lasted only a few months as editor of the *Spokesman* before he sold it, though he continued to work as the paper's printer. On December 22, 1899, he issued the first number of the *Josher* as volume 300, number 52. The four-page paper declared its motto: "Avoid the truth and Prohibition whiskey; one is fatal, the other more so." Much of the paper featured Biggers' cartoons and doggerel verse, as well as satirical comments on local affairs.

Later issues of the *Josher*, still jocular in tone, addressed serious issues such as compensation for Confederate veterans. Biggers also inveighed against abuses of the lease law, which provided bonuses for settling and improving certain public lands to those who subsequently sold the land for profit. Biggers said "the enactment of the lease law was a disgraceful, fuddle-brained, inexcusable error . . ." The *Josher* masthead now called itself "A Very Weakly Paper, Issued Monthly, Devoted to Trouble. Our Motto:—Be Sure You're Wrong, Then Write It." By May 1902, Biggers claimed a circulation of 1,639 for the *Josher*.

In 1901 Biggers published *History That Will Never Be Repeated*. The following year he published a similar history of buffalo hunters and cattle drovers called *Pictures of the Past*. Part 2 of the latter book contained the whole of the earlier one. Biggers published both under the pseudonym "Lan Franks," though it is not clear why. By August 1902, the *Josher* was published in Abilene along with a second paper also "Devoted To Trouble," the *Texas Cleaver*.

Published twice a month, the *Texas Cleaver* continued after the *Josher* folded in September 1902, issued by "One Don by the name of Biggers, Soul Owner and Editor." As its name suggests, the *Cleaver* was stronger and sharper than the *Josher*. Biggers attacked the poll tax and those who supported it, such as the *Dallas News*.

A sheet that is notoriously corrupt from foot slugs to date line and that doesn't attempt to deny that its editorial utterances and news columns are for sale to any one for any purpose, is certainly worthy of high council in this important matter. If the Dallas News is in favor of such gigantic reforms and has the welfare of the people so near its frozen tadpole tempered gizzard why doesn't it advocate the abrogation of the absolute lease law . . . and not continually fill its columns with a lot of putrid misrepresentations written mostly in Austin and dictated, if not paid for, by cowmen whose interest is served by this class of deception?

Biggers asked his readers, "Did you ever stop to think that the voluminousness of the state and Federal statutes is simply inconceivable?" He called that legal accumulation "An Incomprehensible, Multifarious, Multiloquent Mess that Defies Interpretation and Surpasses all Bounds of Utility." But he confided that "these big words are harmless and may be used with impunity and pronounced to suit the taste."

In an article comparing "Kings and Editors" for no apparent reason, Biggers noted there was rejoicing at the birth of a king and sorrow at his death. "But when an editor is born his identity is kept a profound secret for a number of years" and his death produced little grief. Wars between editors only caused amusement, while people ran from kingly wars to avoid conscription. "When an editor's paper goes busted he generally goes to some other town and starts up again," while a dethroned king had no chance of a comeback. Biggers concluded it was "evidently much more pleasant to be an editor than a king . . ."

In 1904, despite his stated opinion of the Dallas *News*, Biggers accepted a *News* commission to write a series of articles about the history of West Texas. The series, which ran in the *News* from January through early April 1905, rehearsed the same material Biggers used in his two previous histories. Issued as a book in 1905, *From Cattle Range to Cotton Patch* was serialized again by the *Frontier Times* in 1943–1944 and reprinted in book form that same year.

Biggers again recounted the slaughter of the buffalo in Texas from 1870 to 1877, which caused "calamity" for the Indians as it "deprived them of a source of independent subsistence—took away their bread, meat, wearing apparel and building material." Biggers retailed the first-person accounts of frontiersmen and buffalo hunters who took up ranching when the herds were gone. A cattle boom dominated the high plains from 1882 to 1886, "a blaze of glory in a world of visions; a riotous feast on the crater of ruin." He gave vivid accounts of the "great die-ups," when thousands of animals perished in terrible winter blizzards.

From Abilene in 1906 Biggers issued several numbers of the *Coyote*, "The Official Howler of the American Desert." The *Lone Coyote* followed in 1908 from Rotan, where Biggers had moved in 1907 to start a weekly paper, the *Rotan Advance*. In the *Lone Coyote* Biggers defined the modern daily newspaper.

A medium the chief mission of which is to declare dividends, disseminate accounts of degrading crime, demoralizing scandal, and shocking casualties; a panderer to the stupid mental cravings of mankind; the champion of partisan politics and a producer of prejudice; a plaything for plutocrats and a stranger to principle; a debaucher of morals; an advertising directory of frauds . . . the megaphone of demagogues; a saint in pretension and a hypocrite in performance; a reeking putrid mess of mankind's filthy conduct, paraded without shame as the triumph of enterprise . . . a fusion of facts, fiction, falsehoods, folly and indigestible bombast; the cheapest excursion route for busy people to migrate to the uttermost realms of ignorance.

Biggers kept up his attack on daily newspapers in another satirical paper he started in 1908, the *Billy Goat Always Buttin' In*, "A Journal of such things as the editor takes a notion to write," "published at Rotan, Texas, every time the signs are right, which zodiac event occurs one to four times each month." Here he criticized the mercenary motives of the daily press and of the news service, "unreliable and colored to suit the policies of the paper."

Biggers had settled into his permanent posture concerning the dailies, protesting their power, warning against their motives, and writing for them whenever he needed money. Another series of sketches based on the tales of old-timers, most published by the *Dallas News*, appeared as a book called *Shackleford County Sketches* in 1908. Biggers regarded them as cautionary parables of greed and ambition in conflict with limited resources and a hostile environment.

Mr. Biggers Goes to Austin

In 1909 Don and Nettie Biggers moved with their six children to Lubbock, where Don Biggers took a job with the Lubbock Commercial Club, forerunner of the Lubbock Chamber of Commerce. He was hired to boost the town, which hoped to attract the Santa Fe Railroad. When his Commercial Club contract expired, he took up farming. Years later, the Biggers' son Clyde recalled how the whole family had planted crops and dug wells, experimenting with irrigation techniques.

To support his agricultural venture, Biggers submitted freelance articles on various subjects to different periodicals. Now that he had a personal stake in farming, Biggers wrote impassioned pieces about unfair farm prices, wasteful marketing distribution of farm products, and why county agents should be authorized to set up local farm co-ops. He would continue to write about these problems for years, mostly in *Farm and Ranch*. Biggers also published profiles of successful and innovative farmers and described how Mexican laborers were exploited by bosses on farms and in the oil fields.

Though Biggers was never a socialist—and would later pronounce socialism "unworkable"—he took the socialist view regarding unrest in Mexico, a discontent that ultimately led to revolution. In a 1911 article entitled "Poor Old Mexico!" Biggers blamed "American and European industrial and financial greed" for "keeping the people of Mexico in poverty, bondage and abject misery."

In 1914 the legislative representative from the district that included Lubbock decided not to run for reelection. Biggers volunteered himself as a candidate. According to one account, Biggers campaigned on a promise to exterminate prairie dogs and a joking platform of self-deprecation. "Don't waste a good man by sending him to Austin," said Biggers. "The country needs good men too much. Send me; I'm already ruined." Biggers won the election.

Don Biggers served in the regular (January 12 to March 20) and the called (April 29 to May 28) sessions of the Thirty-Fourth Legislature in 1915. Official records show that Biggers did cosponsor House Bill 28, "An Act declaring prairie dogs a public nuisance" and calling for their destruction. He also cosponsored a law to declare an emergency on the range and offer a bounty for wolves. And he offered a resolution to allow a Seventh Day Adventist to speak against blue laws requiring Sunday closings.

Biggers also jumped into the fight over state funding for the University of Texas journalism department. Some members wanted to end funding for the school of journalism, which had been established one year earlier. Others wanted to cut off money for the publication of the *Cactus* and the *Alcalde*, the student yearbook and alumni magazine.

"Representative Biggers asserted vigorously that he could not understand why a University which spent $24,000 a year for the support of a school of journalism should not be able to teach the students the intricacies of publishing a self-supporting newspaper and . . . he offered an amendment striking out the appropriation for the distribution of the Daily Texan to the many high schools throughout the state."

After heated debate, his motion was tabled by two votes, "narrowly averting the dispropriation of the Texan." The following day, Biggers objected to the university employing an expert in farm management "and said he had a Mexican back on his ranch who was far better qualified to fill the position than the present incumbent, who he failed to name."

In his late forties by this time, Don Biggers had clearly not mellowed with age. A photograph taken "about 1916" shows his tight jaw, his piercing eyes beneath a receding hairline, and only the faint suggestion of pleasure on his Irish face. Decades later different individuals would remember Biggers differently, but the descriptions have common elements. "Biggers was a small thin man, exceedingly hot-tempered," with "a deep sense of social justice," according to John Lee Smith. Another coeval said, "He was a red-faced, sandy-haired man who chewed tobacco veterately . . ." His son thought him "handsome, tall—five-eleven—straight, dark-complected, aristocratic-looking, with coal black hair and a fiery temper, very confident, very impatient," with many "chances to get rich if he'd look the other way, but he never did." Many such chances were yet to come, for Biggers was about to enter the decade of his fiercest crusades—against state prisons, the oil industry, the Ku Klux Klan, and the governor of Texas.

Biggers quit the legislature in favor of a friend who subsequently won election. He continued as a freelance writer in Lubbock until he decided to follow the oil boom to Eastland County, where he had grown up. In September 1918, he started the *Eastland Oil Belt News*, "Devoted to the Development of the Petroleum, Agricultural and Stockfarming Interests of Eastland and Adjoining Counties." Biggers had come to boost the oil industry and apparently collected a bonus of $2,500 from local citizens to help start publication.

The *Oil Belt News* advertised Eastland's civic achievements and praised the town's development as "one of the greatest transformations of any western town." The paper called for, and organized, a massive antilittering campaign, and the editor joined a commission to draft a city charter. Biggers also spoke up on behalf of Pancho Villa and against those who ridiculed their legislators. Without mentioning his own recent government service, Biggers reminded citizens that legislators made personal sacrifices to serve in Austin. "The legislature is nothing more than a reflection of the public that creates it. By this system of ridicule we have made it difficult to get good men in the legislature."

In a mild preview of his later campaigns, Biggers warned that "the fake oil scheme is abroad in the land, and countless thousands are rushing to the grist mill of graft and pouring their pennies into the slot." He called for better laws to protect against fraudulent promotion schemes. And he excoriated two Fort Worth papers, the *Record* and the *Star-Telegram*, for carrying oil scheme advertising "aggregating perhaps ten thousand dollars. Some of them apparently notoriously fakes . . ." Not yet ready to go further, Biggers related the oil boom to earlier booms in buffalo and cattle. Disqualifying himself from giving anyone advice, he admitted he had not been able to make his own farm of seven years support his family. All he concluded was that "the greatest place to make money and the greatest place to get skinned is right here in this oil field."

In the same issue that carried these remarks, Biggers printed the obituary of his son Dale. Twenty-five years old, Dale had died of an illness while serving in the U.S. Army along the Mexican border. Biggers' other four sons, serving in the army in France, all survived the First World War.

Perhaps Biggers took a cautious approach to oil swindles in 1918 because he was not yet sufficiently motivated to dig deeper. Or perhaps he did not wish to jeopardize his nest egg. Certainly the paper had proved financially successful beyond his expectations. He sold the *Oil Belt News* in July 1919 at a large profit. In the penultimate issue he edited, Biggers said it had been his policy not to carry oil stock or promotion ads. "We turned down lots of money by this policy, but we can look the public in the face when tear shedding time rolls around and truthfully say that we didn't cause their anguish nor contribute to it."

Biggers took a position as roving correspondent for the *Fort Worth Record*. His first assignment, a series on the prison system, appeared in 1919. From the start, Biggers made his bias plain. "The state penitentiary is by far the largest of our institutions marking and desig-nating our lack of civilization. So long as we have jails and state prisons we are not civilized . . ." Biggers analyzed the history and statistics—criminal and fiscal—of Texas prisons. He criticized "two bungled laws . . . the indeterminate sentence law and the parole law," as ill-conceived and unfair. But his harshest attack was on living conditions inside prison walls. "The greatest crime society is committing against its condemned members is tuberculosis, contracted after the victim has been placed in some jail or in the penitentiary."

He continued as a *Record* correspondent from Austin, where he wrote about the legislature. When the Eastland representative resigned his office, Biggers ran for the seat in a special election held February 21, 1920. He ran an offhand campaign, declaring, "I am not an aspirate for the office, but will do my best for the district if elected." He won the race and attended the third and fourth called sessions of the Thirty-Sixth Legislature in the summer and fall of 1920.

Meanwhile, in March 1920, Biggers began publishing the *Olden Advance*, a weekly, out of Olden, despite—or perhaps because—as he had reported in his *Oil Belt News*, "there is no more Olden, so far as official name is concerned. It is Nahoma now." That was the name given by the government when it put up a new post office there. Biggers reprinted a personal plug Hugh Nugent Fitzgerald, his *Fort Worth Record* editor, had run in the *Record*. "Politics has purified Don and he has elevated the political game to a high plane . . . He fights for his convictions, he pays as he goes, he keeps his word, he is loyal to friendship and he is one of the best haters in Texas."

Living up to the accolade, Biggers waged a relentless assault on Thomas L. Blanton, the congressional representative from the paper's district. Ignoring his own admonition about ridiculing legislators, Biggers referred to "Tongue Loose" or "Talk Lots" Blanton. He pressed the attack from the first issue. In May he offered Blanton $250 if he could get an affidavit from any member of Congress that he was a "truthful, honorable gentleman . . . and that his work has been valuable to the country."

Between legislative sessions that summer, Biggers wrote a strong investigative series for the *Ranger Record* about fraud in the Eastland oil fields. Each article was headed: "Something Is Wrong! Who Is To Blame? What Are You Going To Do About It?" On July 8 Biggers wrote, "This series of articles was interrupted some weeks ago because someone 'borrowed' our data." Such sabotage only made Biggers more determined. He implied lawyers, bondsmen, and local officials were in collusion with the swindlers.

In this busy, slightly schizophrenic year, Biggers made an odd decision, even for Biggers. Apparently enjoying his own legislative work, he announced his candidacy for commissioner of agriculture. A lifelong Democrat, Biggers ran on the Republican ticket with a promise, if elected, to abolish the office. The *Temple Mirror* approved Biggers' notion that "the department has outlived its usefulness and that the A&M college and the county agent system have supplanted it." The *Denison Herald,* while acknowledging that "Don Biggers is unique in some ways and acute in many ways," thought it "unreasonable to suppose" he would actually abolish the office. The *Austin American* concurred: "A very cheery and very companionable man is Biggers. He is as ugly as a mud hen, as sharp as a steel trap and no man bosses him . . ." but "offices are created every two years. Offices are never abolished."

When Biggers lost the election he returned to Eastland and threw himself into a thorough investigation of the oil field scandals as a partner in the weekly *Independent Oil News and Financial Reporter.* He angrily refused ads from fraudulent promoters and stubbornly stood up to their threats. His son remembered "plenty of trouble," including several physical fights. When threats of violence failed to stop Biggers, several promoters conspired to buy the paper secretly, using intermediaries to hide their purpose.

But Biggers helped federal agents prosecute the swindles his paper uncovered. Biggers later claimed to have "exposed a total of 126 fraudulent promotion schemes in Texas. Of these 96 were convicted in the federal courts." He furnished authorities with "thousands of letters" from swindled victims to help the prosecution. Then, based on "my experience and observations during that war of exposure," Biggers drafted a Blue Sky Law for Texas. Designed to protect citizens from "promotion schemes, stock gambling schemes and all kinds of schemes wherein leeches prey upon an ever gullible and always to be pitied public," the law was passed substantially as Biggers wrote it.

With the $11,000 he made from running his muckraking oil paper and the $23,000 he got for selling it, Biggers had done well by doing good. But he did not consider a vacation. Having whetted his crusader's appetite for social justice, Don Biggers set out to fight other fights. He soon found them.

In the Limelight

In his detailed history of the period, Norman Brown identifies "the three main issues in Texas politics from 1921 to 1928—the Ku Klux Klan, 'Fergusonism,' and Prohibition." Don Biggers went after all three. As he wrote later, "Having sold the oil paper, having nothing particular to do, I got out two issues of Anti Ku Klux Klan paper, the first newspaper assault on the Ku Klux in Texas." Typically, Biggers did not publish a single anti-Klan paper but several short-lived ventures. Defiantly he set up shop in Fort Worth, a Klan stronghold.

Klan influence in Texas peaked in 1922, with Klan candidates running for major state offices as well as the U.S. Senate. In January, Biggers issued the first number of *Life's ABC's*, which promised to be "Fair, Faithful, Fearless and Clean Withal." Biggers declared his aim "to assign to the limbo of oblivion the demagogues and other public enemies, and to seek to replace them with good men and true, and to help in some small way to remove the shackles of oppression from the wrists and ankles of Liberty." He sounded some familiar themes, protesting the harsh treatment of juvenile offenders at Gatesville Reform School under the title "Should We Beat Them to Death When They Are Young to Keep Them from Growing Up Bad?" He again reminded voters that "if the legislature is composed of intellectual nonentities, the public, famed for wanting something for nothing, is getting its money's worth—nothing for nothing. What does the public expect for five dollars per day anyhow?"

Biggers allowed Tom Arnold, his "General Manager," to write an effusive puff piece, "About the Editor," comparing Biggers to Mark Twain, Bret Harte, and W. C. Brann, among others. The Arnold profile listed Biggers' prominent friends and offered highlights of his journalistic and legislative careers, stressing his reputation for unbuyable honesty even among his opponents. In the second issue of *Life's ABC's*, Biggers took direct aim at the Klan. In an article belittling Klan wizard Edward Young Clarke, entitled "Ku Klux Kleagel Klarke Klucks Kold," Biggers attacked the KKK for "usurpation of government functions, by acts of lawlessness, by engendering hatred, prejudice and paving the way for serious trouble . . . Who the devil are you anyhow . . . that you are ashamed to show your faces?"

In March, *Bigger's Magazine* replaced *Life's ABC's*, but continued to denounce the "Invisible Empire of Wagon Sheets and Wet Ropes." He detailed three acts of illegal Klan violence. While "socialism is a fantasy; democracy as we are applying it is a joke . . . a tragedy." But "the voodoo spirit that lurks beneath the ghost shroud of a ku klux parade" would only lead civilization "into the exact center of an awful mess." What was the prescription to "remove the disease that is poisoning the social system"? Biggers said: "The church must be purged of hypocrites, politics must be cleansed of demagogues or the whole social fabric is doomed, but before these things can be accomplished the people must be educated to be the doctors."

The front page of the following issue featured a Biggers cartoon showing hooded Klansmen with tar, feathers, and a cross chasing "the bootlegger, gambler and chicken thief" around a racetrack while top-hatted fat cats ("oil crook," "beef trust," and utilities) watch with glee from the grandstand and a figure labeled "The Public" points to the Klan saying, "Get *them*. They are the ones that robbed me."

Inside, under a flubbed headline, "BE IT DISTINBTLY UNDERSTOOD," Biggers disavowed any affiliation with the Citizens League, recently formed in Fort Worth to oppose the Klan. "I am with any organization that is fighting the ku klux kraze of konglomeration to that extent at least, but I am by no means necessarily with it any farther." His monthly became *Biggers' Semi-Monthly* in June, with a "Ku Klux Klatter Special" issue. He also attacked evangelist friends of the KKK, including J. Frank Norris, asking, "Can The Christian Spirit be consecrated to cussedness?"

Klan members were not amused. Clyde Biggers remembered his father rushing to their Fort Worth home one day, ordering the family inside. Taking his gun to the porch, Don Biggers said "Some Ku Klux are going to come and run me out of town." Three cars drove up with "KKK" painted on their sides. When five men approached the porch, Biggers told them to get out. "I'll never change." According to his son, Biggers printed the incident in his paper. Biggers continued to issue anti-Klan papers well into 1924, including the *Square Deal* and the *Texas Tail Twister*, with his characteristic mix of ridicule and outrage.

During these Fort Worth years, Biggers began to use an expression that would appear with increasing frequency in his public writing and his private correspondence: "Barnum was right." The meaning of this enigmatic phrase became clear on those occasions when Biggers elaborated somewhat: "But Barnum was right. The American people like to be humbugged." The sentiment revealed Biggers' ambivalence about the democratic competence of the people. Though he often appealed to their judgment and tried to act on their behalf, he frequently doubted whether the "suckers" would ever wise up.

Late in 1924 Biggers accepted a commission to write a history of German colonization in Texas. Nettie and Don Biggers moved to Fredericksburg. Using courthouse records, several previous studies, and interviews with old-timers in the area, Don Biggers quickly produced a book. *German Pioneers in Texas*, "compiled for the Fredericksburger Wochenblatt and Fredericksburg Standard," appeared in 1925.

Biggers found much to admire in the struggles of the principled, industrious colonists. "No higher class citizenship ever immigrated into any country." Opposed to slavery, secession, and capital punishment, the Germans suffered violent persecution for these views during the Civil War. The worst single outrage committed against German settlers, known as the Nueces River massacre, occurred in July 1862 when thirty-five men who were trying to leave Texas rather than join the Confederate Army were overtaken and murdered, including nine who had surrendered. Biggers concluded that "Only great people could have endured what these people have endured, and have done what they have done . . ."

Also in 1925, Biggers helped expose a major scandal in the administration of Governor Miriam Ferguson. Defeated for the U.S. Senate in 1922, Jim Ferguson entered the race for governor in 1924 but was ruled ineligible by the State Supreme Court, based on the terms of his impeachment in 1917. His wife ran in his stead. Placing second in the first primary, Miriam Ferguson faced a runoff election with Felix Robertson, who had the support of the KKK. As Biggers wrote later, "It was strictly a Ku Klux and an anti-Ku Klux fight, with a majority of the voters not enthused over either candidate . . ."

When Miriam Ferguson won the election, her husband published a "Good Will Edition" of his paper, the *Forum*, featuring large ads from banks, newspapers, public utilities, and highway contracting and road machinery companies. "To a discerning person every one of those ads cried out loud: 'Influence for sale,' on the one hand, and 'we are buying influence,' on the other," wrote Biggers. The highway commissioners met in February 1925 to divide the state into districts. They invited Jim Ferguson to attend their meetings. "Contracts were awarded to men or firms who had never before built or maintained roads. . . . One thing they all had in common: they either were loyal Ferguson men or had advertised in the *Ferguson Forum*."

In July, Louis Wiltz Kemp, newly hired executive secretary of the Texas Highway and Municipal Contractors Association, learned about some of the corrupt activities of the State Highway Department. When he presented the charges to Jim Ferguson, the governor's husband accused Kemp of colluding with the Ku Klux Klan to discredit the Ferguson administration. Kemp then met with Attorney General Dan Moody, who filed an injunction to restrain contractors from using State Highway Department equipment on private contracting jobs. Ferguson attacked Kemp publicly, again accusing him of acting for the Klan. In August, Kemp was fired from his job. On August 19, Don Biggers wrote a letter to Louis Kemp: "Have been, and shall continue keeping up with your row with Ferguson. It seems to me that there are elements of real interest and front page stuff in this scrap . . . Where there is so much smoke there must be at least a few smoldering embers, and this little match may start a conflagration."

On August 26, Kemp, who saw himself as the scapegoat in the affair, began to publish mimeographed newsletters, called the *Goat Bleats*, which detailed the irregularities he had found in the state highway contracts. Kemp sent his information to newspapers around the state, but none of them would print it. As Kemp said later, "An odd situation existed in Texas. The State was being robbed of millions of dollars in broad daylight while the newspaper reporters helplessly looked on."

Don Biggers met with Louis Kemp in Austin on September 3. Biggers had persuaded R. T. Glidden, editor of the *Record-Courier*, a weekly paper in Johnson City, to run articles Biggers had written based on Kemp's information. Biggers promised that the paper would print any further information Kemp cared to furnish about the scandal, eliminating the need for *Goat Bleats*.

The *Record-Courier* began an exhaustive series on the highway scandal in its September 4 issue. Long articles by Biggers provided background on the cast of characters and the issues involved. Biggers also summarized material from Kemp's mimeographed circulars and provided cartoons, which usually ran on the front page. As Kemp collected more information, the *Record-Courier* ran it. The revelations quickly gained statewide notoriety. Under a Biggers cartoon labeled "An Executive Session of the Highway Commission," with Jim Ferguson wearing a woman's hat and pulling the commissioner's puppet strings, Biggers aggressively stated the paper's aim. "We don't know whether you like the policy of this paper or not. We hope you do; we don't care if you don't."

Biggers appealed for support and subscriptions to carry the scandal coverage forward. He noted that the *Fort Worth Star-Telegram* had requested some of the scandal material in order to run it. "We under-

stand the daily papers of the state have been threatened with the libel law. But we consider it a great compliment when a great daily
calls on a country weekly for inside 'dope.'"

The subscription drive for the *Record-Courier* succeeded too well.
Requests for the newspaper came in by the hundreds. Biggers later
wrote that "some fifteen persons made a donation of approximately
$100. This money was used to send the Record-Courier to every
county judge in Texas, to many commissioners, to all members of
the house and senate . . . to effectively reach the right people . . ."
The paper's suddenly burgeoning circulation threatened its very
existence. The local advertising that sustained the *Record-Courier*
could not meet the costs of printing so many additional copies and
mailing them to distant subscribers. Those advertisers wanted to
sponsor local news, of no interest to readers in other counties. But if
the paper "attempted to convert to a state-wide journal, it would
lose its local patronage and probably die a quick death after the campaign was over."

Biggers tried to solicit financial support from various sources.
Replying to his appeal, former Governor Oscar B. Colquitt told Biggers that "as my experience has taught me, the man who fights graft
and corruption in high places usually has to do it at his own cost."
Colquitt advised Biggers to try selling the scandal material to papers
outside Texas in order to cover expenses. Biggers had another idea.
He started his own paper, the *Limelight*, to supply all *Record-
Courier* subscribers outside Blanco County with continuing news of
the highway scandals.

Before the *Limelight* began publication early in 1926, Biggers attacked the "Daily Press Vultures" who had come lately to the highway scandal story. In the November 27 *Record-Courier*, Biggers
noted that "today every daily in Texas blares flaring headlines and
reeks with tommyrot editorials" about the crisis. But three months
earlier, when Louis Kemp was struggling to get his story out, those
same papers "were shying around and entirely away from Kemp's
stuff. They were afraid of the libel laws, they were afraid of public
sentiment, and they were afraid of everything including their own
shadows." Biggers blamed this reticence on the fact that "the daily
papers of Texas are owned by corporations and edited by nonentities."

Published weekly in Fredericksburg, the *Limelight* continued to
reveal more details of highway corruption. Two highway commissioners were forced to resign and one contractor was indicted for perjury and swindling, but talk of impeaching Miriam Ferguson never
led to action. Early in 1926, it became clear that the governor, de-

spite her pledge to serve a single term, was preparing to run for re-election. Attorney General Dan Moody, capitalizing on his publicity for the highway investigations, became the favorite of the anti-Ferguson forces, including Don Biggers.

Biggers used his new platform to continue scolding the major Texas dailies. Reprinting one of his tirades against the press, the *Hamilton Record-Herald* called Biggers "An American Matador." The editors ran the Biggers column because, "along with a lot of 'bunk,' it contains some real food for thought. Read it and weep." Biggers singled out the *Houston Chronicle* for particular scorn. "Long after the highway stench had made every decent person sick, the Houston Chronicle still defended Jim. It stayed with Jim when it should have helped the public. It did not quit Jim until it couldn't help the public."

Biggers slammed "Jesse Jones, who ostensibly owns the Chronicle, who isn't anything of a writer but a forceful dictator, and who is one of the big bugs in the oil game . . ." Biggers said no Texas daily had ever criticized oil or any other corporations because "the daily paper is nothing more than a reflex of, and an absolutely dominated part of, our industrial machinery," with profit its only aim. He deplored the "news columns . . . filled with nauseating filth and boosting bombast, its editorial columns with senseless twaddle and its special departments with stereotyped nonsense." Biggers concluded that the dailies were not likely to change, though the people should not stand for it. "The daily paper and the congressional record are the two greatest reflexes of bunk in the world. And the person that takes either seriously is beyond the pale of mental repair."

Through the primary season, Biggers hammered at the Ferguson administration in the *Limelight*. Despite his relentless campaign, Biggers could not help expressing a certain admiration for Jim Ferguson as a political survivor. While calling him "The Forlorn Victim of His Own Folly," Biggers also thought "no one person ever possessed more courage and tenacity" than Jim Ferguson. His fascination with Ferguson would lead Biggers to write a book-length satirical review of Ferguson's political career in 1933. But when the primaries ended, with Moody the clear front-runner, Biggers abandoned his crusade and sold the *Limelight*.

The Slimy Trail of Petroleum

Don Biggers remained active in state and national politics—as critic, candidate, and gadfly—for the next decade. As always, he found time for extracurricular writing in many sorts of journals. In

1926 Biggers published an article attacking "J. Frank Norris—Salvation Specialist." Calling Norris a "Baptist, Fundamentalist, real estate dealer, 'last will and testament expert,' oil scheme booster, politician," and "sensationalist," Biggers explained how Norris beat an indictment of arson for burning his own church. He also accused Norris of swindling an Arlington printer who had gone into debt to produce several issues of the *Searchlight*, for which Norris never paid. He noted that "Norris singled out the Pope of Rome as the blight of the world" and allowed the Ku Klux Klan to use his First Baptist Church of Fort Worth "for political and spiritual purposes."

Biggers explained how Norris had alienated his fellow Baptists with attacks on Baptist institutions and attempts to seize power. He detailed the Norris method of making unproved accusations and using his personal notoriety to overwhelm opponents in the church, the press, and the community. Biggers concluded that Norris and others of his stripe "owe their wealth to the fact that Barnum was right."

In September 1927, Don Biggers announced his entry into the Democratic primary race for the United States Senate. As newspapers across Texas reported, the character of the announcement, like that of the candidate, was "unique, forceful and 'altogether different.'" Biggers declared, "I do not choose to be elected, do not expect to be elected, and could hardly hope to accomplish anything should I be elected." With such low expectations, Biggers figured he was "the only candidate for the office who can go before the people, say what I think just as I see it, and have no fear of the consequences."

His campaign was "based on opposition to all forms of legalized gambling in farm products by boards of trade and exchange." Biggers said he intended to get rid of market manipulators so that "supply and demand will be about the only law needed on the subject of farm relief. Co-operatives and common sense methods can then function." He said he would not need a campaign manager or headquarters and would not seek any donations. "My present plan is to . . . make about fifty speeches, distribute several thousand pamphlets giving a brief but sufficiently complete history of cotton and grain gambling in the United States, and then come home and go fishing."

Biggers offered to support incumbent Senator Earle Mayfield for reelection if Mayfield would agree to speak out against cotton and commodity speculation. But Mayfield replied noncommittally. Mayfield had won election with Klan support in 1922 at the height of Klan influence. The drastic diminution of that influence, combined with Mayfield's lackluster performance in office, left him vulnerable to defeat. Five candidates opposed him in the primaries, hoping to get enough votes to challenge Mayfield in a runoff.

One of the aspirants for Mayfield's Senate seat was U.S. Representative Tom Connally. Connally announced in January 1928 and began a long campaign, attacking Mayfield's Klan background. Biggers declared his own withdrawal from the race in favor of Tom Connally. Connally finished second to Mayfield in the first primary vote, forcing a runoff.

Jim Ferguson, though he had lost to Mayfield in the 1922 contest, now decided to support him. As Biggers put it, "Ferguson didn't support Mayfield enthusiastically, but he abused Connally most uproariously." Ferguson's support proved disastrous to Mayfield, thanks largely to the efforts of Don Biggers. Biggers "was the one who put Senator Mayfield in a most embarrassing situation in regard to a hotel room conference between Mayfield, Ferguson and Mayfield's friend."

"Mayfield's friend" was A. P. Barrett, of the Louisiana Light and Power Company, one of Mayfield's largest campaign contributors. The three men met in Barrett's hotel room, room 428 of the Stephen F. Austin Hotel, in Austin. As Tom Connally wrote in his memoirs, "The obvious assumption was that the three men had concluded a financial deal regarding the election." Connally did not mention Biggers by name in his autobiography, calling him "our mutual friend." " . . . I had our mutual friend come to my headquarters . . . and make an affidavit of what he had learned at the Austin hotel." "Room 428!" became the battle cry of the Connally campaign. Connally told a crowd in San Antonio that "Ferguson and the power magnate and Earle are all in the same bed, and it's a single bed at that."

Connally beat Mayfield in the runoff by more than sixty thousand votes. John Lee Smith later recalled that Biggers "was able to write a good part of Connally's campaign literature . . . which helped with Connally's election." Connally told Clyde Biggers, "I could never give Don anything." Biggers apparently refused Connally's offers of jobs as postmaster and sheriff. Tom Connally was grateful to Biggers but wary of this man of oddly variable means who passed up offers of patronage. Connally's career and writings reveal a straightforward, pragmatic politician, ill-equipped to fathom the complexity, the irony, and the absolute need for independence that characterized Don Biggers.

Throughout Connally's four terms in the United States Senate, he maintained an odd epistolary relationship with Biggers. He replied soothingly to whatever issues might have provoked Biggers to write,

though he often failed to understand what Biggers was driving at. He
sent Biggers birthday gifts or money every year. Biggers passed these
donations along to others and reported this to Connally, who sent
more the following year as if trying to repay a debt Biggers did not
even acknowledge existed.

"But there were other complications in the good year 1928,"
Biggers wrote. The nomination of New York Governor Al Smith, a
Catholic and a "wet," as the Democratic presidential candidate
deeply divided the party in Texas. Large Prohibition and anti-
Catholic factions bolted the Democratic party in favor of Herbert
Hoover, the Republican candidate. Biggers was among these
"Hoovercrats."

He estimated that "we Democrats who are for Hoover are about
30 per cent wrong, but that is 30 per cent better than if we were for
Smith . . . I am trying to salvage at least 30 per cent of my self-
respect, vested rights and political independence." But such talk of
percentages must have seemed small comfort to Biggers, who was
now in league with some of those whom he most despised, including Prohibition activist J. B. Cranfill. With Republican funds, Cranfill printed five hundred thousand copies of his weekly *Southern Advocate;* he showed Democrats how to split their ticket and vote
Republican for Hoover but Democratic for all other candidates.
J. Frank Norris campaigned vigorously against Smith because of his
Catholicism, invoking the specters of "foreign control," destruction
of religious freedom, and the persecution of the Dark Ages in his
emotional tirades.

Perhaps his loathing of such political allies contributed to Biggers'
foul mood when he attended the Democratic National Convention
in Houston. In the lobby of the Rice Hotel, Biggers got into a fist-
fight with a New York delegate who made a "slurring remark about
Texas." Biggers knocked the man down and had to be restrained and
hustled away by several of his friends.

Biggers rejected the "blind bridle Democracy" that produced
Smith's presidential nomination, but he lost his tenuous affinity for
Hoover shortly after the election. Biggers experienced a similar dis-
enchantment with Governor Dan Moody. Since riding Louis Kemp's
highway scandals into office, Moody had revealed himself to Biggers
as a tool of corporate interests, particularly the oil industry.

By 1928 Biggers had embarked on his most ambitious project, a
book-length exposé of the oil industry, from the first discovery of oil
to the present day. He called his study "The Slimy Trail of Petroleum." Biggers concentrated his attack on the Standard Oil Company and recent events in Texas. He issued one chapter in 1928 as a

separate circular entitled *University Oil Land Scandal*, but it failed to make any money. Nervous about the safety of "The Slimy Trail"—and that of its author—he gave the manuscript to a friend for safe-keeping. Unable to pay for publication, Biggers ran the book as a serial in 1930, a chapter a week in the *Record*, his own newspaper. Biggers had started the *Record* specifically to oppose the ambitions of Moody's would-be successor, Ross Sterling.

"There was plenty of jockeying, confabbing and conferring all during 1929, preparatory to the gubernatorial campaign of 1930," Biggers wrote. Moody wanted a third term, but the "interests and elements" who backed him decided on Sterling. A successful lumberman, banker, and oilman, Sterling had helped organize Humble Oil.

With the discovery of the great East Texas field, oil glutted the world market, driving prices down as low as ten cents a barrel. As one Humble Oil executive said later, "We had to let a president of Humble quit to become governor to establish proration (production control)." Sterling acted to protect the larger companies against the onslaught of free enterprise. Biggers thought that "As a citizen Sterling was above an average; as a business man he had his limitations; as a statesman he fell below zero."

Biggers published the first issue of the *Record* in Austin on February 20, 1930, "Not Trying to Keep Any Politician's Record Straight, but Showing How Crooked Most of Them Are." Biggers declared that "our mission is not to destroy, except to the extent that it is necessary to clear away rubbish, and expose rotteness to make room for a better, more beautiful and substantial structure." He ran stories and cartoons about the legislature and introduced the first installment of "The Slimy Trail of Petroleum, . . . the romantic, the tragic, the heroism and rascality of one of the world's most important commercial products." Discussing the race for governor, Biggers said that "So Far Only Ferguson and Mayfield Have Said Anything Worth Reading or Hearing."

Concentrating his venom on Sterling and Moody and the oil interests they represented, Biggers once again found himself in the awkward position of supporting the Mayfield and Ferguson forces by default. "We Are All Working for Corporations," said one anti-Moody Biggers headline, "but Most of Us Are on the Wrong Side of the Payroll." Biggers agreed with the *Ferguson Forum* that "The evil of prohibition discussion is that it invariably sidetracks every other question and passion . . . Just now the question of getting something to eat and wear is far more important than a row over something to drink." He ran a front-page cartoon labeled "Same Old Tune, Same

Old Artist" showing "Big Business" as an organ grinder, cranking out "Bunk" and more "Bunk" on an instrument labeled "Daily Press," with five monkeys—"corporation lawyer," "state legislator," and other elected officials—assaulting the pockets of a stunned "G.P." (general public).

Biggers used the *Record* to criticize the political coverage of the major Texas dailies, including the *Dallas Morning News,* the *San Antonio Express,* and the *Houston Chronicle.* "As an economic proposition, I don't see how these dailies can print so little news for so much money, even at five cents per copy . . ." He saved a special sneer for the *Houston Post-Dispatch,* "Sterling's official organ and expensive plaything," which "certainly pulls some amusing bunk and inconsistencies, or thinly veiled confessions, in its editorial stupidity."

Biggers endorsed ex-Klansman Earle Mayfield for governor, but Sterling faced Miriam Ferguson in the runoff election. Moody supported Sterling as expected, while Biggers, backed into a corner, reluctantly came out for the Fergusons. When Sterling finally won the governorship, Biggers stopped publishing the *Record* and left Austin in disgust.

From Lampasas, where he moved in 1931, Biggers waged an unsuccessful race for congressman-at-large. Then he moved to Stephenville, where he operated a print shop. Still vigorously opposed to Ross Sterling, Biggers gave his lukewarm support to the Fergusons' attempt to stop Sterling's reelection in 1932, an effort that led to Miriam Ferguson's second term as governor. From Stephenville, in 1933, Biggers published several issues of the *Bombardier,* "A Monthly Magazine Devoted to Frank Discussion of Public Questions."

"It is not our dream, scheme nor plan to reform or revolutionize, but to give you facts that you do not get from corporation controlled publications, particularly the daily press . . ." Biggers denied that he had any "pet political theories, nor pets of any other kind . . ." He attacked the public utilities, including the Southwest Gas Company and Texas Light and Power. "Old Commodore Vanderbilt, daddy of the American system and methods of big business, was credited with the statement: 'The Public be damned.' His public utility offspring still adhere to the parent's creed."

By June the *Bombardier* had run out of steam and money. "Now It's Up to You," Biggers told his readers. About his monthly Biggers wrote, "We didn't expect to make any money out of it. Neither do we propose to continue it indefinitely as an expensive pasttime. If you want the paper pay for it . . ." But his now frequent repetition that

"Barnum was right" indicated Biggers expected no popular uprising to halt the abuses of the utilities, the dailies, or the politicians. He suspended the *Bombardier* and devoted his energies to the August publication of his book about the career of Jim Ferguson.

Our Sacred Monkeys, or 20 Years of Jim and Other Jams (Mostly Jim), the Outstanding Goat Gland Specialist of Texas Politics, promised "A Thousand Chuckles and a Thousand Facts, Showing the Amusing Humbuggery of the Whole Business, Particularly Since Jim Broke into the Game in 1914." Biggers began with a quick survey of Texas political figures in a forced attempt at lightheartedness. "Come, folks, let us take a look at the monkeys. We will not have to go to the zoo. We will just get a hand-mirror and pass it around.

"Some races of people have sacred elephants, some have sacred cows, and others have sacred chickens. In this country we have sacred monkeys, but we call them political leaders.

"And we send missionaries to the countries where they have sacred elephants and sacred cows and sacred chickens to tell the heathens of those countries about our wonderful civilization and great achievements."

As Biggers detailed the life and fortunes of Jim Ferguson, the satire turned bitter. Essentially faithful to the facts, Biggers rendered the main points of Ferguson's life in a disparaging, sarcastic tone. But shining through the scorn was a grudging admiration for Ferguson's ability to survive as a political power. In the end, Biggers muted his condemnation of Ferguson. "Jim is our greatest political comedian. He is good for laugh stuff only. He doesn't belong in the heavy villain parts . . ." In an atmosphere of high political crimes, of "graft, waste and infamy" with regard to land fraud and abuses of natural resources, "Jim Ferguson [is] guilty of nothing more than a misdemeanor in any case, and for the most part [is] innocent, or at least not guilty on every count." Biggers, the Barnum disciple, placed more blame on "the people, the victims of these grafts, penalized for permitting themselves to be grafted."

In the vague conclusion to his curious look at Fergusonism, Biggers promised a more scathing look at the real culprits of political crimes. That promise went unfulfilled. Biggers' confusing tone of voice resulted from his failure to resolve his own ambivalence about the meaning of Jim Ferguson's career. Ferguson may have betrayed his supporters, embraced hypocritical positions, and forged alliances with those he had previously denounced. But Biggers understood Ferguson's motives. He had committed similar sins. In several political and editorial campaigns, Biggers had sacrificed his own principles to expedience. Despite his vigorous condemnation of the Ku

Klux Klan, Biggers had backed former Klansman Earle Mayfield for senator and governor. He had made common cause with Prohibitionists and the Catholic-hating J. Frank Norris against the national Democratic ticket. And despite his outrage at the highway scandals of the mid 1920s, Biggers had turned against Dan Moody, who policed that corruption, to support the Fergusons, who had permitted it. Don Biggers had charted his own course through the thicket of Texas politics, but it was a way few others could follow.

Do Not Go Gentle

Though he had favored the election of Herbert Hoover in 1928, Biggers soon denounced the Republican administration and backed Roosevelt. In 1937, after Roosevelt's reelection, Biggers wrote an unpublished book manuscript, "Our Twelve Billion Dollar Juggernaut," denouncing New Deal bureaucracy. In 1936, he ran for the state legislature as the representative for Hood and Erath counties. Instead of his usual satirical campaign style, Biggers made a sincere effort. He traveled extensively, made speeches, received endorsements from prominent individuals, and circulated posters. He promised to consolidate commissions to save money and to raise taxes on oil, sulfur, coal, and other "exploited resources." "I have just two words in my platform: Common Sense. I make to the people but one pledge: If elected I'll use common sense, no matter what proposition comes before the legislature." It was the hardest race he had ever run, but Biggers lost the election, his final attempt to gain public office.

Biggers published a single issue of the *Passing Show*, a periodical dedicated to denouncing the state's plan for an expensive celebration of the Texas Centennial. He called the "Centennial 'Racket' a Reckless Waste of Public Funds." Biggers wrote to members of the Centennial Committee, including J. Frank Dobie, writer, folklorist, and faculty member at the University of Texas. At the height of Centennial fever in 1937, he told Dobie he was "sick to death of everything connected to the Centennial." Dobie replied in conciliatory tones and continued to receive letters from Biggers on various subjects for many years.

In 1939, Don and Nettie Biggers moved from the small community of Fischer's Store to El Paso. Biggers apparently left town after a fierce argument over a traffic accident with a deputy sheriff, who swore out a warrant charging Biggers with disturbing the peace. Their children helped Nettie and Don buy a house in suburban El

Paso. At seventy, the Biggers were broke and Don was in poor health. "I am a constant sufferer from hernia and have no money for an operation," he wrote one old friend from El Paso. "For some months I have been sorely troubled with a sore on my left cheek. I have no money to pay for treatment and probably wouldn't so waste it if I did have. I have about decided that my erasure would wipe another naught off the blackboard of life."

Biggers was down but not out. His health improved enough to take advantage of the automobile the Biggers children bought their parents. "Dad always had an itchy foot," in the words of Clyde Biggers. "Him and mother never seemed to be happier than when it came time to pile into the car and take off for greener pastures, make new friends or renew acquaintance with old ones." Don had never learned to drive. Nettie was the pilot for the couple's numerous extended drives. They roamed as far as California but spent most of their time driving around Texas, visiting family and friends or renting homes and apartments for short periods. Nettie put most of her energy into painting. An amateur painter much of her adult life, Nettie had exhibited her landscapes in galleries and shows. Don kept busy writing about current affairs.

He was no longer able to issue his views in his own publications. Instead he wrote letters by the hundreds—to politicians, old friends, and journalists. As he wrote one friend, "I know the west, the land swindles, the booms and the busts. But I don't feel like writing it." Many of Biggers' comments on various issues appeared in Letters to the Editor columns of newspapers, large and small, throughout Texas. He maintained contact with friends of his youth and with politicians he had known personally, such as Senator Tom Connally. But Biggers did not hesitate to offer unsolicited opinions to influential strangers.

The letters revealed his continuing interest in public questions at all levels, from small-town gossip to the thorniest international problems. Biggers subscribed to *In Fact*, a crusading newsletter begun by George Seldes in 1940 to criticize the press. He wrote governors and senators, past and present, including Dan Moody, Morris Sheppard, and Ralph Yarborough. He offered advice to Homer Rainey, president of the University of Texas.

Biggers thought W. Lee O'Daniel, who won the race for governor of Texas in 1938, to be "the most pussillanimous political swindle of the age, and his supporters the most monumental ignoramuses and simpletons that have ever given proof of their incapacity, and his financial backers the most infamous and corrupt bunch . . ." In another letter he referred to O'Daniel as "O'Donkey," a "four flushing flour fakir" who had "surrendered himself to the influence and control of powerful and corrupt agencies."

In 1938 Texas Congressman Martin Dies was named chairman of the House Committee on Un-American Activities. The goal of the committee was to find out about communist and fascist activities in the United States. But some people, including Don Biggers, thought Dies and his committee were a greater threat to America than the subversives they sought. Biggers sent some damaging information about Martin Dies to Washington syndicated columnist Drew Pearson. Pearson was grateful. He wrote Biggers, "If you have any other dope on Dies, we would like to have it . . . Rest assured your letters are read with great interest."

Occasionally some event would move Biggers to break briefly back into publication. When the Truman administration offered postwar aid to Greece and Turkey in the late 1940s, a furious Biggers printed a one-page satirical flyer titled "The Pigtown Purifier." Biggers saw Truman's $400 million aid offer as "a corruption bribe to a gang of crooks in Greece and Turkey" and a "fascist fraud."

"The purpose of this 'aid' bribe is to landlock Russia, and stop Russian commerce, not Communism. Why lie about it except for Big Business reasons?" Biggers announced he was not going to worry about anything, though he thought that the "UN" stood for "Unlimited Nonsense." Biggers also admitted after all that he was not Barnum, just one of the crowd. "I have a Fellow Feeling for all Suckers. I'm One of Them, Too."

Biggers reserved much of his comment on national and world affairs for his letters to Tom Connally. Their delicate relationship, based on the unspoken sense of Connally's obligation, seemed to bestow a special license on the already unbridled pen of Don Biggers. On August 1, 1950, with American troops already in Korea on behalf of the United Nations, Biggers wrote Connally. He said he lacked faith in the United Nations, since "any organization that seeks to compel, rather than influence, is doomed to failure.

"If the world, and the fullness thereof, was made in six days, with one day for preparing the way for Sunday law violations, it was entirely too much of a rush job, resulting in more imperfection than perfection. If the first man was made of clay the wrong material was used, since man has, with rare exceptions, developed into a storm of mental dirt. But out of this dirt great fruits may yet grow. Fraternally and sincerely . . ."

Four days later Biggers sent Connally another long letter. He described the charitable uses to which he had put several of Connally's gifts of money. He told a story of some unemployed young people he had met, and concluded it would be better to give young men "work right here at home" instead of employing them in foreign countries with deadly weapons. "Meanwhile booming implements of death in Korea drown the wise warning of Washington. 'Avoid entangling alliances.'"

Before August ended, Biggers wrote Connally yet another letter. In this one Biggers told a sarcastic tale of how the Korean War had started. A U.S. church missionary in Korea "(denomination immaterial)" told stories of the American Revolution, the Declaration of Independence, and the fight for freedom at Valley Forge, inspiring the Korean people to fight for their own freedom. But Biggers' third letter crossed a reply from Connally in the mail.

Calling Biggers' second letter "full of wisdom and good sense," Connally wrote, "Your observations regarding Korea and the sacrifices which American boys and American people pay are timely and to the point. Be assured that I am doing whatever I can to bring about . . . a triumph for our army. I am always glad to hear from you." Whether or not Connally truly misunderstood Biggers, his response illuminates their odd, wary relationship.

Later that autumn, Biggers wrote a friend that he doubted "there ever will be a real reform at the ballot box; too many filth nurtured juvenile minds in the heads of adults . . . I pity the heedless, brainless herd, but damn those who deceive, betray and abuse them." In 1953 he wrote a similar letter to Dobie, in which he said, "Oliver Goldsmith and Barnum were both right. And while the country perishes congress piddles, and the people absorb poisonous propaganda, indifferent to and ignorant of the doom that looms by reason of impoverished and vanishing soils and water shortage."

Dobie wrote back telling Biggers to "Cheer up!" But Biggers had fought too long and lost too many battles to throw off his mood of cynical despair. Even his victories seemed short-term, as those saved from oil fraud promptly fell victim to land swindles and crooked politicians gave way to officials who simply served the corporations. The many publications he had issued all died. The many guises he had taken on—Billy Goat, Josher, Coyote, Bombardier—had all fallen away. He had changed locations and causes and political allegiances too often to have any but distant admirers. And even the faraway friends misunderstood his irony and feared his temper.

In 1955 Nettie Biggers had to be hospitalized in Houston. Upon her release, Nettie and Don moved in with their son Earl in Aransas

Pass. Nettie longed to return to the Texas Hill Country, where she had spent fond summers sketching and painting. The elderly couple lived in several rented homes there until 1957. On a visit back to Aransas Pass, on November 16, Nettie Lee Biggers died. Don Biggers joined her on December 11, 1957. His fight was finished.

3. A Rational Radical

We do not have a great deal of sympathy for those good folks
who think things are in an awful mess but they don't know
what to do about it. Some go so far as to say that you can't
do anything about it, which to us is a deadly heresy.

—*John C. Granbery*

When John Granbery started his monthly magazine, the
Emancipator, in 1938, he was sixty-three years old.
Journalism became his final refuge. Granbery had been
forced out of earlier careers as a Methodist pastor and a college professor. His outspoken, radical views clashed with the prevailing or-
thodoxies of the religious and academic institutions for which he
worked.

"To only a very limited extent are we free to choose our own
course," he wrote in the *Emancipator*'s first issue. "When one door
is closed to us, another opens. It may not be what we wanted, but
we must make the best of it. I love to preach, but one must have a
pulpit. I love to teach, but one must have a 'chair.'" Granbery would
continue to preach and teach in the *Emancipator* to the end of
his life.

Unique among iconoclastic journalists, Granbery was a trained
scholar with several advanced degrees, including a doctorate in philosophy from the University of Chicago. A student of ancient and
modern civilizations, Granbery wrote a college history text. He
traveled in Europe, the Middle East, and Latin America and knew at
least nine foreign languages. Ironically, he ventured into journalism
to lobby for international understanding as the world was falling
apart.

Granbery was fated to preach tolerance in one of the least tolerant
periods of the twentieth century—during the fascist domination of
Europe, the Second World War, and the American red scares of the
late 1940s and early 1950s. He fought against xenophobia, racism,
bigotry, censorship, and the unreasoning fear that produced them.
His calm voice provided a rational counterpoint to the shrill accusations and atrocities shouting from newspaper headlines.

Granbery's activism was more than editorial. He was a chronic
joiner and organizer for causes he advocated. He constantly empha-

The Rev. Dr. John C. Granbery, Jr., in his forties, at
about the time of his service in the First World War.
(Courtesy of Eugene C. Barker Texas History Center,
University of Texas at Austin.)

A Swastika Flies at Southwestern

It is a real swastika shown above and Saturday it adorned the once-peaceful main building at Southwestern university at Georgetown. Saluting the mysteriously-placed banner in true der fuehrer style are a group of leading Southwestern students. Among them are Don Scarbrough, second from left, editor of the Megaphone, student publication; Norman Stafford, fourth from left, business manager of the South-

western U. magazine; and Dor Mann, fifth from left, president of the student body.

The students are saluting the emblem in fun, but university officials sensed an undercurrent of feeling about the dismissal of Dr. John C. Granberry from the faculty, as the reason for the flag. Dr. Granberry, head of the departments of philosophy and sociology, has been identified at times with the socialist movement.

Students salute a swastika, protesting Granbery's firing
from Southwestern University, May 22, 1938.
(*Austin American-Statesman* photo, courtesy of Eugene C. Barker
Texas History Center, University of Texas at Austin.)

sized the necessity for like-minded individuals to work together to ameliorate social ills. In the "Emancipator Fellowship," a regular feature of his magazine, Granbery offered a forum for the exchange of ideas and addresses among progressive thinkers worldwide.

Long before he began the *Emancipator*, Granbery had played an active role in state and local politics. He wrote frequently about the need for equality and served for years on the Commission on Interracial Cooperation. He did not hesitate to address his concerns directly to individuals involved in making policy, from the president and the governor to local officials.

His social and political activism arose directly from his deeply abiding Christian faith. Granbery's father, a Methodist bishop, exercised a profound influence on the future crusader for human rights. Granbery later remembered that in the sermons he heard as a youth, including those of his father, "the emphasis was seldom on doctrine as such but nearly always on religious experience. From the days of Wesley, we were told, Methodists did not insist on specific doctrines but founded their movement on experience."

From this early commitment to Christian activism, strengthened by seminary studies at Vanderbilt and graduate work at Chicago, Granbery never wavered. He would expend much ink and energy in the *Emancipator* defining his beliefs. He tried to get at the truth of issues and individuals beyond the facile labels, name-calling, and hair-splitting that distracted and dissipated the forces of change. Granbery preached inclusion, not exclusion. He rejected communism but reached out to communists and atheists who sincerely desired social justice. He defended Christian belief but denounced Christians who practiced intolerance.

Granbery endured constant criticism from many of the factions he hoped to unite. He noted that fundamentalists disliked his interest in Social Security and other liberal matters, while leftists complained "because we believe in religion as a vital power in individual and social life, and because we do not utterly condemn the church." Granbery thought his own position could not be adequately described by terms such as *liberal* or *progressive*.

My favorite explanation of my own philosophy is . . . the word *radical* . . . I am not a reformer . . . I want to go the whole way. Half-way measures, superficial remedies, compromises, do not appeal to me. This position is forced upon me by acceptance of Christian philosophy. Now is the axe laid at the root of the tree. Ye must be born again. Seek ye first the Kingdom of God. No man can serve two masters. Ye cannot serve God and mammon.

If any man be in Christ, he is a new creature. Old things are passed away. Behold all things are become new. What communion hath light with darkness? I saw a new heaven and a new earth. Here are absolutes. There are no compromises, no qualifications, no exceptions.

Granbery did not believe radicalism necessarily signified a position to the political left or right. He acknowledged his own causes were often on the left, but noted that "extremes of Left and Right tend to meet," as the pact between the totalitarian governments of Hitler and Stalin illustrated. "If the radical point of view lands me far to the Left, I can take it. On the other hand, I can think of two instances in which it throws me with the conservatives." He was referring to his "old-fashioned belief" in monogamous marriage, with a single standard of morality for both sexes, and his opposition to the consumption and sale of alcohol.

Academic freedom was a cause dear to John Granbery's heart, an understandable concern for a man fired from two Texas universities. Granbery campaigned vigorously for the rights of independent voices on college faculties, especially on behalf of Homer Rainey, who was fired from the presidency of the University of Texas during purges of state institutions in the 1940s. He exhorted Christians, especially the Methodists, to lead efforts on behalf of minorities, the poor, and the dispossessed. He deplored the false Christianity of those who used religion to justify their own aggrandizement.

Granbery eschewed the easy answers, so popular with demagogues of the 1930s and 1940s. Before America entered the Second World War, Granbery cautioned that the country must avoid the reactionary aftermath of the First World War. He despised Hitler but was more worried about Hitlerism at home, the fascist, anti-Semitic tendencies in our own country, our own hearts. During the war he reminded his readers and his radio listeners that we were fighting totalitarianism, not the German or Japanese peoples, with whom we shared a common humanity.

He fought for full equality for women and for blacks. He promoted international cooperation, with particular emphasis on Mexicans, Mexican-Americans, and others in our own hemisphere. He encouraged farmers and laborers to organize in order to secure economic justice. A dedicated internationalist, he lobbied for a strong United Nations to preserve world harmony and prevent war. He criticized the jingoistic press, which served entrenched interests instead of the people. He attacked incompetent, insincere, and dishonest politicians at all levels of government, often confronting them directly by letter and printing their replies—or noting their evasions—in the pages of the *Emancipator*.

During the anticommunist fervor of the late 1940s and the reign of McCarthyism in the 1950s, Granbery preached against paranoia. "We are distressed to find open-minded, intelligent, progressive thinkers in terror lest someone call them 'Communists.' . . . If The Emancipator were unduly disturbed whenever it is called 'Communist,' our lot would indeed be an unhappy one." Granbery's political stands did not go unnoticed. The Minute Women, a right-wing anticommunist watchdog organization headquartered in Houston, included Granbery's name on a list of two hundred Texans "known to be 'brazenly' associated with subversives."

Granbery's equanimity never turned to despair, despite the many threats to the freedoms for which he fought. He remained steadfast in his belief that "our primary problem is to think the thing thru; then it is up to us in an imperfect world to take the most effective steps possible toward realizing as much of the ideal as conditions admit." Granbery did not feel "called upon to support the status quo, and [was] sure that a dynamic civilization must have doors wide open for change, new ideas, experimentation."

When Granbery died at seventy-eight in 1953, writer and university professor J. Frank Dobie said of him, "I haven't known many nonconformists who remained so serene and reasonable." The editor of the *State Observer* said, "Dr. Granbery's life was one of perpetual warfare, despite the fact that he was a man who had an overwhelming love and desire for true peace." Granbery's faith in his beliefs enabled him to tolerate many points of view except those that sought to limit, on any basis, the rights of others. Though his writing displayed anger as well as wit, Granbery never violated his own principles. He was a man and a journalist who practiced what he preached.

Heeding the Call

John Cowper Granbery, Jr., was born June 15, 1874, in Richmond, Virginia, where his father served as pastor of the Methodist Broad Street Church. The next year, the elder Granbery accepted a position at the newly founded Vanderbilt University in Nashville, Tennessee, to teach philosophy and theology. John and his five older sisters lived in Nashville until their father was elected bishop in 1882.

Late in his life, John Granbery called his father "the most modest, unselfish, pure-minded, and saintly man I have ever known." The parallels between the lives of father and son prove the sincerity of his admiration. In 1848, the year he graduated from Randolph-Macon College at nineteen, the elder Granbery engaged in a public debate with the president of the college about the slavery question. Despite his Virginia upbringing, the young man argued in favor of abolition.

Though opposed to slavery and to war, he joined the Confederate Army as a chaplain. Wounded, the future bishop lost an eye and was captured by the enemy. Released after a brief internment, the elder Granbery harbored no resentment against his captors. After his election to bishop in May 1882, he undertook missionary work including supervision of the Methodist Church in Brazil. In September 1890, Bishop Granbery founded a college in Juiz de Fora, Brazil. Fifty years later, the bishop's son proudly noted that Granbery College was still going strong.

Bishop Granbery's internationalism, his pacifism, and his opposition to slavery were embraced by his son, along with his vocation. "At about the age of 16 I became convinced that I was called to preach. There was no doubt in my mind about the 'call.' My father was pleased with the decision." Granbery enrolled at Randolph-Macon in 1895 to prepare for three years at Vanderbilt. In 1897, while studying for his bachelor of divinity degree at Vanderbilt, Granbery was ordained in the Methodist ministry.

Granbery later described the School of Theology at Vanderbilt as "liberal" but "in a transition stage, a curious mixture of the old and new. Questions as to the historicity of Jesus, his deity, and the authenticity of his teachings worried me no little. Such matters never came up in class." Granbery was impressed by a guest speaker from Chicago, a social worker at a settlement house who "intimated that a big social revolution was about to take place. An explosion might occur at any time in Chicago. I did not know what he was talking about, and was eager to find out."

Bishop Granbery thought his son had studied enough and ought to preach, but the young man was determined. "My years spent at the University of Chicago were not consecutive. I would drop out for a period and serve small charges as pastor on modest salaries" in Virginia, West Virginia, and Kentucky. Granbery recalled that "during the first year of my married life I served five churches widely removed; had, of course, to keep a horse, and roads were terrible." Granbery married Mary Ann Catt, known as "May," on January 22, 1903. He did not receive his doctorate from Chicago until 1909.

For a man "working under the urge of an intellectual, moral and spiritual necessity," as Granbery described himself, the University of Chicago was almost too stimulating. He took courses in seven departments. Besides the Greek and Hebrew he learned at Vanderbilt, Granbery acquired French and German to aid in his quest for the historical Jesus.

Though he devoted most of his time to Biblical history, Granbery also studied sociology with social reformers Jane Addams and Florence Kelley, and with Albion Small, the minister who had founded the department. He also took a number of courses in philosophy. "By confining my studies to a specific field, keeping my mind and mouth shut as to embarrassing questions, and standing apart from the social struggle, I might have occupied a comfortable professor's chair or filled with success a well-paying pulpit." But such mild acquiescence was not in his nature.

Granbery found sociology inadequate to explain the spiritual roots of human conduct. He turned to philosophy. At Chicago then, "the philosophy of pragmatism was rampant, but never for one moment did I fall for it." He likened his studies with John Dewey to Isaiah 28 : 20: "'For the bed is shorter than that a man can stretch himself on it, and the covering narrower than that he can wrap himself in it.' In a sense we are all pragmatists, but as an ultimate philosophy I found it superficial, meeting the needs of neither head nor heart."

It was his close historical study of Jesus that allowed Granbery to reconcile the troubling contradiction between scientific method and religious faith, between reason and belief. Despite exhaustive textual analysis of Old and New Testament sources, Granbery concluded the historical Jesus was only available to us in the "thought-world" of our own time. "Suppose we undertake to peal an onion with the idea that after removing this layer and then another, finally we'll get to the heart of the onion. Really the onion is the whole." The frantic effort to "get back to primitive Christianity" was "unhistorical and shortsighted." The various layers of interpretations of Jesus and his teachings in various eras were part of a natural and necessary process, proving that revelation had never ceased. An inspiring example of a religious scholar who put this revelation into practice was "the great missionary, Albert Schweitzer."

Granbery's doctoral dissertation, *Outline of New Testament Christology: A Study of Genetic Relationships within the Christology of the New Testament Period*, traced different conceptions of Christ through New Testament periods. Published in 1909, the book was used as a text at Chicago. Extending the lessons of his research, Granbery had resolved the separation of the supernatural from the natural. "I discovered that miracle belonged to a prescientific age; it was a 'wonder,' and not a denial of casual [sic] relationship in our world order." Such reasoning allowed Granbery to believe both in evolution theory and biblical miracles, a point of view popular with neither his colleagues in the ministry nor his activist liberal friends.

His studies completed, Granbery returned to rural pastorates in Virginia and West Virginia. He quickly realized that the kinds of questions he had grappled with at Chicago "had little direct bearing on the work of the Virginia circuit-rider." His interests in psychology, philosophy, sociology, and radical social reform provoked hostility among his parishioners and his colleagues.

May Granbery would later recall her husband's sermons as "so searching and direct that he left official boards a little worried. All the evils and injustices were looked after and something done about them. It made church-going not altogether comfortable at times." Granbery spoke publicly on women's rights and Prohibition, chaired the West Virginia Child Labor Committee, and organized the first Wilson Club of West Virginia. In 1912, when he denounced the "foul bossism" of two important local leaders, the conference of his church at Barboursville arranged to have him transferred out of the state.

At his next pastorate, in Paintsville, Kentucky, in addition to his church duties Granbery was offered the temporary presidency of Sandy Valley Seminary. In 1913, he gave an address at the seminary, characterizing the teacher as "a pioneer, a leader, one who breaks new tracks, the high priest of progress." Kentucky Wesleyan College awarded him a doctor of divinity degree in 1913. Granbery thought it "inevitable" that he should be called to education, with its chance for "prestige" and "influence that I had not known before. But I was still a man apart: a 'higher critic' and evolutionist, probably a Socialist, a radical, a dangerous character with pro-labor, interracial and revolutionary theories."

Despite his dangerous tendencies, Granbery was offered the presidencies of Sandy Valley and of the Holding Institute in Laredo, Texas. Instead he accepted an invitation from President Charles M. Bishop to join the faculty of Southwestern University at Georgetown, Texas. The Granberys moved to Georgetown in September 1913. Granbery acted as head of the education department for one year. The next year he became head of the Department of Sociology and Economics. He quickly stirred up trouble.

Southwestern University already had problems before John Granbery arrived. Founded by the Methodists in 1873, Southwestern had been an important center of revivalism and the leading Methodist university in Texas. But in 1910, the Methodist Conference decided Georgetown was too rural and remote to serve the educational needs of the church. Some factions argued for the removal of Southwestern to Dallas or Fort Worth, while others fought for the school's local survival. These internecine struggles were resolved by moving Texas Christian University to Fort Worth and by upgrading Texas Wesleyan University in Dallas and renaming it Southern Methodist University. Southwestern remained in Georgetown, but with most church attention and money now directed to SMU, the smaller institution began to suffer a financial hardship it would feel for decades.

On November 15, 1914, Granbery addressed the Texas Conference of Charities and Corrections at Travis Park Methodist Church in San Antonio concerning "The Church and Social Service." Praising Jesus as "among the radicals of history," an "innovator" with a "revolutionary message" to reverse the order of human conditions, Granbery concluded that "the churches have largely failed to realize the character and opportunity of their social mission." He conceded the church some "credit for progress in temperance reform," but decried its passivity in stopping "the evils of child labor," a problem about which "I have found more interest and co-operation from labor unions than from churches."

Granbery told his listeners, "We cannot save society simply by saving individuals one by one, because there are no mere individuals. We are all bound together by psychic bonds . . . Society and the individual are so related and inter-related that they must be saved together." The First World War already underway showed the impotence of the uncommitted church. "Institutional, dogmatic Christianity has failed—has certainly failed—to prevent the terrible European conflict now raging."

The next morning, the *San Antonio Express* published a front-page story with the headline "Minister Says Christianity Has Failed." In Dallas, the editor of the *Texas Christian Advocate,* the official organ of the Methodist Church in Texas, ran a front-page editorial demanding Granbery's immediate expulsion from Southwestern and from the church. Granbery was stunned. "Thinking that he had been misled by the daily paper I sent him the manuscript of my speech, but he came back with the charge that it was worse than he had supposed."

The *Advocate* editor, George Clark Rankin, printed attacks on Granbery by other ministers and pressed the case for Granbery's ouster to the Methodist hierarchy. Angry church members wrote Southwestern officials that Granbery should be fired because, as one man wrote, "so revolutionary are his views . . . that his usefulness as an instructor is gone . . . Southwestern cannot afford to endorse his position." Granbery tried to switch the debate to the issue of free speech, but church officials warned him against stirring up "trouble where peace and harmony existed," and to "let things alone." When Rankin died on March 5, 1915, the controversy died with him.

Freedom Is Not Academic

In 1917, as his father had, the pacifist Reverend Dr. John C. Granbery, Jr., went to work on a battlefront. Under the auspices of the YMCA, Granbery served as a chaplain for Allied forces in Europe. A projected one-year tour of duty turned into three, as Granbery ministered to American, French, and Greek troops. May Granbery recalled her husband's work "with the Greek Army where he planned an educational program so successfully that it was taken over by the government." Greece decorated Granbery twice for distinguished service.

When Granbery returned to Texas in 1920, he found that "a dark cynicism had settled down like a pall on the nation." He set out to rally the forces of progressive change, but encountered suspicion and misunderstanding. Recounting his overseas experiences to a convention of Houston schoolteachers in January 1921, Granbery compared the illiteracy of American soldiers to the better education of their European counterparts. He praised the valor of U.S. troops but argued that higher educational standards would improve their reading skills and eliminate their penchant for obscenity and petty theft.

One of the teachers in the audience objected to this insulting portrait of American fighting men. Her protest provided the *Houston Post* story with a headline and a lead: "J. C. Granbery, described to several hundred Houston school teachers as a professor of sociology at Southwestern University, discovered Saturday afternoon it was unsafe to hurl anathema at American soldiers in front of Houston women." As a result of this speech, the American Legion began an investigation of Granbery's political beliefs.

At the State Democratic Convention in San Antonio, in September 1922, Granbery was appalled to find the party lining up behind Earle B. Mayfield, the Klan candidate for governor. The night before the convention opened, he met with other anti-Klan delegates to present a resolution "condemning religious intolerance" and other alleged Klan principles without mentioning the Klan by name. The caucus rejected the resolution as too mild. Concluding he had "gotten in the wrong pew," Granbery walked out of the meeting, afraid the anti-Klan forces would destroy the convention.

He was most deeply shocked by the Methodists and Prohibitionists who supported Mayfield. Granbery tangled with Atticus

Webb, head of the Anti-Saloon League. The League's publication, *Home and State*, attacked anti-Klan candidate George E. B. Peddy for being a "wet." Granbery denied the charge, but the League refused to budge. The Methodists also stuck with Mayfield, a 1900 graduate of Southwestern. Granbery denounced the church alliance with the racist, anti-Catholic Mayfield in terms that angered Klansmen. May Granbery recalled the violent result.

> Threatened with a tarring and feathering because of his opposition to the Klan which had taken over the Democratic Party in the state lock, stock and barrel, the Professor found at his door one evening a young six-footer armed with a gun who offered to sleep on the front porch as a protection. I was thoroughly sold on the idea, but the Professor would have none of it. Rocking our house and breaking our kitchen window satisfied the Klan's spirit of violence for the time being. And the Professor actually took the stump for the candidate opposed to the Klan and helped materially in breaking its hold on the State.

In 1924 Granbery again opposed the Klan candidate for governor, Felix D. Robertson. Though no admirer of former Governor James Ferguson, Granbery supported Miriam Ferguson because she ran against the Klan. Once again the Methodist establishment and the Anti-Saloon League came out for the Klan candidate. Granbery thought he would "probably never get over the effects of the allegiance of the Church with the Klan. What the church is going to do with me does not concern me the least, but I am troubled about what *I* am going to do with the Church."

Both Klan and church groups began to press Paul W. Horn, president of Southwestern University, for Granbery's dismissal. The Women's Missionary Society of the Methodist Church in Taylor, Texas, publicly charged him with "most willfully maligning the ministry of Texas." Granbery responded that Methodists and Baptists had desecrated their churches by admitting hooded Klan members to their services, but that his indictment clearly did not include all ministers. Nor did Granbery endear himself to church members with public utterances, such as his well-reported sermon in San Antonio about the "despiritualizing influence of the absorption in business pursuits" which caused businessmen to form "mammoth schools, classes and brotherhoods" in misguided attempts to reclaim their souls. When the Taylor Missionary Society continued to demand his dismissal, Granbery decided to offer his resignation the following June.

Southwestern did not force Granbery to leave, though his position was increasingly tenuous. But his friend and supporter Paul Horn invited Granbery to join him at Texas Technological College, a newly opened state school in Lubbock where Horn had just been made president. The job offered more money and an apparent escape from denominational squabbles. Granbery resigned from Southwestern in June 1925 and moved to Lubbock in September to head the history department at Texas Tech.

Granbery quickly organized a forum for discussion of liberal ideas among like-minded students and faculty, including the Reverend Bradner Moore, rector of the college Episcopal church, and Jack Boyd, secretary of the Tech YMCA. All three men believed in the need for political reform to right economic wrongs. They sponsored socialist speakers to express their views on campus and in Granbery's classes. Granbery coauthored an introductory college history text, the purpose of which was clear from its opening paragraph: "Movements for social and political reform are necessarily weak and faulty when they are not based on an understanding of history."

Lubbock was a pious, orthodox community, dominated by conservative Baptists and home to smaller, more rigorous sects—not a congenial atmosphere for radical thought. When hard times came upon the area in the late 1920s and early 1930s, Lubbock hosted emotional mass revival meetings. At one such meeting, where Paul Horn also spoke, an evangelist proclaimed that "'All our troubles—hard times on the farm, our present drouth, all—are caused by sin. Every drouth-stricken community in the United States experiences drouth because of the sin of that community.'" As the historian said who quoted these words, "Two views of life, two types of mind had met in Lubbock. Conflict could hardly be avoided." John Granbery stood at the center of that conflict.

Early in 1930, the Reverend R. C. Campbell came from Belton to be pastor of Lubbock's First Baptist Church. He soon located the enemy of religion in Lubbock at Texas Tech. In the summer of 1931 Campbell preached a series of sermons "ostensibly on the modern dance, but in fact condemning practically all forms of contemporary thought and action." When the editor of the student newspaper, *El Toreador*, took issue with Campbell in print, despite a disclaimer from the Tech administration, the battle was joined.

Campbell was elected president of the Lubbock Ministerial Association in January 1932. Feeling community sentiment on his side, Campbell preached a sermon charging "a department head and a group of professors associated with him" on the Texas Tech faculty with "teaching atheism and infidelity." The *Lubbock Morning Ava-*

lanche gave the sermon front-page play, along with a rebuttal by President Paul W. Horn, who promised to investigate.

The story continued in the newspaper all week as Campbell reaffirmed his accusations and students denied them. By February 12, when the *Avalanche* revealed "Horn Finds No Foundation for Charges of Atheism," the charge had dwindled to one professor. Though Granbery had been named by neither side, he was known to be Campbell's target. The Sunday *Avalanche-Journal* of February 13 reported a new development as "Frank Norris Takes a Hand in Tech Case." The Fort Worth pastor, brother-in-law of Lubbock school superintendent Marcus Homer Duncan, sent President Horn a questionnaire to be answered by all Tech faculty. The six questions asked about belief in the literal infallibility of the Bible, the divinity of Christ, the Virgin Birth, the Resurrection, evolutionism and creationism, and any "public or private sympathy toward Sovietism."

Norris campaigned against Granbery on radio broadcasts and in the *Fundamentalist*, threatening to pressure the Appropriations Committee of the legislature about funds to state colleges. Norris offered the history text coauthored by Granbery as proof of the professor's apostasy, since one chapter was sympathetic to evolutionary theory. The Tech administration resisted the Norris attack. Tech students demonstrated outside Campbell's house and protested to the *Avalanche* for their right of free speech and good town-gown relations. But the death of Paul Horn in the spring of 1932 removed Granbery's most powerful defender.

In June 1932, the Texas Tech Board of Directors failed to renew Granbery's contract. Moore, Boyd, and others were also dismissed for allegedly exposing students to communist-affiliated organizations. Granbery protested the board's "militant religious fanaticism" in vain. At age fifty-seven, in the middle of the Great Depression, John Granbery was out of work.

Granbery beat a strategic retreat. He decided to visit his sister Ella Granbery Tucker in Brazil. Ella and her husband worked as missionaries and teachers, carrying on the work of Bishop Granbery, who had died in 1907. John and May Granbery spent two years working and traveling in Brazil. John quickly learned Portuguese and later described his life there as one of "studying, lecturing and organizing," where he "came into contact not only with the more familiar aspects of life, but also with Socialists, Anarchists, Communists, Nazis and Fascists."

Back in Texas in 1934, short of money and options, Granbery reluctantly accepted a standing offer to return to Southwestern. Financial conditions there had deteriorated badly. The Southern Association of Colleges and Secondary Schools had put the college on probation because of its low endowment and faculty salaries. Granbery had to settle for a monthly wage of one hundred dollars plus board for him and his wife. He signed a nine-month contract, refusing a permanent position.

Aside from the poor living conditions, Granbery faced problems from a new president, John W. Bergin, appointed in August 1935. Bergin had little academic training. His greatest interests were football and fundraising. Though Bergin began to improve Southwestern's financial position, he made no move to raise faculty salaries. Granbery lost his Lubbock home and went into debt, his poverty aggravated by poor health.

His fragile situation did not prevent Granbery from speaking out publicly on issues he thought important. On April 22, 1936, he addressed a campus rally of two thousand students at the University of Texas at Austin, part of a nationwide "strike for peace." "Orators Damn War and Makers of Munitions at Peace Strike," *The Daily Texan* said of the event.

"'God damn war.' With a rising voice, Dr. John C. Granbery, Southwestern University professor, repeated the phrase half a dozen times to drive the conclusion of his speech tight into the minds of the audience . . ." Granbery explained that the phrase "was not profanity. It was a prayer" from the Reverend Harry Emerson Fosdick, who had taken it from Walt Whitman.

"Bulky, big-headed, bald, Dr. Granbery spoke jerkily as he searched for words, spoke without passion, but spoke emphatically." Granbery told the students that protesting war while upholding the capitalist system that promoted it was dealing with the matter superficially. He said "the abolition of war requires a fundamental change in our economic structure." Neither his economic views nor his Whitmanesque opening prayer improved Granbery's standing with President Bergin or members of the Board of Trustees.

As Southwestern began to recover financially, Bergin decided to get rid of Granbery and two other faculty members. He notified the three professors in February 1938. Students protested the dismissals in sufficient numbers to force a reconsideration of Bergin's action by the Board of Trustees. The board met in May to allow the three men to present their cases. The board members reversed two of the three decisions but voted to fire Granbery.

Students at Southwestern demonstrated their anger at Granbery's dismissal by hanging a Nazi swastika, "emblazoned on a large black flag, between two windows on the second floor of the Administration Building." An outcry from Texas liberals heartened Granbery but did not restore his job. In the first issue of the *Emancipator*, Granbery quoted the American Civil Liberties Union report on his case. "No reason was given by the college administration, but it was long understood that his liberal activities had marked him for trouble. The American Association of University Professors is investigating the case."

He was fired but he was free. And still full of fight. Describing several years later "How the Emancipator Started," Granbery recalled that while "in college work," he and May had made their home a center for informal gatherings of students, faculty, and others. "The groups did not in general represent a particular philosophy, cause or theory . . . Everyone was free to express himself frankly." Visitors to the town or the campus were often invited to attend.

"Due to circumstances . . . closely connected with the liberal influence of such groups, all college relations of the future editors was broken off." In order not to be silenced but to maintain a fellowship "through which they and their friends might find expression," the Granberys decided to create an open forum in the pages of a monthly magazine.

Emancipation from What?

In 1938 a sense of crisis assaulted liberal sensibilities on many fronts. In September, when the *Emancipator* first appeared, Neville Chamberlain assured Hitler in Munich that the German seizure of Czechoslovakia would meet with no resistance. Nationally, conservative Democrats had turned against the New Deal. Roosevelt loyalists such as liberal Congressman Maury Maverick of San Antonio lost their offices. Martin Dies, of Texas' Second Congressional District, became chairman of the House Committee on Un-American Activities and searched for subversive influences in and out of government.

Texans elected W. Lee O'Daniel as their governor. O'Daniel, owner of the Hillbilly Flour Company, was famous for radio programs advertising his product and featuring sacred and hillbilly music. His declared political platform was the Ten Commandments and "all his speeches contained endorsements for Hillbilly Flour." Despite his folksy image, O'Daniel's closest friends and advisers were oilmen, bankers, and other corporate leaders. One historian, George Norris Green, pinpoints O'Daniel's ascent as the moment "in 1938 when conservative, corporate interests took over the state, once and for all, perhaps permanently. They launched the Establishment, a loosely knit plutocracy comprised mostly of Anglo businessmen, oilmen, bankers, and lawyers. These leaders—especially in the 1940s and 1950s—were dedicated to a regressive tax structure, low corporate taxes, antilabor laws, political, social and economic oppression of blacks and Mexican-Americans, alleged states' rights, and extreme reluctance to expand state services."

John Granbery stood in precise opposition to every item on this agenda. "I stand for a philosophy that is definite and positive," he told his earliest readers. "Call me a crusader, call me a propagandist, if you like. But do not call me a neutral." Granbery called for the emancipation of education, religion, and industry. He wanted to rescue "our schools from the control of special privilege," to "save the Church from the reproach that religion is the opiate of the people," and to promote democracy among workers and farmers through "unionization and collective bargaining."

Ever the patient teacher, Granbery stated and defined his principles over and over again in the pages of the *Emancipator*. "If one believes the Negro has no soul, the Jews should be persecuted, Communists and Socialists should be run out of the country, the Pope is an anti-Christ and freedom of speech and press should not be tolerated, then The Emancipator will interest him no more than he interests us." He combined philosophical and spiritual arguments for his social beliefs with pointed campaigns for or against specific policies and individuals. As for his enemies, Granbery quoted Psalms: "May the net they spread ensnare themselves, into their own pit may they fall."

He deplored the defeat of Maverick and the election of O'Daniel. He scolded the Methodist publishing plant in Nashville for opposing unionism. And he rebuked the religious press for shunning controversy in favor of "small church news, harmless articles on doctrinal subjects and powerful editorials against liquor and racetrack gambling." Granbery admitted he did not know whether his "liberal, independent magazine" could survive. He appealed for support, the beginning of a constant, sometimes desperate, supplication for funds. "We entered upon this venture as an act of faith. We had no money to put into it, and we have none now."

Granbery immediately began unceasing calls for justice for "Texas' Stepchildren," the Negroes who made up 15 percent of the state's population. He maintained exchanges with black publications and reprinted their editorials. He fought against racism in housing and education and advocated abolition of the poll tax. He protested unfair treatment of blacks in the criminal justice system in and beyond Texas. As a member of the Texas Commission on Interracial Cooperation, Granbery protested the paltry funding for graduate education at Prairie View A&M, the only state-funded Negro college. Eventually Granbery would adopt an ingenious economic argument against segregation to augment his frontal attacks on racism in the press, the schools, and the church.

The *Emancipator* proclaimed its feminist stance on its masthead, which listed John C. Granbery and May C. Granbery as editors and publishers. May's column, "Woman's Outlook," ran in every issue throughout the life of the magazine. "Woman's Outlook" featured interviews and profiles of outstanding women in various careers and discussions of women's issues. John offered congratulations to women who ran for offices held by unworthy men whom other men would not oppose. The Granberys ran or reprinted articles by noted feminist leaders such as Minnie Fisher Cunningham. Several of the *Emancipator*'s regular correspondents were women, including Nora K. Rodd. Rodd's "Canadian Letter," which ran for more than a decade in the magazine, reflected Granbery's belief that international understanding is necessary for human progress.

Reader response to the *Emancipator* was decidedly mixed. "Friends have been generous with advice, but most of it has been of a negative character, how not to do it," wrote Granbery after a year of publication. "Had we followed one tenth of it, there would have been no magazine." But a former admiring reader of *Brann's Iconoclast* thought Granbery's writing showed "a depth of learning and a grasp of principles far transcending that of the famous Brann."

To help make ends meet, the Granberys spent the summers of 1939 and 1940 in San Antonio, where Granbery taught a variety of courses at the University of San Antonio. As the summer of 1941 approached, John and May Granbery decided to move permanently from Georgetown to San Antonio. "Our home is opposite the science building and the men's dormitory and one block from the main building . . ." The professor and his wife were back on campus.

Even before the move to San Antonio, the *Emancipator* changed from "An Independent, Forward-Looking Journal of the Southwest" to an expanded constituency "of the Americas." Granbery cultivated exchanges with religious and political publications in Mexico, Cuba, and several South American countries. He translated articles and editorials from these journals for his own magazine. But Granbery's "Pan-Americanism" resisted sentimentality. Based on his exposure to Brazilian dictator Getulio Vargas, Granbery cautioned readers that "when Latin-American countries do lip-service to democracy and promise collaboration with the United States, they may not mean just what we think they mean."

Early in 1942, as America entered the Second World War, Granbery wrote, "Yes, we are 'pro,'—British, French, Greek, Italian, German." Denouncing Hitler and Mussolini, Granbery wanted Americans to distinguish between evil leaders and their peoples. He advised a San Antonio radio audience that the best response to the crisis was "to observe the spirit of the Declaration of Independence that says that all men are created equal. History knows no more brutal and unjust treatment of any race than Hitler's persecution of the Jews."

He pleaded for tolerance of Jews and blacks. Of Latin Americans he said it was "rather absurd to speak of them as Mexicans. They are not aliens . . . 100,000 of these Latins live here in Bexar County." He spoke against condemnation of all Japanese or Germans. "A large proportion of my listeners at this moment have German blood . . . There is no sounder . . . more constructive element in our population." Characteristically Granbery quoted the Bible to remind his audience, " 'God has made of one blood all nations to dwell on earth.' "

Granbery wanted to extend the fight against the dictators to a broader front. "When the British Government is fighting for democracy, let it be a democracy that embraces India. Let the high-sounding principles of France extend to her concentration camps and suppressed minorities . . ." Granbery did not want the obvious barbarities that necessitated war to obscure the ongoing struggle for human rights, as he said in 1940. "Let not the semifascist, capitalistic politicians and aristocrats, who are running things in the so-called democratic countries, suppose that after they get Hitler whipped and Stalin put in his place, they are going to continue in power."

The politicians Granbery saw serving repressive capitalism could be defeated only by education and organization. Promoting an effective alliance of progressive elements in schools, churches, labor unions, and minorities remained Granbery's constant goal. He had no illusions about that effort. He had helped to start many such groups. "We have spent hours making constitutions. In some instances no meeting was held after the first." He blamed these failures on exhibitionists and on those who fled when a crisis arose. Nor could any constructive organization "hold together on general principles . . . There must be a specific issue."

While he sympathized with the communist advocacy of racial equality and justice for workers, Granbery rejected communism for its godlessness and its uncritical view of Stalin and the Soviet system. He had long pondered the irony that many fundamentalist religious sects, filled with "masses of the unemployed, partially employed, and underprivileged," were in league with right-wing politicians. "What a power for sweeping democratic movement there is in these 'fanatical' religious bodies! At present they are curiously allied with capitalistic reaction, but their adherents are among the most exploited victims of capitalism . . ." Granbery wondered how these exploited masses might be led to "wake up to realities."

O'Daniel had run his gubernatorial campaign rallies like fundamentalist revival meetings. J. Frank Norris compared O'Daniel to Moses, who could "lead the nation back to the fundamentals of God and home." Granbery deplored this "pious showmanship." He described the Bible reading, hymn singing, and evangelistic speechmaking at O'Daniel's inauguration. "Now there's no denying that people of Texas in general fall for this sort of thing." Granbery admitted he also enjoyed it but warned the new governor, "that there's a limit to the amount that the people will take. Pious phrases are no substitute for truthfulness, fair dealing and statesmanship."

O'Daniel believed otherwise. Granbery wrote the governor "courteously but emphatically expressing disapproval of certain of his policies. His secretary replied that the Governor greatly appreciated our support and endorsement of his course. So that was one of the deluge of letters he gets in his favor!"

Granbery referred to "O'Daniel in the Lions' Den," but unlike the biblical character, "Governor O'Daniel is in a hot spot on account of his own folly and faithlessness to the people of Texas." Granbery called for a tax of five cents a barrel on oil for the permanent school fund. He noted that the Louisiana tax was eleven cents a barrel. "Why should Texas sit helplessly by and witness the vast bulk of her natural wealth leave the State to enrich others and leave ourselves impoverished?"

O'Daniel's plans for the Texas educational system did not include increased investment. He and his supporters wanted more control, especially over the universities. They viewed certain teachings as a threat to "Americanism" and their own well-being. As the Dies committee undertook to smoke out subversion in all segments of American life, Texas officials took particular aim at the University of Texas campus, partly in concert with Dies. John Granbery, living in political exile from academe, once again took up the cause of academic freedom.

The Trojan Horse in America

Martin Dies became chairman of the newly formed House Un-American Activities Committee (HUAC) in June 1938. The committee was supposed to investigate subversive activity and propaganda within the United States. But when public hearings began, Dies and his committee allies used their forum to condemn their political enemies, including prominent members of the Roosevelt administration.

Dies quickly discovered that the testimony of committee witnesses often made national headlines. Committee witnesses were not subjected to cross-examination or required to substantiate any of their accusations against groups or individuals. Dies found communists and "communist fronts" in New Deal programs and labor unions. "Even the Boy Scouts, the Camp Fire Girls . . . etc., came in for suspicion under the head of organizations whose activities increase international understanding." The Dies committee pioneered the techniques later known as McCarthyism, using former communists as witnesses and pronouncing people guilty based on their membership in certain organizations or on evidence "too sensitive to reveal."

Granbery joined those who found the Dies committee itself to be un-American. He called it "cancerous," "a tool of reaction," and "a travesty," intended to "smear the Roosevelt Administration and to throw suspicion on every honest Liberal who is working for a better world." Granbery thought Dies should be given no more money. Instead, "appropriations should be sought to investigate his Committee."

Buoyed by the conservative press and favorable public opinion polls, Martin Dies decided to run for the U.S. Senate from Texas in the special election of 1941. He preceded his candidacy with charges of communism in Texas schools, including his alma mater, the University of Texas. The Texas Senate formed its own "Little Dies" committee in January 1941 to assist the investigation. Challenged by University of Texas President Homer Rainey to produce evidence of his charges, Dies waffled and then backed down. The "Little Dies" committee quickly folded.

President Rainey, a believer in academic freedom, was on a collision course with the University Board of Regents. As the chairman of that board said later, "a certain definite political activity was started about the year 1940 . . . to eliminate from our institutions of higher learning so-called radical teachers." O'Daniel's appointees to the board increased the pressure on Rainey to fire professors, tenured or not, whose ideas some regents found "un-American." Rainey refused.

In 1942 a Dallas millionaire with close ties to the regents held a rally to promote his view that a forty-hour work week undermined the American war effort. Four University of Texas economics in-

structors, denied the chance to address the rally, held a press conference afterward to protest. The UT regents fired the instructors,
bypassing President Rainey. The regents also wanted to fire the individual responsible for putting a John Dos Passos novel, *The Big
Money*, on an English reading list. They settled for banning the book
over Rainey's objections.

Granbery understood the nature of the struggle at the University
of Texas. He traced the start of "the epidemic of Texas purges" to his
own dismissal from Texas Tech in 1932. The legislature's investigation of communism at the university was "ludicrous and insincere,
but do not for a moment suppose that this farce failed to serve its
purpose. The few members of the Faculty who once spoke out occasionally on controversial subjects are now rarely heard from." Granbery took up the cause of the fired economics professors.

He found an ally in his battle for academic freedom in J. Frank
Dobie, longtime UT faculty member. Dobie, a 1910 Southwestern
graduate, had a national reputation as a writer and collector of folklore. He wrote a weekly newspaper column printed in many Texas
cities. Granbery called him "the only free-lance on the teaching staff
of any tax-supported institution of learning in Texas." He reprinted
many of Dobie's columns in the *Emancipator* and the two men
maintained a cordial epistolary friendship.

In August 1943, Dobie reviewed the recent actions by the UT regents "to suppress freedom of speech, to get rid of liberal minds, and
to bring the University of Texas nearer to the status of Fascist-con-
trolled institutions of learning and farther away from the democratic
ideal of free and inquiring minds." The regents had tried to censor
the *Daily Texan*, fired three economics professors, forced the resignation of a law professor, and then fired the university's public relations officer. "Certain regents are after Rainey's scalp. There is no
secret about that." Dobie thought this current threat to academic
freedom more serious than that posed by Governor Jim Ferguson in
1917, as it was "against principles and not against individuals . . .
against all whose outspoken political and economic beliefs are contrary to those that seem comfortable to reactionary millionaires and
corporation lawyers."

Granbery reprinted Dobie's column and wrote the regents to ask if
Dobie had misstated anything. He also wrote Texas Attorney General Gerald C. Mann, charging the UT Board of Regents with malad-
ministration and betrayal of public trust. Granbery printed Mann's
reply—"I am unable to be of assistance to you in this situation"—in
the *Emancipator*. No official response—or lack of it—surprised
Granbery. "I have been watching the Texas Legislature for thirty

years, and do not recall a single occasion on which interest was manifested in academic freedom except to curtail it."

In his October 1944 issue, Granbery predicted Homer Rainey's imminent dismissal from office. On October 12, President Rainey presented a long list of grievances to a general faculty meeting. On November 1, the regents voted to fire Rainey, offering no reasons for their action. UT students went on strike and marched by the thousands to the capitol, to no effect. Frank Dobie, back from a year of teaching in wartime England, told a Texas Senate committee the University of Texas regents "have built a Maginot line around the institution with the purpose of keeping out ideas . . . It will be about as successful as the real Maginot line," a series of French fortifications the Germans simply circumvented to invade France. Dobie said, "Having academic freedom at the University of Texas is as easy as having freedom in Europe under Hitler's New Order."

Granbery announced his own appointment to the UT Board of Regents by Governor Coke Stevenson, but it was only an April Fools' joke. "The report is premature or exaggerated, or a hoax." In the spring of 1945, Granbery seriously began to push Homer Rainey as a candidate for governor. Part of Granbery's method was to name and describe those he saw as enemies of progressive thought.

He had already published a revealing list of "O'Daniel's Angels," including all who had contributed more than one hundred dollars to the former governor, now U.S. senator. Granbery received a telephone threat "that they were going to kill him for publishing the list of O'Daniel's Angels." As the campaign for Rainey's gubernatorial candidacy heated up, Granbery published detailed sketches of the regents who had fired him, outlining their various corporate connections.

Regents, former regents, and Rainey's four conservative opponents for governor attacked Rainey for promoting homosexuality, racial integration, and dissemination of obscene matter on campus. In fact, Rainey had not attempted to integrate UT and had cooperated with investigations of alleged homosexuality. The obscenity charge related to the Dos Passos novel. One regent published a pamphlet with selected quotes from the offending book to demonstrate its foul language, putting him in the odd position of disseminating material he had labeled obscene. The pamphlet included quotes from two Dos Passos novels not assigned at the university.

Rainey finished second in the election, then lost badly in a runoff to Beauford Jester. Shortly after Jester's victory, Granbery vigorously protested the reappointment of two regents "who betrayed the educational interests of the people of Texas. They so mismanaged the

University as to cripple it as a genuine institution of higher learning . . . And after their wretched betrayal they are rewarded with reappointment!" The American Association of University Professors
blacklisted the University of Texas (until 1953) for abridging free
speech. But no protest or censure checked the regents from their
course. In 1947 they found a way to drop J. Frank Dobie from the
faculty, silencing their most outspoken campus critic. The conservative victory was complete.

Granbery did not let defeat deter his commitment to academic
freedom. In 1951, the Texas House voted 130 to 1 to fire UT economics professor Clarence Ayres, a faculty member since 1930.
Granbery thought this action, "striking at the heart of the University, should not be described as clownish, for it is wicked . . ." He
kept *Emancipator* readers aware of national trends, noting which
universities required loyalty oaths or punished professors for expressing their political views.

Granbery spoke up for the right of teachers to choose their textbooks. He took particular issue with the "Puristic Houston" School
Board banning of the textbook *American Government* by conservative Oregon author Frank Magruder. The Houston board dropped
the book on the basis of a single paragraph that said United States
capitalism was "subject to increasing governmental control" due to
increased social complexity. "The country is capitalistic with strong
Socialistic and even Communistic trends," Magruder had written.

"The Houston School Board is afraid that insidious seeds of socialism and communism may be planted in the minds of the children by the book," Granbery wrote. On that basis the children
should be kept from reading Houston's daily newspapers, "which report these trends constantly. Pupils should certainly not be permitted to see the Congressional Record." Granbery thought Houston's
action added to the "curious reputation" of Texas nationally, and
wondered "What kind of folks constitute the School Board in Houston anyway?" He would soon learn the answer.

The censorship, purges, and other abridgements of civil rights in
the schools of Texas and elsewhere stemmed from the national fear
enunciated clearly by Martin Dies in his 1940 book, *The Trojan
Horse in America.* "The experience of this generation, more than
that of any other," wrote Dies, "has demonstrated that the enemies
within a country constitute a peril as great as any foreign foe."

Though Dies gave up chairing HUAC in 1944, the committee
gathered fresh momentum in the uncertain early days of the atomic
age and the cold war. Committee investigations ended a number of
careers and launched others, including that of Richard Nixon, and

led directly to the excesses of Senator Joseph McCarthy. Granbery opposed each successive version of HUAC and scorned McCarthy, whose power continued unchecked until after Granbery's death.

The Methodist minister turned editorial prophet had warned that the hardest part of winning the Second World War would be avoiding the reactionary aftermath of the First. As he began his fourteenth year of publication, Granbery noted that "during the first half of the period covered by The Emancipator the big question was that of Fascism, and during the second, Communism . . ." He took pride in having opposed "these alien ideologies" as an intelligent person, not an "emotional, hysterical, non-discriminating and ignorant dogmatist, whose puny mind can conjure nothing but repression, persecution, denunciation, suspicion and character-assassination."

Granbery clearly aimed these demeaning epithets at "small-minded rabble-rousers like Senator Pat McCarran . . ." and "the execrable Joe McCarthy." He thought "the greatest danger that the United States faces . . . is the defeat of our own ideals . . . Mediocrity is a greater enemy than is Russia." But conspiracy proved a more appealing and durable adversary than mediocrity. The potency of Martin Dies' metaphor was apparent in 1962, when FBI Director J. Edgar Hoover told a House committee that "the U.S. Communist Party was a 'Trojan Horse of rigidly disciplined fanatics unalterably committed to bring this free nation under the yoke of international communism.'" Hoover was sounding an alarm about communist influence on civil rights leader Martin Luther King.

John Granbery fought for his radical ideals on many fronts through the embattled 1940s and early 1950s. As he moved among local, national, and philosophical issues, from precinct fights to the meaning of existence, lashing out against segregation, intolerance, and superficiality, Granbery resembled a one-man bucket brigade at the conflagration of the American promise. "There's so much to do and so little time in which to do it," he acknowledged. "Some folks have been unkind enough to suggest that perhaps [this editor] can't do very much after all about saving the world. Well, he will have to have some help, to be sure."

New Deckers, Not New Dealers

Though John Granbery lost many battles, he never considered giving up the fight. Despair was the only real defeat. "I am weary of hearing about what terrible times these are," wrote Granbery in 1944. "We cannot shut our eyes to violence and cruelty and injustice, but this is also a great day in which to live, and we are glad to be alive."

Granbery told his readers how he spent his seventieth birthday. "I once thought of a person seventy as old. Surely not now!" He rose before six and bused across town to teach a three-hour summer class in American government at a Catholic college. Just before noon he presided as chairman at a meeting of the Bexar County Democrats. He had lunch with the "Mayor of San Antonio in a committee to discuss postwar planning." Back home to read his mail and "take few minutes of rest," he phoned out a long telegram "regarding a fourteen-year-old Negro boy to be executed in South Carolina the next day."

Granbery kept an afternoon appointment with the director of the Texas Farmers' Union, met his wife for dinner at a hotel, and attended an evening meeting of the Open Forum, "reaching home about eleven. Not much time to think about one's birthday, yet I could not escape the awareness. This day was hardly typical, for it was fuller than most. But it is something like that. And it is mostly pleasant."

In 1943, fed up with "the old machine system" in city politics, Granbery ran for mayor of San Antonio. "My appeal is to self-respecting, independent, intelligent voters who wear no man's collar, who are disgusted with the low type of politics that is our disgrace. We have got to make a start somewhere." Declaring himself with labor and against big business, he gave a series of radio talks to support his unlikely candidacy. Lacking money and organization, Granbery did poorly. "The vote for the writer was almost negligible," he wrote later. "The answer was unmistakable. The time for change had not yet come." But Granbery did serve on the committee for the Twentieth District of the Democratic party.

Granbery always maintained his active membership in the Democratic party, faithfully attending meetings and conventions on all levels and reporting the proceedings to his readers. Party precinct conventions provided a valuable opportunity because "in the United States we have little direct democracy." Sadly, after years of attending these gatherings, he had "realized what a farce they are, due to neglect and indifference on the part of the majority of the people." Summing up one such uninspired meeting in 1948, Granbery wrote, "It was our unpleasant duty to report that the first Democratic Convention of the year in Bexar County was found lacking in sincerity and firmness."

Granbery had a particular disdain for Democrats who turned against the party principles. "We prefer an honest, liberal Republican to a reactionary Democrat." He despised the Texas Regulars, "the anti-democratic, special-privilege element" that opposed Roosevelt and took control of the party machinery in 1944. "The editor is proud to have had a part in the struggle" to defeat the Regulars, Granbery wrote. "In 1948 the Texas Regulars became the Dixiecrats, and they too were defeated, not without a struggle." Granbery felt betrayed by Senators Tom Connally, and especially the erstwhile liberal Lyndon Johnson, for joining the "demagogues and peanut politicians" in reaction to Democratic party initiatives, including civil rights legislation.

Abetting the political and social forces of reaction, in Granbery's judgment, were the daily newspapers. The big newspapers were not "merely on the side of Big Business; they are Big Business." The three San Antonio dailies, "all with the same philosophy," served as perfect examples of this disheartening trend. Two of the three were owned by the same management. The third belonged to the Hearst chain. "People who are exposed only to the reading of these papers have little chance to think outside of the narrow limits prescribed." Their positions were clear and unchanging: "Anti-Roosevelt, anti-Mrs. Roosevelt, anti-New Deal, anti-labor, anti-socialist, anti-communist." Only the Hearst paper's "supernationalism and isolationism" set it apart from the others.

During the 1944 presidential campaign, Hearst's *San Antonio Light* opined that the only support Henry Wallace brought to Roosevelt's fourth-term ticket was "COMMUNISTIC support." "What a lie!" responded Granbery. "Hearst journalism reaches low levels of degradation. Hearst has always been cynical. He has a poor opinion of popular intelligence. To use the word COMMUNISTIC (capitals his) for the millions of Americans who admire Mr. Wallace . . . is worse than downright stupidity. It is a falsehood put forth to catch the poorly informed people who do not know the meaning of the word 'Communism' but think it must be something awful. The vast majority of these millions are not Communists, and Hearst and the wretched stooges who are paid to write for him his lies know they are not."

The days of the free press in America were already over, in Granbery's view, undermined by economic development. "Personal journalism yielded to the corporation and the chain. Emphasis shifted from information to entertainment, from enlightenment to a variety show." Enriched newspaper owners became estranged from the reading public as competition disappeared and even large cities were left with a single newspaper. Surviving owners "associated with bankers, utility operators, manufacturers . . . at the Chamber of Commerce, clubs and rich suburban estates." Advertisers did not have to pressure publishers, since "the point of view is already that of those with whom one lunches."

Newspapers abused their trust by suppressing vast amounts of news and reporting the rest with bias. "It seems strange to us that in the light of the tremendous responsibility resting upon the newspaper, there is so little sense of obligation to give the news truthfully." For newspapers to express their editorial opinions on controversial issues was fine, "but when the news is slanted and twisted so as to make a misleading impression, that constitutes unethical conduct as we see it."

Mass media offended Granbery's professorial sensibilities because they failed to make use of their vast potential to educate. Granbery thought that radio could provide "a fine educational service . . . But the ignorance of announcers is astounding. They appear not to have been anywhere, and to have no familiarity with German, French and even Spanish." If stations could not employ well-educated newscasters, then they ought to make them study, said Dr. Granbery. "The matter is serious because the public is being wrongly educated on a colossal scale." He urged editors of smaller newspapers—the "country weeklies"—"to exercise their prerogatives to write editorials taking stands on issues to guide and instruct their readers." Granbery could not understand editors who did not express their opinions. That was the *Emancipator*'s raison d'être.

Granbery attacked Texas dailies for their racism. He blasted the San Antonio papers for failing to publish pictures of prominent Negroes, and "especially to avoid giving pictures where whites and Negroes are in the same group." He accused the *Dallas Morning News* of printing phony letters to the editor purportedly written by blacks, though "these alleged letters from Negroes . . . would be written by no honest, self-respecting and intelligent Negro of our acquaintance." Granbery's satire "White Supremacy, a Defense of the White Race," appeared in the *Nation*. Supposedly written from the view of a white supremacist, the essay protested discriminatory laws against blacks and others because such laws implied that whites needed special advantages to compete successfully with blacks and Jews. Not all of Granbery's readers appreciated the essay's ironic intent.

To fulfill the mission of the *Emancipator* as an open forum, Granbery read widely and shared his findings—from state, national, or international sources—with his readers. He resumed exchanges—interrupted in wartime—with many Latin American publications. He subscribed to national liberal magazines such as the *New Re-*

public and the *Nation,* to which he submitted letters or occasional articles. Granbery hailed the founding of George Seldes' *In Fact,* in 1940, a periodical designed to criticize the mainstream media and to publicize stories they missed or suppressed. He praised or argued with Seldes over the years. When Seldes stopped publishing in 1950, citing the "apathy among American liberals," Granbery blasted the decision in an article entitled "APATHY: WHY 'IN FACT' QUIT AND WE DON'T."

Granbery monitored the daily papers of Dallas, Houston, and San Antonio and wrote many letters to their editors, some of which prompted editorial replies. He included items in the *Emancipator* from black, religious, and labor publications. Granbery commended the work of "liberal free-lance newsmen" Stuart Long and John McCully, who published weekly insider reports on the Texas Legislature. And he constantly urged support for the liberal Austin weekly *State Observer,* edited by Paul Holcomb. The two editors often reprinted each other.

By 1948, in the tenth year of the *Emancipator,* Granbery could report that his independent monthly reached subscribers in every state of the union and twenty foreign countries. Most out-of-state American readers lived in New York and Washington, D.C., "not on account of subscriptions but of exchanges and various agencies." Brazil and Canada led the foreign subscription list. About half the copies mailed went to Texas cities, mostly San Antonio, Dallas, and Austin. Granbery made sure prominent Texans living out of state received their monthly sermons. His 1951 subscription list included Vice-President Alben Barkley, Representative Lloyd Bentsen, and United States Attorney General Tom Clark, as well as U.S. Senators Tom Connally and Lyndon Johnson. Granbery continued to feel an urgent need to spread his message of tolerance and reason, as the ideals of his church and his government came under attack during the red scare.

Is There a Pink Fringe in the Methodist Church?

The orchestrated furor began in 1950 in Houston, where "a group of laymen from Houston's Methodist churches created the city's first Red Scare–era anti-Communist organization: the Committee for the Preservation of Methodism." One of the Committee's primary goals was to rid the church of its national affiliate, the Methodist Federation for Social Action (MFSA). Founded in 1907, the MFSA emphasized industrial and economic reform, world peace, and social justice. John Granbery had long been a member.

Anticommunist authors in the 1930s, including one Methodist minister, had accused the MFSA of having close ties with the Communist party. In 1947 the Scripps-Howard newspaper chain ran two exposés about the ties of the MFSA to communism. The allegations appeared in six articles in the Houston *Press.* Hoping to offend neither faction in his Houston fold, Methodist Bishop A. Frank Smith tried to weather the storm in silence, earning enmity from both sides.

In 1948, HUAC issued a pamphlet, *100 Things You Should Know About Communism and Religion.* Written in question-and-answer form, the pamphlet expressly condemned the MFSA. As Granbery said later, despising HUAC's inaccuracy as much as its intent, "Here by innuendo and the formulation of questions, individuals and groups of the Methodist Church are smeared with communism, including 17 bishops. This report was dated 1948 . . . but it cited the Epworth League, which went out of existence in 1939."

In February 1950, a *Reader's Digest* editor attacked the MFSA as "Methodism's Pink Fringe." The article appeared the same month that Senator Joseph McCarthy gained national attention with his Wheeling speech about communists in the State Department. The timing of the article and the large circulation of the *Digest* caused great concern among Houston's Methodist community, which included some of the city's most powerful individuals, such as Jesse H. Jones and Hines Baker, president of Humble Oil. Baker agreed to chair a committee appointed by Bishop Smith to look into the allegations against the MFSA and report to the Texas Annual Methodist Conference in June.

Baker's committee and the Methodist Conference condemned the MFSA and demanded its disaffiliation from the Methodist church. The Methodist Federation for Social Action ignored the directive. As the outbreak of war in Korea spurred further fears of communist influence, MFSA opponents in the church formalized their cause by creating the Committee for the Preservation of Methodism in December 1950. Their express goals were to stop "the spread of Socialistic and Communistic theories in our church" and to oust the MFSA.

In 1951, using the *Reader's Digest* term, the Committee for the Preservation of Methodism published a thirty-five-page booklet, *Is There a Pink Fringe in the Methodist Church?* The group printed fifty thousand copies and distributed the booklet nationally. One response was a meeting in Chicago of thirty-three conservative Methodists from several states in October 1951. They formed the Circuit Riders to combat radicalism in the church. The vice-president of the

Circuit Riders was a prominent Houston member of the Committee for the Preservation of Methodism.

John Granbery called the Committee for the Preservation of Methodism "the most reactionary, sinister and un-Christian movement of which we know in the Methodist Church." The *Pink Fringe* booklet appalled Granbery with its conclusion "that there is a pink fringe, and the thing to do is to rid the Church of all this 'pink' leadership, which includes bishops, editors, pastors, educators, and others" by name. Granbery thought this "blacklist" contained "some of the most devoted, eminent and useful bishops and other leaders of the Church."

Many of Granbery's good friends and kindred spirits within the church appeared on the Committee's blacklist. Bishop G. Bromley Oxnam, of Washington, D.C., a particular target of the Houston organization, was a longtime Granbery ally. The editor had praised Oxnam frequently over the years. In 1948, Granbery ran in the *Emancipator* an essay by Oxnam entitled "Methodists on Communism, Civil Liberties and Race," in which the bishop called for increased democracy throughout society as the best way to offset the growing threat of communism.

Granbery acknowledged the "militant and determined" efforts of certain "powerful Houston laymen" to banish social activists from the Methodist church. But he thought that others who were "not so powerful" had been "sucked in and used" by the Committee for the Preservation of Methodism. He accused this small group of having "intimidated" the 1950 Texas Annual Conference to "adopt an incongruous, contradictory, and absurd" condemnation of the MFSA. Granbery said the Conference had only adopted "this poorly written hodgepodge . . . as a compromise with the hope that the matter would be disposed of and settled . . . a vain hope."

The most astounding aspect of this movement is that following the sane and correct statement that the Church as such is not committed to any specific economic system and cannot allow any special group to use it, these laymen insist that the Methodist Church must come under their own domination in support of the laissez-faire, "free-enterprise" system of capitalism, purging as subversives those who do not accept their economic interpretations. Fortunately this is an affront to intelligence and Christian loyalty that self-respecting Methodists will reject, but it can stir up dissension and unhappiness. As for "Circuit Riders," the writer of these lines is a real circuit rider of the old kind in a literal sense . . . We do not need to have these self-appointed critics to tell us what Methodism is.

Granbery suffered no illusions about the perfection of the Methodist church. He had kept up a steady stream of criticism over the years about institutional racism and antiunionism in church businesses. He often denounced the harmless irrelevance of religious publications and the platitudinous mediocrity emanating from church pulpits. But now he found himself vigorously defending the modest impulse toward equality and tolerance that existed within Methodism.

The attempt to discredit and dismantle social activism in the church was a personal threat to Granbery. He had always believed that those who truly understood their Christian commitment would feel compelled to help others, especially the underprivileged. When he moved to San Antonio, Granbery learned that Methodists spent about one hundred thousand dollars annually on social welfare programs. But there was no cooperation, no coordination, among the various agencies. Granbery was instrumental in establishing the Methodist Council of Social Agencies to provide efficient oversight for the many charitable boards and agencies. He interpreted antisubversive "super-patriotism" as a rationalization to continue the exclusion of minorities and the poor from full economic enfranchisement.

In an article entitled "Is This Perjury?" Granbery wrote, "I have a confession to make. I have signed a loyalty oath." By state law, in order to teach Greek at an evangelical school he had to swear he was not a member of any group deemed subversive by the attorney general or the State Department. The problem was that "those lists were not furnished me and without a great deal of research I have no means of knowing what those organizations are." He did know that HUAC had cited the Epworth League of the Methodist church "as Communistic or at least under suspicion, and almost as a child I was connected with that. Moreover about 17 Methodist Bishops are under criticism; my father was a Bishop . . . and I respect these men and am indeed under their jurisdiction." Confessing he had also signed petitions and sent money to various causes, some of which might be suspect, Granbery ended: "Page Senators Nixon and McCarthy!"

A number of readers asked Granbery why his name did not appear "on the blacklist of subversives in the Methodist Church. It must have been because we are such 'small potatoes' in the Church as to be unworthy of mention." But Granbery emphatically associated himself with "these forward-looking leaders who have been grossly insulted."

In 1951 the Minute Women of the USA established a local chapter in Houston. Dedicated to defending traditional American values, the Minute Women favored continued racial segregation, the repeal of income tax laws, the abolition of labor unions, and the withdrawal of the United States from the United Nations. They helped launch an all-out offensive against the Houston Independent School District in 1953–1954. The Minute Women also compiled a twenty-five-page list of "*Individuals from Texas Reported as Having Been Affiliated with Communist or Communist-Front Organizations.*" Among some two hundred Texans "known to be 'brazenly' associated with subversives" was Dr. John C. Granbery, Jr. Granbery might have felt honored by this mention, but the list was not published until three years after his death.

Facing the Sunrise

The *Emancipator* was never self-sustaining. When asked how he was able to keep going without any subsidy, Granbery pointed out that "there is no overhead. The editor receives no salary. Only the printer is to be paid . . ." John and May Granbery lived on a small annual retirement stipend from the Methodist church that barely covered their modest living expenses. Subscriptions to their monthly could not pay the printing costs and they took no advertising.

Though he taught a variety of subjects—Latin, Greek, philosophy, ethics, history, government, and the Bible—part-time at several institutions, Granbery did not get a permanent teaching appointment anywhere. His jobs were temporary, in evening or summer sessions. Nor did he fare better as a preacher. In 1949 Granbery noted that "I have been connected with a local church of over 5,000 members for about eight years." He had volunteered to teach Sunday School, even as a substitute on short notice, but "I have never been called upon, nor have I been invited to preach in that church. . . . I am still greeted by the glad-hander with these words: 'What's your name? Are you a visitor in our city?'"

Early in the life of the *Emancipator* Granbery noted, "It is not easy to wield a shining sword in one hand and a tin cup in the other . . ." He knew his editorial independence "will mean only the freedom to become extinct unless we have the means of livelihood. 'Give me liberty or give me death!' we cry, and sometimes we think we stand a good chance of getting both." In one attempt to earn money, the Granberys offered their "Personal Service" in providing counsel, lectures, book reviews, classes, coaching, foreign languages, papers, and travel talks, among others. "Do you need help? Whatever your problem, come to us. We may be able to help directly. If not, we can probably direct you to the proper sources. Ask the Granberys." A few years later the Granberys offered "Some One To Talk To," at five dollars a sitting. What return these solicitations yielded is unknown.

"How Free Is the Emancipator?" asked a Granbery article title. He acknowledged that the magazine's economic bondage "at times neutralizes all the other freedoms." After "Six Delightful Years" of publishing, the editor said, "we must confess that many a time we have been on the edge of the precipice . . . Writing and assembling material are pleasant. It is only the business end that has sapped our strength." Over the years, in spite of economic hardship and his pleas for funds, Granbery peppered his magazine with many expressions of faith that somehow the *Emancipator* would be able to continue.

He knew his faith was not taken altogether seriously by others. When the Granberys began their monthly, friends were sympathetic, but "there was perhaps not one who really believed that we were going to make a continuing success of the enterprise. Some bluntly said so, while others tried to break the news gently." Granbery appealed for money on behalf of other magazines as well as his own, including the *Texas Spectator*, a liberal Austin weekly.

"If our democracy is to function effectively, our people must have access to the news and its interpretation and analysis," Granbery wrote. Convinced such access was unavailable in the large daily newspapers, he thought "the tremendous importance of an independent press, even though the circulation be comparatively small, is obvious." He pleaded with his readers to support "such journals as the Observer and Spectator of Austin and of course, The Emancipator, and this is not as a favor but as a necessity."

In April 1945, Granbery announced that "a generous friend has contributed five thousand dollars to the Emancipator," enabling the magazine to clear off its many debts. The "announcement" turned out to be only an April Fools' dream. "But we had fun dreaming it. Forgive us!" Four years later Granbery was still writing dream letters in his magazine, addressed "Dear Mr. Multimillionaire," asking for financial assistance.

Then, in September 1950, a real letter was sent from Austin to solicit funds for the Granberys and their magazine. Signed by six union leaders, including Paul Sparks of the AFL and J. J. Hickman of the CIO, the letter lauded the *Emancipator* as a nonlabor publication that had fought the fight on labor's behalf. Calling Granbery the

"Dean of Texas Liberals," the union leaders pointed out his personal sacrifices. They sought birthday contributions on the thirteenth anniversary of the magazine to "help free this good friend from his money trouble so that he can continue to speak out in behalf of us all."

On October 28, 1950, John and May Granbery attended a banquet in their honor at the Driskill Hotel in Austin. One hundred and fifty-five guests paid $1.75 a plate to hear testimonials to the Granberys from ministers, journalists, and other "luminaries." The couple was presented with a bank account "of over $2200." Describing the banquet and the gift, May Granbery recalled how "we had got into such a deep hole that early in the fall we considered . . . selling our home and belongings . . ." She did not say whether they considered giving up the *Emancipator.*

His precarious financial condition was only one of several pressures on Granbery. After five years of keeping his monthly publishing schedule, Granbery noted ruefully that he missed the world of "books, of ideas, of poetry and meditation, of abstract thinking." "Often I wish I might withdraw from all political activity," he admitted in 1945. He fantasized about "declaring myself an absolute independent unable to work with any group," or else working with "some minority group that repudiates capitalism and its evil works and thereby avoids responsibility for what is being done in this wicked world." But Granbery's conscience did not permit him to abandon the frustrating labor of practical political activism.

By 1949, Granbery had to face the reality of his own deteriorating health. He suffered a heart attack, which forced him to slow his pace. He remembered with wonder and gratitude his many years of good health. "Just a few months ago I did not know what the medical terms thrombosis and occlusion meant." Granbery quoted from the Gospel of John: "We must work the works of him who sent me, while it is day; night comes, when no one can work." He spent three weeks in bed. "But for me the night has not yet come . . . My work is far from complete . . . My mind is clear . . . I am tremendously interested in what is going on in the world and enjoy doing my part."

When he felt sufficiently recovered, Granbery continued his active ways. Serving as the San Antonio United Nations Committee chairman, Granbery declared that "World Government is an ultimate goal. We are all for peace, and the only road to the kind of peace we deem worthwhile is that of freedom." He published a comparison of the United Nations and the U.S. State Department in terms of budgets and staff sizes.

In 1950, the UN, with a staff of four thousand, had a budget just over $41 million. That same year, the U.S. State Department, with twenty-one thousand employees, would spend more than $250 million. Noting that the United States gave $16 million to the UN, or about 40 percent of the UN's total budget, Granbery concluded that "our contribution to the United Nations is about 6.7% of what the State Department spends this year."

Granbery continued to hammer away at the "high cost of segregation." He cited the case of Heman Sweatt to help prove his contention that "the policy of separate and equal education for Negroes in Texas is prohibitive." Sweatt, a black man, had tried to enter the law school at the University of Texas. The school responded by setting up a separate facility for blacks, which meant a separate law school for a single student. By 1948, the University of Texas black law school had moved to Houston and expected fifteen students. Citing three U.S. Supreme Court cases decided against the separate but equal doctrine, Granbery reiterated that "in such fields as education and transportation the economy of the southern states cannot stand up under a policy of separate and equal facilities honestly administered." If legislators would not act for moral reasons, perhaps they could be persuaded on economic grounds.

Senator Joseph McCarthy gained national attention in February 1950 by charging there were fifty-seven card-carrying communists in the State Department. In the March *Emancipator,* Granbery pronounced McCarthy more dangerous than Benedict Arnold, a "cowardly character-assassin hiding behind Senatorial immunity who is spreading before the world falsehoods regarding men and women whose patriotism and purity of motive are unintelligible to his low wit." Granbery saw McCarthyism as the main issue in the November 1950 elections, "a policy of crying 'Communism' for political and personal advantage, and smearing with the Communistic taint one's opponents in absence of any truthful argument." He was particularly distressed by the "low methods" used in the Senate victory of Richard Nixon in California "against the intelligence and courage of a woman above his political level. We thought better of the people of California."

When the Republicans nominated Nixon as their vice-presidential candidate in 1952, Granbery was "surprised and disappointed." Nixon "seems to be proudest" of "his service in connection with the House Committee on Un-American Activities." Though Granbery favored Stevenson, he thought "General Eisenhower is a fine man, worthy to be President . . ." but "the sanity of an informed person who does not shudder at the thought that Richard Nixon may some day be President of the United States should be called in question."

Glancing at the 1952 U.S. Senate race in Massachusetts, pitting John Kennedy against Henry Cabot Lodge, Granbery was circumspect. "Kennedy's voting record in the House is excellent but he appears to us to be something of an opportunist in whom we cannot put much confidence until he is further proven."

Though McCarthyism made Granbery feel angry and embattled, it did not dull his wit. In response to local versions of McCarthyism, Granbery called San Antonio "a patriotic city; we might say superpatriotic. Witness our long and frequent parades." He made a sarcastic demand for an investigation of the San Antonio symphony for playing music by a Russian composer and warned against "another invasion from those dangerous communistic radicals, the Quakers."

As he had done for years, Granbery reminded his readers that "fear is the most distressing and deadening of all ills . . . we have no fear of Communism, of Russia . . . of any man or group of men, of things present or of things to come. We do not even fear that someone will cancel his subscription."

Granbery continued to scrutinize the activities of the Texas Legislature, which he sometimes described as "Opera Bouffe." He called the Texas senators "clowns" when they failed to authorize women to serve on juries. He also referred to Texas House members as "clowns" when the legislature resolved to urge Texans in Congress to work for the impeachment of William O. Douglas from the U.S. Supreme Court.

The May 1953 issue of the *Emancipator* contained Granbery's postmortem of the San Antonio City Council elections, which he characterized as "a triumph of ignorance and prejudice over enlightenment and intelligence." On the back cover was an announcement signed by May Granbery: "At the very time that the material for this issue of The Emancipator was about to go to press, its founder and Editor-in-chief was stricken with another heart attack and slipped quietly into the regions beyond . . ."

The final issue of the *Emancipator*, in June, was a memorial. Organizations and individuals eulogized John Granbery who had died at 78, passionate for justice to the end. Jewish rabbis and Catholic bishops joined poets, educators, journalists, and political leaders in mourning the passing of an iconoclast motivated by love and reason.

Six months before he died, Granbery wrote an article entitled "It's Time for a Change." "It's always time for a change. Panta rei, said the old Greek philosopher: everything flows. All is in a state of flux. Where there's life there's change. The status quo, if continued, is death." John Granbery fought for the changes he believed in, not despairing his losses but taking the struggle itself as his victory.

4. The Printer Who Fired Both Barrels

What is news? . . . if somebody wants something in the paper more
than you do, it's not news, it's advertising . . . if somebody does
not want something in the paper, that's news, and if somebody
is determined that you shall not print it, that's hot news, indeed.

—*Archer Fullingim*

Archer Fullingim published a weekly newspaper in the small
East Texas town of Kountze from 1950 to 1974. The largest
circulation he ever claimed for the *Kountze News* was only
1,800 copies. But the influence of this small country paper belied
that modest figure. Fullingim's outspoken editorials were reprinted
in the *Texas Observer*, the *Dallas Morning News*, and a number of
Texas weeklies, and read in the White House.

Ronnie Dugger, editor of the *Observer*, pronounced the *Kountze
News* "the best weekly newspaper in Texas." Dugger wrote: "I guess
Archer Fullingim is the closest thing in Texas the law still allows to
William Brann." J. Frank Dobie said he subscribed to the *New York
Times* but seldom read the editorials, "but I read the editorials of the
Kountze News every week, and I doubt there's another editorial
writer in Texas who puts as much juice and vinegar, common sense,
fire and laughter into his editorials as Archer Fullingim . . ."

Even his editorial enemies at the *Dallas Morning News*—a newspaper Fullingim attacked frequently and vehemently—acknowledged that the *Kountze News* was "one of the most widely quoted
newspapers in the state." By the time he retired from publishing,
Fullingim had been written up in *Life* and *National Geographic* and
appeared on the nationally broadcast "Tomorrow" show on NBC. In
1975 a book of selections from his twenty-five years at the *Kountze
News* received favorable reviews and an award from the Texas Institute of Letters.

When John F. Kennedy, one of Fullingim's heroes, got the Democratic presidential nomination in June 1960, Fullingim began sending him the *Kountze News*. But he wondered whether Kennedy ever
read it. In 1961, Fullingim wrote to Pierre Salinger, President Kennedy's press secretary, to ask. Salinger replied: "Let me assure you
that we do read the Kountze News and we are delighted to be receiv-
ing it. I am sorry we haven't told you so before . . ." After Kennedy's

The Printer in his habitat. Archer Fullingim in the pressroom at
The Kountze News, 1975. (Courtesy of Roy Hamric.)

An ailing Fullingim, with eyepatch, at his office door, 1975.
(Courtesy of Roy Hamric.)

assassination in 1963, Fullingim sent his paper to the new president, "and Lyndon Johnson always got one until Arch got mad at him one day and cut off the White House."

Fullingim earned the respect of journalists and politicians with his blunt, colorful prose and his passionate opinions on a wide range of subjects. In his front-page editorial column, "The Printer Fires Both Barrels," Fullingim let fly at politicians, corporations, or newspapers he saw working against the interests of the common people, even when "the people" he represented disagreed with him. He mixed barbed social commentary about racism or criminal justice with recipes for cooking armadillo and reminiscences of growing up poor on a cotton farm in West Texas.

With equal vehemence, The Printer might indict American foreign policy or the cooking at a Kountze cafe. Regular readers learned that Fullingim loved poke salad, Elvis Presley, and the environment, but hated the John Birch Society, the phone company, and the *Beaumont Enterprise*. But whether Fullingim's editorial focused on the latest "Playhouse 90" television drama or a speech by Joseph Weldon Bailey at a Confederate picnic in 1912, certain themes remained constant.

Politics was The Printer's passion, whether local, state, or national. Early in his tenure at the *Kountze News*, Fullingim asked readers to be "charitable to his mania for taking sides in national politics. That is his one big fault and he can't help it. After all he's an eccentric old bachelor and perhaps should be forgiven if he gets fired up over politics. Maybe that's fun to him."

Fullingim's fun was not always shared by the politicians he criticized. When The Printer stopped printing, U.S. Representative Charles Wilson said, "Archer Fullingim has retired—now Texas politicians can breathe easier." Fullingim had referred to Wilson for years as "Timber Charlie," to imply the legislator's subservience to lumber companies. When Kountze suffered pollution in its creeks, Fullingim labeled Mayor John Blair "Dirty Water" Blair. And among the demeaning nicknames he coined for politicians, Fullingim is credited with being the first, in the mid 1950s, to call Richard Nixon "Tricky Dick."

In Fullingim's view, except for James Allred, Texas had not had a decent governor since James Stephen Hogg, before the turn of the century. He never forgave Democratic Governor Allan Shivers for supporting Republican presidential candidate Dwight Eisenhower ("Holy Ike") in 1952. Fullingim attacked Shivers and each of his successors in their turn for serving corporate interests against the interests of the people. None enacted the educational, environmental, or welfare legislation the state needed. None had the nerve to levy appropriate taxes on gas and oil companies or other corporations instead of leaning harder on the average citizen.

Fullingim thought most of the daily and weekly newspapers of Texas full of reactionary propaganda for the conservative establishment. He blamed the *Dallas Morning News* for helping foster the climate of hatred that resulted in the assassination of John Kennedy in 1963. He scorned the *Beaumont Enterprise* for its silence concerning regional environmental issues. He feuded with the editor of a nearby weekly and even with one of his own columnists. But Fullingim also reprinted editorials from papers he admired.

Fullingim became best known for his prolonged crusade to save the Big Thicket, a dense tropical hardwood forest in Southeast Texas. The creeks, swamps, and sandy uplands of the Thicket are home to a variety of plant and animal life, including hundreds of species of birds and flowers, some of them endangered. In 1750 the area was estimated to have covered more than three million acres. By the time Fullingim moved to Kountze, near the heart of the region, the Big Thicket consisted of about 435,000 acres and was rapidly disappearing.

Bears, panthers, and many types of birds that had once lived in the Thicket were gone, victims of encroaching civilization. Overharvesting by lumber companies, who cleared the Thicket to plant fast-growing pines as cash crops, threatened the very existence of the Big Thicket. Fullingim fought the timber interests, pressured the politicians, and helped rally support among local residents who feared losing their jobs with the lumber companies and from environmentalists anywhere who might help the cause.

The *Kountze News* ran pictures of Thicket flowers and creatures and reminiscences of older residents. The paper documented the destruction of the wilderness and the complicated political fight to save it. Fullingim ultimately ran a quote from Chief Crazy Horse on his masthead: "Man does not sell the earth upon which he walks." Fullingim made the case for preservation in a number of ways, and provided a platform for others. He backed Senator Ralph Yarborough's efforts to involve the federal government, which finally met success in 1975 with the creation of an 84,500-acre Big Thicket National Preserve.

Reviewing the book of Fullingim's selected writings in 1975, Molly Ivins found that "perhaps the most fascinating theme" in the collection was "Fullingim's struggle with his own racism." Ivins thought "sociologists interested in the roots of racism" could learn from Fullingim's public and painful change from his segregationist stance in the 1950s to his identification with blacks by the late 1960s. In his final years at the *Kountze News*, Fullingim transcended his heritage to become a strong advocate of integration and full civil rights for all.

As the social issues of the 1960s involved The Printer's imagination, he came to examine several of his own long-standing assumptions. A veteran of the Second World War, Fullingim began the decade as a loyal supporter of the U.S. war in Vietnam. But he came to believe Vietnam was a mistake and called for American withdrawal. He spoke up in favor of student rebellion and the long hairstyles on men that incensed so many of his readers. And he condemned the state's harsh penalties for the use and possession of marijuana, arguing that long prison terms harmed pot smokers more than their habit did.

Cranky, opinionated, and stubbornly old-fashioned, Archer Fullingim continued to grow and change into old age. He held to his views in the face of fierce opposition, but did not flinch from admitting his mistakes. A literary man with a folksy manner, he looked on world affairs from a small country town and offered an honest, personal response to events large and small. Over the years, Fullingim's weekly column—quirky, independent, forthright—provided his readers with a valuable, endangered resource, like the untamed and untidy wilderness he fought so long and vigorously to protect.

Buzzard Watcher and Wanderer

Archer Jesse Fullingim was born May 31, 1902, "at a place called Decatur, Texas, which is the county seat of Wise County, and my parents were born there and my grandparents fought Indians there." His father, Alfred, born in 1862, worked for the railroad and on Panhandle ranches. In 1884 he drove cattle up to Montana, where he stayed to work for the Montana Cattle Company. Returning to Texas in 1893, Alfred married twenty-one-year-old Mahala Ball. They had eight children, seven of whom survived.

Archer spent his earliest years helping his parents raise cotton on the family farm. More than half a century later, the editor of the *Kountze News* would describe vivid childhood memories to his readers. "We lived on a hill . . . on one side of Catlett Creek and Uncle Charlie lived on a rise . . . on the other side. Between our house and the creek was a field on the slope and in the bottom was our apple and pecan orchard." Uncle Charlie, a Confederate veteran, kept peacocks that Archer and his brother Ford loved to chase.

Fullingim recalled it was "about 1910 when I saw my first Gyp-

sies . . . and I had been warned many times by my parents to run if I
saw the Gypsies coming, but I had no intention of running . . . I
wanted to see if they would try to steal me as my folks assured me
they would." Besides this precocious urge to travel, Archer acquired
an early interest in politics. "All I remember about the year 1912
was that Woodrow Wilson was elected president." Archer rode three
and a half miles to town in a buggy to get the newspaper with a big
picture of Wilson on the front page. "So when I was ten years old I
felt strongly that the Democratic party was the greatest thing on
earth, except the Methodist Church . . . My father was a man who
talked politics. I acquired all his prejudices against Republicans."

Remembering his childhood late in life, Fullingim emphasized the
pleasures of youth, not the pain of poverty. He wrote about making
cane syrup, pulling his grandmother's mare out of a bog, and attending the annual Confederate picnic. The family rode to the picnic "in
a carriage that we called a hack" pulled by their two roan mares,
Chicken and Dolly. His father would fill up two water buckets—one
with lemonade and the other with barbecued beef—at a cost of fifty
cents each. One memorable year "I saw my first movie. One scene
showed a train coming straight at the audience. Every seat emptied
and people ran over each other to get out of the way."

In 1916, drought forced the Fullingims to sell their land. The family loaded their possessions on a train and traveled to Lynn County,
in the wheat lands of far West Texas. Archer attended three different
high schools that year. But less than a year later, the continuing
drought forced the Fullingims to move again, this time "to Cottle
County in a covered wagon, leaving the terrible drouth of the South
Plains behind us. Everything was green in Cottle County in 1917,
but in 1918 the drouth hit . . ." Archer and his father loaded their
plow into a wagon and set off with horses and mules on a long, dis-
couraging search for any farm work they could find.

"During the drouth of 1917–1918, fried rabbit was our principal
meat . . . We had a barbed wire 100 feet long and we would twist
them out of prairie dog holes." The cold rainy autumn of 1918 reminded Fullingim of "the opening sentence of 'The Fall of the House
of Usher.'" His mother was ill with appendicitis in a hospital at
Quanah, fifty miles away. His father was with her. Archer was left in
charge of his three younger brothers and his youngest sister. "I never
did finish high school. I dropped out in the spring of 1918 to ride the
middle buster, the planter . . . I went directly from the cotton patch
to college, without a high school diploma, and I had to take entrance
exams."

In the fall of 1919, Archer's parents decided to enroll him in Decatur Baptist College. But he had to help harvest the cotton crop first. On the plateau overlooking Salt Creek, "we'd be picking cotton by sunup. I had a strong back in those days, and although I wore knee pads, most of the time I was on my feet and stooped over. At noon, we'd rest an hour, and that's when I became a buzzard watcher." In November, the harvest complete, Archer's father took him to enroll in college.

At the strict Baptist school that Fullingim called "the oldest junior college in the world," the newest student felt very uncomfortable, awkward, unathletic, and poorly dressed. "I had lived on a farm all my life and never had known more than 50 people, and here I was thrown into association with at least 200 strangers . . . potential enemies and I developed an instant antipathy and contempt."

His English teacher, Bernice Neel, taught young Archer to appreciate good poetry and literature. She encouraged his writing. "Maybe at the age of 17 or 19 somebody like Miss Neel is going to happen in everybody's life. The person, not especially meaning to, turns you the way you go after that. Mine went the writing way." Fullingim graduated from Decatur Baptist College in 1921 and went back to the family farm. He also taught school, to earn money for university.

"In 1921–22 I taught school with my sister Lena . . . at a two-teacher school at Green Valley. The next year, I taught school at Lone Star, a two-teacher school about three miles from our home on Salt Creek." Fullingim taught the older students, from fifth grade up. He remembered the fierce sandstorms that hid the sun and blew sand into the schoolhouse "through the roof, window cracks, door cracks and various holes in the building . . . We would use a hoe to move it into piles and then shovel it into the coal scuttle, carry it outside and dump it."

During his teaching days, Fullingim bought a Corona portable typewriter to type up stories he had written in longhand and send them to popular magazines, but without success. The young teacher "tried to inspire, incite and encourage" his pupils. But when one dissatisfied father removed his son from the class, Fullingim took it as further "evidence that I failed fundamentally as a teacher. I just wasn't cut out to be a teacher."

In the fall of 1923 Fullingim enrolled at the University of Oklahoma to study English and journalism. He chose Oklahoma, where his four younger siblings would eventually follow, instead of Texas "because we lived 180 miles from Norman and 480 from Austin." Fullingim recalled that "when I told my father I was going to the

University of Oklahoma, he said, 'You won't learn anything in the Indian Territory, up there amongst them gut-sucking Indians.'"

Fullingim worked his way through university by writing essays for other students. "I used to charge 'em $1 a theme, and a lot of 'em would be in class with me and I'd make straight B's and they'd make straight A's," he told Willie Morris in 1958. He also worked in cotton fields near campus, where he could hear the roar of the football crowd from the stadium. Later Fullingim thought, "I made a mistake in studying journalism at the University." He had hoped that practicing journalism would improve his writing enough that he could realize his true ambition—to write fiction. "What I did not know was that if you worked for a newspaper you would have time for nothing but journalism."

"After I got my degree I wandered north into Kansas and ran into the wheat harvest." Fullingim labored two weeks in the fields and was beaten by the owners, who thought he was a union organizer. He wrote up his experiences and took the story to the editor of the *Wichita Eagle*, "the biggest and oldest daily in Wichita, Kansas. I got a job that lasted three months, and my boss sent me to the Arkansas City Traveller, a small daily in Southern Kansas. I stayed there until Christmas."

Then Fullingim decided to see the world. He hopped freight trains to follow the tour of the Polish pianist Ignace Paderewski, which led him to Florida and a job as music critic for the *Miami Herald*. In Miami he signed on a merchant ship headed for the Far East. "Travelling was almost an overpowering passion with me . . ." he said later. Within a year of graduating from university in 1925, "I had spent six months in Florida, six weeks in Cuba, six weeks in Japan, passing through the Panama Canal en route." When the ship returned to British Columbia, Fullingim got off and worked his way south. He picked apples in Washington, potatoes in Oregon, and cotton in California's San Joaquin Valley.

In 1927 Fullingim got a job at the *Shafter Progress*, a weekly paper in the foothills of the Sierras, near Bakersfield. "I told the owner, when the snow on that mountain there melts, I'm leavin', and I did." Fullingim went to San Francisco, then to Carmel. "There was a writer I thought the world of then—Robinson Jeffers . . . He was stayin' at Carmel and I guess I made a hit with him . . . cause I ended up stayin' a month." Then the wandering writer headed home to Cottle County to help his family with the cotton harvest. Except for his U.S. Navy service in the South Pacific during World War Two, and a few brief vacations, Fullingim would spend the rest of his life in Texas.

The Printer Comes to Town

"When I lived in Galveston the first six months of 1928, working on the paper there, I finally came to refer to it as 'a running sore set in a muddy sea,' but nevertheless I liked Galveston then and still do." Fullingim got a reporting job on the *Galveston Tribune*. "At that time three families ruled (and ruined) Galveston . . . the Moodys, the Sealys and the Kempners . . . I was a Moody Menial because I worked on the newspaper they owned." After an unsuccessful attempt to ship out from Houston to Europe on a merchant vessel, Fullingim found an editorial job at the *Panhandle Herald*.

In 1929, he moved to Pampa, twenty-eight miles from Panhandle and fifty-eight miles north of Amarillo, to work for the *Pampa Daily News*, where he would remain for thirteen years. "I worked on the editorial staff . . . but I wrote durn few editorials. Mostly I was a reporter, a feature writer, a columnist and held the title of city editor, meaning that I took the copy off the Associated Press wire and edited it . . ." When Archer's father died, in 1931, his mother and two of his brothers, Alf and Henry Will, came to live with him in Pampa.

"I probably held my job mainly because I had my mother and brothers to support, not because I was any great shakes as a newspaperman." His young brothers went to high school in Pampa, where they played football. "That intense football period in my life lasted about six years . . . Whenever we lost, my considered opinion was that it was either the coach's fault or the referee's fault, proving that I was about like all the other parents, then and now." Archer sent Alf and Henry Will through the University of Oklahoma.

He remained in Pampa throughout the depression of the 1930s, glad to have a way to support his mother and brothers. Besides editing wire copy and writing articles bylined "Roving Reporter," Fullingim wrote a regular column of anecdotes and local gossip entitled "People You Know." Commenting about "Henry" P. Rainey, the new president of the University of Texas, in January 1939, Fullingim opined that "the president of the University is the most powerful man in Texas."

When the United States entered the Second World War and local boys were drafted into the armed forces, Fullingim filled his column with items about where the area men were serving. He printed excerpts from letters the boys wrote home. He was a booster for blood drives, bond drives, and other patriotic activities. He urged young men to volunteer to fight. But, as Fullingim wrote later, readers began to wonder why he did not go. "When I was 30 I looked 20 and when I was 40 I looked 30. So I would lie about my age and it caught up with me. People would say, why don't they draft Fullingim, the draft-dodger!"

In July 1942, Fullingim exhorted young men to "Join the navy and help Texas win the war! The navy is running short of men . . . Join the navy and free the world!" Two weeks later he informed his readers that he had joined the navy himself, but not "on the spur of the moment or as a publicity stunt." He said he had tried to volunteer a month after Pearl Harbor, but the navy turned him down. Now the county draft board had run out of men classified 1-A and relaxed their requirements.

Fullingim thought he was physically fit. "I can out-walk anybody in town half my age; I don't have a bay window. I have enough teeth. My eyes are good enough . . . All I have is hay fever and that's the reason I picked the navy." If the navy would not have him, he would get in the army. His mother would be fine, living with his sister in Galveston. "I have been sitting at this desk for 13 years, and of course I will hate to leave Pampa, but who doesn't?" A few days later he wrote about taking his physical examination in Dallas. A week after that he was gone.

Fullingim never returned to Pampa, not even in 1966 when he visited other Texas Panhandle towns. "I didn't go to Pampa because for one thing I didn't want my old friends to see my gray hair and bay window. Besides nearly all the people in Pampa that I liked a whole lot are either dead or rich, and both groups depress me."

Before reporting to the navy in 1942, Fullingim visited his grandfather's brother, "Uncle Bunch," in Oklahoma. The old man, in his late eighties, told Archer he wanted some "Jap ears." He reminded Archer about how many Yankees his Uncle Jess had killed in the Civil War. "The Fullingims have made their mark in every war," said Uncle Bunch. "I've set my head on gettin' them Jap ears. If you bring them back I'll know that you smelled the patchin'. I'll know that you made your mark."

As a gunner's mate, Fullingim served two years in the South Pacific. He traveled to New Caledonia, to the Solomon Islands, and to New Zealand, "My favorite of all places where I spent 30 days on a 'rest' tour . . . I flew from Howe Island in the Admiralties to Bougainville, to Guadalcanal . . ." Jumping with a full pack off a landing craft at Manus, one of the Admiralty Islands, Fullingim injured his back and legs. "But I did not go to sick bay at the time . . . what with sick bay being full of malaria and jungle rot cases."

In June 1944, Fullingim was sent to a hospital at Pensacola, Florida, to recover from his injuries. The navy made him an officer. "A lot of people might be tempted to call it a battlefield commission, but I ain't gonna call it that. I didn't see any fightin' and the Navy was the longest vacation I ever had." Released from the hospital, "I wrote manuals on how to fly the SB20 3, 4 and 5."

When the war ended, Archer Fullingim came back to Texas. He visited his brother Alf, who lived in Silsbee, near Kountze. Archer had made up his mind to edit his own weekly paper, but Hardin County already had one weekly and could not sustain another. He found a newspaper for sale in Normangee. Archer bought the *Normangee Star* in 1946 and ran it for three years. "Normangee had the most fascinating people on earth and in 1949 I sold the Star to the man I bought it from and came back to Silsbee to my little house. In 1949 I wrote a book about Leon county and had the best time of my life . . ."

Later Fullingim gave slightly different accounts of his literary year. In 1958 he showed Willie Morris two manuscripts and said he wrote "two books in fifteen months." "This book was about a hillbilly singer, I know more about hillbilly music probably than any man alive." Three years later Fullingim said his book was about "what you might call authentic 'old country boys and girls' (not the phony kind) and politics. I know more about politics than any other subject so I wrote about it."

Though vague about the content, Fullingim was firm in believing that "that book has been the biggest thing in my life. I had the happiest time of my life writing it. Sometimes I would get up and run around the house three times to calm myself down." He thought it was the only time in his life he had done exactly as he pleased. Even if the book were never published, "I will say that the time I spent on it has justified my existence—in my humble opinion." His book never did get published.

While Fullingim finished his manuscripts, the local weekly paper ceased publication. Among the classified ads in the *Dallas Morning News*, Fullingim noticed a complete print shop for sale in Paris, Texas, for $845. He bought the shop, loaded it on a truck, and drove it to Kountze, the seat of Hardin County, in the heart of the Big Thicket. A census Fullingim cited in his first issue showed the population of Kountze to be 1,654. The editor rented a room and set up shop, hoping his gamble would be able to make him a living.

The Frightened Fifties

The first issue of the *Kountze News* appeared September 14, 1950. Besides the census, the four-page paper mentioned the second test drilling for oil in the county and urged the paving of the town's main street. But the big news was the paper itself. Fullingim introduced himself as a man who "has been wanting to come to Kountze for five years, and now that he's here he is as happy as a cow in a pea patch." He printed up six hundred copies and gave them away for six weeks at the post office. When he acquired six hundred subscribers at two dollars each, he knew the *News* would survive.

In January 1951, Fullingim took the final plunge. He bought a "Blue Streak Model 31 Linotype . . . The new machine cost $9,000 and the editor hocked everything in sight to make the down payment . . ." Besides detailing the sums he owed the Merganthaler company and the bank, the proud editor boasted that his new machine "has 30,000 parts, most of them moving, and we know how to fix 10 if they get out of order." He invited his readers to an open house to see it.

The technology of Fullingim's mechanical pride was old-fashioned when he bought it and increasingly antiquated as the years passed. More than one visitor marveled at Fullingim's ability to compose his editorials directly on the Linotype. "That takes confidence," as Leon Hale wrote. "It's kin, at least, to carving words in stone, since the words were cast directly into metal type." After Fullingim's death, longtime *Kountze News* columnist Gordon Baxter tried without success to get The Printer's equipment to the Smithsonian Institution.

The editorials that would make Archer Fullingim famous were absent from the *Kountze News* in its earliest years. The Printer's style, and perhaps his opinions, evolved gradually as he settled into his chosen hometown and his chosen role as political and social commentator. Fullingim concentrated on local gossip, anecdotes, and the activities of local organizations. He explained his weekend absences from town to visit his mother in Galveston. When Mahala Fullingim died at seventy-nine on February 24, 1951, her son wrote a lengthy obituary.

Columns entitled "I Heard" or "I Saw" resembled Fullingim's "People You Know" column in the *Pampa Daily News* with informal comments or observations, some of them merely jokes, such as his story about the local barber: "I Heard: Continued speculation about Goat McDonald's new car. While the juke box ground out Lefty Frizzell's 'Mom and Pappy Waltz' over in the Nip N' Tuck Tavern where the temperature was trembling at 104 degrees, I heard some wise guy say that Goat left one of those places . . . investigated by the Kefauver committee, with 20 G's one night recently and that the money paid for that new Chevy was just chicken feed to Goat."

Fullingim showed an early interest in the environment, praising certain gardens, exhorting his readers not to dump their garbage on the highways, and protesting thefts of dogwood and honeysuckle by visiting tourists. Toward the end of his first year in Kountze, Fullingim boasted in print about the dependability of the *News* and its community emphasis. He had only used "canned news" (i.e., wire stories) in two issues.

In one of his earliest political skirmishes, Fullingim attacked Jack Neil, a local radio station owner who was running for Congress. He thought the constant promotion of Neil's candidacy by the station's disk jockeys violated "the spirit of FCC political regulations" if not the letter of the law. He kept after the station owner for weeks, telling him, "Neil, you may be a sharp operator, but I voted for hillbilly music one time (O'Daniel) and look how O'Daniel did? Besides, you ain't no real hillbilly."

When the primary results showed Neil the winner, Fullingim decided "that if this printer had kept his big mouth shut Jack Neil would not have carried Hardin County. He probably would have got skunked in Kountze if I hadn't chewed out Neil about three times. . . . I probably drummed up more votes for Neil than he would have got otherwise. Next time, I'll jump on the man I'm for— but there'll be no next time. For never, never again will I take sides in a political race. I am humiliated and put out. But I still think— never mind what I still think. I ain't gonna say what I think never, never again." Two weeks later he endorsed Jack Brooks for Congress.

From his earliest days at the *Kountze News*, Fullingim strove for a light, humorous touch. He wanted to separate his paper from "The big daily press of Texas which has become habitually sourpuss Republican." Eventually he advertised Kountze on his masthead as "The Town with a Sense of Humor," a description perhaps more wishful than accurate. In an article entitled "Big Lies Printed Only When News Is Scarce," Fullingim said that though he aimed to publish the facts, in almost every issue "some big lie gets into print. If it ain't about politics it's about football. However, it should be emphasized that the editor only prints big windies when he's too ornery to go out and get the news. Or when a big lie sounds better than the truth."

Fullingim liked to use bold oversized headlines, of the type reserved for cataclysmic world events, to announce odd or trivial matters. Perhaps the best-known example is: "He Knocks Toe Nail Off Getting to Bed!" Some other *Kountze News* headlines over the years included: "Mad Fox Chases Woman on Top of Icebox," "Man Laid Up in Bed and Drank Stolen Whiskey," "Carolyn Has Pink Beehive Hair-Do," and "Hound Dog Suckles Pig."

With some exceptions, Fullingim avoided discussion of serious issues in his newspaper for years. His editorial column did not appear on a regular basis until 1956. Fullingim's desire to get well settled in his new home, and to maintain the solid support of advertisers and subscribers, probably accounted for part of his initial reticence. Another reason for this slow start may have been because the issues of the 1950s did not fully develop until midway in the decade.

In his autobiography, Theodore H. White wrote that "the strange fluid decade of the fifties did not begin until . . . 1954, to be precise. And ended only in November, 1963, with the assassination of John F. Kennedy. That decade incubated not only the problems, but the abundance, the vitality, the passion that exploded in the tormented sixties."

White chose several seminal events of 1954 to make his case, including the surrender in Vietnam of French forces at Dienbienphu in May and the Geneva conference in late June, at which Secretary of State John Foster Dulles agreed to protect the South Vietnamese in that newly partitioned country. As a result of that decision, Americans were fighting and dying in Vietnam twenty years later. Also in 1954, the United States Supreme Court, in Brown v. the Topeka Board of Education, outlawed racial segregation in American public schools. That Court action began the modern civil rights movement in the United States, with its massive demonstrations, widespread violence, and sweeping legislation over the following fifteen years, and with the legal and social consequences that continue to evolve.

By mid 1954, Senator Joseph McCarthy reached the height of his power. By year's end he was censured, his career in ruins. White also pointed to the 1954 congressional elections. "That was the last year in our time that Republicans would enjoy control of both houses of the U.S. Congress." The frustration resulting from this prolonged inability of the Republicans to propose and enact legislation continues in Congress almost forty years later.

Though Kountze lay far from any seat of power or flashpoints of radical change, Archer Fullingim eventually became deeply involved in the debates over Vietnam and civil rights. More immediately, Fullingim spoke out against McCarthyism and the reach of red scare tactics into Texas politics. As a self-styled "brass collar Democrat," he opposed Republicans at all levels on principle. But in the early 1950s Fullingim discovered a more insidious enemy—nominal Democrats with the conservative instincts of Republicans, fronted by a man he detested, Governor Allan Shivers.

Fullingim criticized Joseph McCarthy for his "perjury" and for the "political lynchings that he calls campaigns." He thought McCarthy's "ominous and daringly false accusation . . . that the Protestant clergy form the greatest pro-Communist group in America" showed the Wisconsin senator to be as great a menace to Protestantism and democracy as any communist. When the right-wing Houston Minute Women tried and failed to have their own alternative candidate elected president of the state PTA instead of the majority choice, Fullingim blew up. He berated "the Texas metropolitan press, including the Beaumont papers," for praising the six hundred "conservatives" at the PTA convention as opposed to the three thousand "liberals." "For any time the Beaumont paper puts quotation marks around the word 'liberal,' it goes on to imply that 'liberal' and 'Communist' mean one and the same thing . . ." But his Kountze readers knew "that our two delegates . . . Mrs. Mickey Marshall and Mrs. Harold Willis . . ." were not "liberals with quotation marks. They are simply good PTA workers, good mothers and good Americans," like the other delegates, "except of course the school-wreckers from Houston . . ."

In April 1954, a group of Texas oil millionaires who supported Senator McCarthy invited him to speak at the San Jacinto Monument near Houston. Fullingim thought the idea of McCarthy at the site of a crucial battle in the Texas war for independence from Mexico was "doubly repulsive if one will reread the Texas Declaration of Independence . . ." because McCarthy "has denounced everything Texians fought for . . ."

Fullingim said, "It must be depressing to live in Houston . . ." where the Minute Women ran roughshod over the public schools and the Bill of Rights, where "patriotism is the scoundrel's last refuge and . . . Anti-Communism is the scoundrel's first defense . . ." Oil millionaires like Hugh Roy Cullen, "the McCarthy stooge," browbeat the city with the help of the daily press. Fullingim thought the *Houston Post* had been "made callous by the reeking atmosphere of McCarthyism, murder (Houston leads the nation in homicides) and Republican propaganda . . ." Fullingim was locating his political enemies and learning the language of attack. His enemies would prove to be at least as dependable as his friends.

Brass Collar Democrat

When Governor Beauford Jester died in office, in 1949, Lieutenant Governor Allan Shivers became the chief executive of Texas. Shivers won an easy election in 1950, but soon came into conflict with the federal government over the rights to offshore oil in the Gulf of Mexico. Backed by conservative oilmen, Shivers argued for state control of "the tidelands." The Truman administration, supported by a 1950 U.S. Supreme Court ruling, claimed federal jurisdiction.

The 1952 Democratic presidential candidate, Adlai Stevenson, did not support state ownership of the tidelands. But Dwight Eisenhower, the Republican candidate, did. Shivers lined up with conservative Dixiecratic Democrats behind Eisenhower. At Amarillo, in the fall of 1952, for the first time in Texas history the Democratic convention endorsed a Republican for the presidency.

Fullingim had already decided Stevenson was "a great man." With Stevenson as president, "the armadillos will be safe for another four years and . . . another general can fade away." The armadillo remark referred to hard economic times, when the poor had to hunt wild game for food as Fullingim had hunted rabbits. Someone Fullingim called "a DED (Disgruntled Eisenhower Democrat)" accused him of voting not for Stevenson but "'agin' Hoover and a depression and armadiller-chasin'.'" Fullingim replied: "Voting against the Depression? Shoot no! I'm still voting against Reconstruction! What the Republicans did to the South between 1865 and 1932 makes the last 20 years of Roosevelt and Truman look like hog-heaven."

When Shivers announced for Eisenhower, Fullingim thought "old Allan ripped his britches when he said . . . he was going to vote for Ike, but that he was still a 'Texas Democrat,' a label Allan himself invented, and which really means 'Shivercrat,'" a word Fullingim thought would come to be held in contempt, like "Hoovercrat." Shivers' vote for Ike was also a vote "for that malicious smear specialist Richard Nixon," whose "sinister and merciless" look gave Fullingim a "fearful feeling."

He worried about Ike dying in office, leaving Nixon and McCarthy in charge. "Between the two, they could start a reign of terror." Nixon had not explained his personal finances. "In my books he's a crook!" Fullingim thought the Republicans would kill prosperity. He wouldn't be able to make his Linotype payments. "I'd have to go back to Buglar cigarettes and going without underwear." He titled this article "How Do You Like Your Armadiller—Fried or Baked?"

When Shivers ran for an unprecedented third term in 1954, Fullingim called him "a dictator." "He rules the state with a hand of iron, and who rules him? Millionaire Republicans and money grabbers." The *Kountze News* constantly attacked Shivers and repeatedly called for his resignation because of the scandals during his administration that sent Land Commissioner Bascom Giles to prison. When Price Daniel declared for governor in 1956, Fullingim denounced him as "the dear, dear friend of the boys who've been running Texas into the mud and slime for the past 10 years," including the lying financiers who "libelled" Homer Rainey.

Fullingim supported the unsuccessful gubernatorial candidacy of Ralph Yarborough in 1952, 1954, and 1956. In 1957 Yarborough won the U.S. Senate seat vacated by Governor Daniel. A senator until 1971, Yarborough would prove a crucial ally in Fullingim's long battle to create a Big Thicket wilderness. The Printer blamed Yarborough's 1956 defeat—"the closest Governor's race in Texas history"—on a "front page boycott" against Yarborough "by most of the big city newspapers, including the Dallas, Fort Worth, San Antonio, and Beaumont papers . . . In Houston, where the newspapers . . . covered his campaign as well as it did Daniel's, Yarborough won."

Early in 1954, The Printer announced that the paid circulation of the *Kountze News* had reached one thousand. Serving the communities of Kountze, Honey Island, Sour Lake, Silsbee, and Village Mills, the *News* circulation reached 1,200 by September 1956. "News Has Followed Crowd, It Decides on Its 6th Birthday . . . The News has always followed the paths of progress in Kountze . . . In fact, we have followed the people in everything from collard greens to Ralph Yarborough."

But in 1956 Fullingim's editorial policy became much more aggressive. In February, he began weekly publication of his column "The Printer Fires Both Barrels." His premiere target was a Fullingim favorite, a newspaper editor—"Beau" Beaumier of the *Lufkin Daily News*—who supported a "corrupt" politician—Attorney General John Ben Shepperd. He called Beaumier's "1,000 word alibi" for Shepperd "a brazen bucket of synthetic hog slop that is routine procedure these days on the editorial pages of the decadent daily press." The next month "Both Barrels" moved to its permanent place on the front page and acquired the striking logo of a smiling hunter blasting a double-barreled shotgun.

Fullingim's continuous wide reading included other Texas weeklies. He enjoyed the independent editorials in the *Canyon News*, the *Ralls Banner*, and the *Tulia Herald*, whose rants "against P. Daniel and A. Shivers make our puny remarks look like love-making." The Printer was happy to learn that his was not "the only paper in the state which would denounce the parasitic swindlers at Austin." Fullingim especially admired H. M. Baggarly, liberal editor of the *Tulia Herald* in a conservative Panhandle town. He often quoted Baggarly in the *News* and occasionally reprinted entire *Tulia Herald* editorials in "Both Barrels."

The *Texas Observer*, a liberal statewide weekly published in Aus-

tin, ran an article called "Country Editors," quoting Fullingim and
Baggarly on the results of the 1956 Yarborough-Daniel race. Fullingim thought the campaign had "vindicated" Yarborough. "So
what do we have to look forward to under Daniel? Coverup, grab and
greed . . ." By 1958 the *Observer* was calling Fullingim "a latter-day
William Cowper Brann" and interviewing him at length. The *Observer* continued to run *Kountze News* editorials on various subjects
over the years, soliciting articles from The Printer even after he
retired.

Fullingim had no respect for the men who governed Texas. They
allowed the corporations, especially the oil and gas companies,
"with high profits and ability to pay the most taxes," to evade their
responsibilities. "Under the corporations Texas has become the
32nd state in the U.S. in education with respect to the amount paid
teachers . . ." Fullingim wrote in 1959. "Now these corporations
want a retail sales tax." Instead of James Stephen Hogg, who cur-
tailed the power of the railroads as governor in the 1890s, Texas suffered under governors like John Connally, lackey of the "Big Rich."

All Connally wanted was more power "to destroy the public
school system . . . to keep his foot on the necks of the old folks . . .
to operate the universities for the sole benefit of big business and
radical right wing conservatives . . ." and "to veto more medical
schools for the state . . ." according to Fullingim in 1965. Like most
state legislators, Connally ruled on behalf of "Big Money and his
rich friends who finance his campaigns, but he is not for us poor
white trash."

Fullingim despised John Connally with the special malice he reserved for Republicans disguised as Democrats, like Allan Shivers.
Eventually Connally did change his political party affiliation, serving as a Republican in the Nixon administration. The Printer also
maintained his loathing of declared conservatives, calling Barry
Goldwater "the most useless, futile, frantic man in America, with
John Tower running him a close second." Fullingim attacked Tower
in print on many occasions. But in 1966 he endorsed Tower's reelection to the U.S. Senate because "at least he admits he's a Republican,
while his opponent, Waggoner Carr, does not, though he is . . ."

During the presidential campaign of 1964, still bitter at the assassination of John Kennedy, Fullingim explained why he thought
Barry Goldwater should be the Republican nominee: "If you have an
eediot in the family there's no use telling him to get under the bed
when company's coming. Put him right out on the front porch and
let him slobber and gibber and run off at the mouth where everybody
can see him and know the worst right off and what to expect. Once

the nation and the world knows just where Barry stands, the better off we will be. Let's get Barry and the John Birchers out of our system once and for all and the only way to do that is to nominate Goldwater for president."

Concerning Lyndon Johnson, Fullingim altered his opinion drastically more than once. In 1956 he supported Johnson's favorite son presidential candidacy. He received friendly letters from the senator—"Dear Arch . . . I know who my friends are, of course, and I am proud to count you as one of the best . . ."—which he printed in his newspaper. But within two years Fullingim declared, " . . . I've had enough of Lyndon Johnson . . . I've had enough of his betrayals."

In 1959 The Printer responded to a Johnson form letter, telling the senator in his column that "there are a lot of brass collar Democrats who used to worship the ground you walked on, alongside FDR, but who now feel sick when they think of you . . ." Fullingim urged Johnson to quit trying to stay in "the middle of the road" and "take sides." "Come on over, man . . . and side in with the people of this world who are striving for a better standard of living, the starving, the victims of dictatorships, the revolutionaries, not to forget the rank and file of the country."

During Johnson's presidency, Fullingim supported his civil rights and poverty programs but deplored his handling of the Vietnam War. In March 1968, when President Johnson announced his decision not to run for reelection, Fullingim said, "I felt kind of sorry for LBJ while he was making that speech, saying he was going to back down in Vietnam and wasn't going to run for president . . . Watching LBJ on TV was like watching a man dying." But if he felt sorry for Johnson, Fullingim felt even sorrier for himself, considering the political choices remaining.

"We have Bobby [Kennedy], who a year ago I hoped would be president but who now nauseates me. We have [Eugene] McCarthy, who I don't understand even a little bit. I don't want either one of them for president and [Vice-President Hubert] Humphrey is about as inspiring as a turnip. George Wallace is a racist, and I'd just as soon vote for the Ku Klux Klan. On top of all that Nixon looms as the Republican nominee, and I would not vote for Nixon under any circumstance."

But when Nixon won the presidency, Fullingim professed "distinct relief." "The Democratic party had become thoroughly discredited . . . mainly because of the Vietnam war . . ." Fullingim was also gratified that "for the first time in 30 years Texas is cut off from Washington. We have no pipeline to the White House. Nobody can now . . . aid and abet the conservative establishment in Texas as did

LBJ." He attacked the Republicans for prolonging the Asian war they had decried when the Democrats were in office.

In 1973 Fullingim said: "Nixon hasn't changed a bit. He's a dictator at heart. What Nixon is doing is simple. He's taking money from you and giving it to the rich. His priority is not you but the defense contractors." A year before Nixon resigned the presidency in disgrace, Fullingim called the Watergate break-in and cover-up "probably the worst official crime of the century because it tried to destroy the two-party system." The Printer didn't think the young men involved in the Watergate conspiracy should be jailed—only the president, who inspired their "debauchery." He had a similar reaction to the My Lai massacre, the murder of Vietnamese civilians by U.S. soldiers, advising that Lieutenant Calley should be pardoned and Nixon put on trial.

Archer Fullingim heated up tons of lead in his Linotype to berate local, state, and national politicians. In league with the politicians against the common people was the Texas press, which suffered, in his view, from a sickness. "This sickness is the daily press' devotion to special interest corporations and monopolies and its hatred of small business, workers, the indigent and what it refers to as 'liberal and labor.'" Fullingim devoted a lot of energy to analyzing the symptoms of journalistic maladies and prescribing specific, sometimes drastic, cures.

Hatemongers and Calamity Howlers

In 1958 J. Frank Dobie wrote Fullingim that he was the best editorial writer in Texas because "You are not afraid to be honest." Dobie, whose weekly comments appeared in Austin, Houston, Fort Worth, and San Antonio papers, complained that he had to "keep quiet on strong beliefs, for if I said what I believe politically these papers would all stop taking my column." Later, informing Fullingim he had quoted "Both Barrels" on Price Daniel, Dobie added, "I would have preferred to quote some of your more damaging remarks . . . [but] He and Shivers and all the other old-line republican reactionaries are such sacred cows to the Texas press that the newspapers won't print even a joke about them."

Fullingim knew the dailies had always supported the rich and powerful. "The bitterest enemies of Hogg in 1900 were the Dallas News, the Houston Post and the San Antonio Express, three papers which have always lined up with the corporations, against the plain people . . ." When John Connally beat Don Yarborough in the Democratic gubernatorial primary in 1962, Fullingim noted that "only one of 125 daily newspapers and six of 600 weekly newspapers in Texas actively supported Yarborough . . ." He thought the reason "for this blanket endorsement is that the papers, most of which endorsed Nixon for president in 1960, want the situation in Austin to stay as it is. They want Texas to remain in the hands of the Shivercrats and lobbyists," with no help for education or the aged.

The average citizens of the state were being continuously misled by "the professional Texans, and these include newspapers, chiefly conservative, part-time Republican journals like the Beaumont Enterprise." These professional Texans liked to claim that Texans governed themselves, held conservative values, had the best schools, and wanted no federal aid. But the truth was "that the oil lobby rules Texas and has for years and nobody admits it . . ."

Forty miles south of Kountze, Beaumont had morning and afternoon papers, "whose stilted editorials are glaring carbon copies of each other," in Fullingim's view, full of "absurd, exotic and unrealistic thinking . . ." He disapproved of the way the "Beaumont papers hate unions and that they are not unionized . . ." The Printer was certain that "No Beaumont newspaper is ever going to win any Pulitzer prize for exposing or even explaining the puzzling situation existing in the district courts or in the courthouse in Beaumont." He berated the Beaumont papers for predicting "that prostitution, gambling, saloons, sales of liquor to minors will continue in Beaumont and Port Arthur. They will continue as long as the press puts the responsibility on the people instead of the officers who are elected to enforce the law."

For years Fullingim "jokingly referred to the Beaumont morning paper as the 'Louisiana Enterprise'"—or simply the "La. E."—since he thought it served the interests of wealthy western Louisiana landowners more than its Texas constituency. Eventually Fullingim considered "changing the name of the E. from Louisiana to Shivers. It's just not fair to Louisiana . . ." The Printer reckoned that "the good people of SE Texas have the good sense to vote exactly opposite to the E. editorials, and to ignore the radical right wing slanted news." But if the *Beaumont Enterprise* gave Fullingim a sour stomach, the *Dallas Morning News* made his blood boil.

In 1961, Fullingim heard about the John Birch Society, a rightwing group that wanted to impeach U.S. Supreme Court Chief Justice Earl Warren. Fullingim studied up on the organization and concluded that "the real aim of the John Birch Society" was to "wipe out all social legislation, including the income tax," leaving the rich Society members "sitting just dandy with the rest of us working for them at a dollar a day or being carted off to the gas chambers."

As Fullingim saw it, "Dallas is the mecca of conservatives, right wingers, Birchers, etc. and the Dallas News is the Bible of the John Birchers; its news columns and editorial page are devoted to attacking federal spending of all kinds." After President Kennedy's assassination in Dallas in 1963, Fullingim increased his attacks on "the Dallas News . . ." for "always egging on radical right-wing haters . . ." He called the Dallas morning paper "the conscienceless, snaffle-toothed harlot for the corporation lobbyists, John Birchers, Kennedy haters and war mongers."

The *Dallas Morning News* had changed drastically since the death of its longtime editor and publisher, George Bannerman Dealey, in 1946. Sober, conscientious, and civic-minded, G. B. Dealey developed the *News* in his own image. With a circulation of more than one hundred thousand in the early 1940s, the *Dallas Morning News* aspired to be the Texas paper of record. But Dealey's son, Ted, who took charge of the *News* when G. B. died, was a different sort. As one historian of the *News* put it, "Ted Dealey was a red-baiter, a supporter of Joe McCarthy, an unforgiving opponent of the United Nations, an enemy of social welfare and unions and federal aid, and so was his newspaper."

In October 1961, Ted Dealey attended a White House luncheon with eighteen other Texas editors. After a briefing by President Kennedy, several editors offered their best wishes. Then Ted Dealey read a prepared statement: "The general opinion of the grass-roots thinking in this country is that you and your administration are weak sisters . . . We need a man on horseback to lead this nation, and many people in Texas . . . think that you are riding Caroline's tricycle."

Fullingim joined the general condemnation of Dealey's remarks, saying the publisher "made an ass out of himself recently by telling President Kennedy to his face in Washington that Kennedy has no 'grass roots' support in Texas. This was disputed by nearly every Texas publisher who attended the dinner . . ." But of the two thousand letters the *Dallas Morning News* received about the incident, seventeen hundred expressed approval.

When Adlai Stevenson, U.S. ambassador to the United Nations, visited Dallas in October 1963, he was mobbed, spat upon, and hit over the head with a placard. The Printer opined that "the John Birch-loving Dallas Morning News has created the climate that has inspired such uncivilized behavior. The Dallas Morning News is in the same position as Governor Wallace of Alabama who continually shouts the racist hatred that results in bombings."

On November 22, 1963, visiting Dallas against Stevenson's advice, John Kennedy read an advertisement addressed to him in the *Dallas*

Morning News. Bordered in black, the full-page ad read: "Welcome Mr. Kennedy to Dallas . . . A city that will continue to grow and prosper despite efforts by you and your administration to penalize it for its non-conformity to 'New Frontierism.'"

The ad asked twelve rhetorical questions accusing the president of being soft on communism, including "Why have you scrapped the Monroe Doctrine in favor of the spirit of Moscow?" John Kennedy handed the ad to his wife and said, "Oh, you know, we're heading into nut country." Three hours later he was shot to death in the plaza named for G. B. Dealey.

Fullingim was devastated. Only a few months earlier, he had written that "personally, I regard John Fitzgerald Kennedy as the greatest president I've lived under and I began life under Theodore Roosevelt." He lashed out at Dallas, "a city now universally acclaimed as the hate capital of the world . . ." He thought "the hate has been building up for years in Dallas, under the leadership of The Dallas Morning News . . . The trouble in Dallas was that the stable minds incited the unstable minds to violence." Fullingim wondered: "Will the shocking murder of the President lessen the hate, will it bring the hate-mongers to repentance . . . ?"

Fullingim made an effort to repent of his own hatred—for Goldwater, the John Birchers, and other radical right-wing Republicans— "because by hating them it puts me in the same class with them. I'm going to have to admit that I have been harboring pure D hate. . . . And I'm even going to try to quit hating Dallas and that is a big concession." He thought Kennedy would ultimately be ranked as great a president as Lincoln, "because like Lincoln he was hated by the right people—the bigots, the racists, the greedy-guts and the professional patriots."

Fullingim's effort to moderate his emotional distaste for the radical right wing was quickly unsuccessful. He soon returned to slamming Goldwater and "Useless" John Tower. When Richard Speck murdered eight nurses in Chicago in 1966, generating a nationwide revulsion, Fullingim found it significant that "The nurses' assassin lived in Dallas from the time he was four years old, he grew up there . . . He is a product of Dallas. He also probably read the Dallas News which has done so much to create the climate that encourages assassinations."

It would not have surprised Fullingim to learn that another aspiring presidential assassin grew up in Dallas. John Hinckley, Jr., was eight when Kennedy was shot. Hinckley graduated from Highland Park High School. On March 30, 1981, in Washington, he shot and wounded President Ronald Reagan.

In 1967 The Printer confessed, "I am addicted to reading the radical right wing conservative editorial page of the Dallas Morning News which is the leading hate-monger in the hate capital of the world." He said he did not believe what he read there, nor could it convince him, "but I read it to learn what the enemy is thinking and doing, even though it makes my blood boil and gives me the heartburn." This attack was too much for *Dallas Morning News* writer Frank Tolbert, who used his own column to reply.

Tolbert and Fullingim had enjoyed cordial relations over the years. Excerpts from Tolbert's column had appeared in the *Kountze News.* The two journalists had carried on a mock feud about whether or not panthers scream. Tolbert even ran several "Both Barrels" pieces to fill his Dallas column when he went on vacation—before the Kennedy assassination. But now Tolbert objected to Fullingim's "weekly tantrum" for "repeating that tired cliche that Dallas is the 'hate capital' of the world." According to Tolbert, Dallas was remarkably free of hatred, while on the other hand "from reading Arch's newspaper, you get the idea that Kountze . . . is well-stocked with 'haters.' And Arch is egging them on."

But Fullingim continued to award Dallas "hate capital" honors, partly because of the immoderate jail sentences given offenders such as the "long haired youth who was sentenced to five years in the pen for wearing the United States flag on the seat of his pants. In recent months Dallas juries have meted out several sentences to blacks for 1,000 years and over . . ." The Printer thought the *Dallas News* "editorials are so full of hate it's a wonder there aren't more assassinations in Dallas," and that the "collection of hate letters" the *News* published showed that "there are 50,000 potential assassins in Dallas."

In 1973, the *Dallas Morning News* acknowledged that "Editorial writers on the Dallas News get a kick, in several senses, from the columnizing of another News, Arch Fullingim of the Kountze News . . ." Calling The Printer "one of our more constant and involved readers," the Dallas editorial said "Editor Fullingim is a master of good, old-timey journalistic indignation, often swinging from the floor with both fists, rarely restrained by inhibitions, prudence or facts to the contrary . . ." To Fullingim's charge that "the Dallas News seems to inspire all the kooks to blow their brains in letters . . . ," such as the letter writer "who urges that all possessors of marijuana be shot," the *News* editorial writer thought "one man's kook is another's sage, and vice versa . . ."

A few days later, *Dallas News* columnist Robert Baskin, responding to a letter from Fullingim, called him "sprightly" and patronized his politics. Startled by this sudden attention, Fullingim admitted, "It scares me to death to see my name in print in the Dallas News." He decided to "quit writing letters to the Dallas News. The La. Enterprise is a good paper to write letters to. It ignores you."

Fullingim thought Dallas the center and symbol of all that was wrong with America. But a sanctuary from that modern madness lay close at hand, in the dark, mysterious heart of the Big Thicket. The Printer went walking there often to renew his spirit, to get what he called "that Holy Ghost feeling." When he learned the existence of the Thicket was threatened, Archer Fullingim roused himself and his readers to fight for its preservation.

The Big Noise in the Big Thicket

During his earliest years at Kountze, Fullingim took the forests of Southeast Texas for granted. He appreciated the natural beauty but felt no sense of urgency or spiritual siege. In 1958, musing on Hardin County's first hundred years, Fullingim praised the legacy of folklore about bear hunts in the Big Thicket. He did not lament the absence of the bears.

But he did express an early concern about the possible extinction of the ivory-billed woodpecker. Because of its large size (twenty-one inches long) and colorful red, white, and black markings, the ivorybill was a favorite with bird-watchers and hunters. Was the ivorybill extinct or still there to be glimpsed in the depths of the Thicket? Fullingim would come to make the search for an ivorybill one of his life's goals. Some readers identified The Printer himself with this colorful, oversized, all-but-extinct bird.

He ran pictures of threatened bird species—including the ivorybill—and exhorted parents to teach children not to shoot birds. "The forests are dependent on the birds for survival. Only birds can control the billions of insects that destroy the trees. Hardin County is dependent on the forests." Including permanent residents and migrating flocks, the Big Thicket was home to about three hundred species of birds, or about one-third of all bird species in the United States.

In 1961, Governor Price Daniel proposed a state park of about five thousand acres in the Big Thicket. Fullingim's report of this proposal emphasized Daniel's ignorance. "The way the governor envisions the park, it would be enclosed in a cyclone fence 10 feet high and would be a refuge for bear, deer and turkey. Thousands of bear flourished in the Big Thicket but none has survived. Also the wild turkey has vanished."

Fullingim thought Daniel's proposal "was suggested at this time for political gain." He predicted that if the park were located where Daniel proposed, "it would be an extension of the Daniel ranch," in Liberty County. Fullingim thought that creating a state park "would kill the very thing we want to preserve. . . . What is needed is to preserve the Thicket as it is." The Printer was still sanguine about the "selected cutting and replanting of timber" by the lumber companies. "The big companies now never cut a tree unless they plan to put one back in its place." He would soon realize the timber companies were harvesting old hardwoods and burning away irreplaceable underbrush to plant row upon row of fast-growing pines as cash crops, turning the wilderness into a plantation.

By the following year, Fullingim had learned the truth about replanting and realized his precious wilderness might really disappear. He began trying to arouse support to save it. "Now that the eventual extinction of the Big Thicket appears not only possible but highly probable, the time has come to make a realistic, scientific evaluation of the storied Thicket. We need to know if the Big Thicket is worth preserving . . ." He educated his readers about the destruction of hardwoods and underbrush with fires and poison sprays, and admitted that "the argument we put up two years ago . . . to let the land companies keep and preserve the Thicket because they are the best custodians, will not pan out." He urged readers to ignore right-wing talk of government encroachment and support a national wilderness in the Thicket.

The Printer called for practical action: "First of all we should petition the department of agriculture to grant no more permits to spray, and second, we should ask the federal government to set aside at least 75,000 acres in the heart of the Big Thicket as a wilderness area." He warned his readers that the half-dozen lumber companies that owned 85 percent of the land in Hardin County would act only for their own profit. "The Big Thicket is doomed unless we do something."

Quoting Fullingim extensively, Ronnie Dugger took up "the Fight for the Big Thicket" in the *Observer* in August 1963 with a long article. The *Observer* would remain Fullingim's ally in the push for a Big Thicket wilderness, running numerous articles by Pete Gunter, a college professor who became president of the Big Thicket Association. Gunter pointed out that the idea of a Big Thicket national park went back to 1927, when the association was founded. By 1937 the association was pushing for a forest preserve of 430,000 acres. The Second World War sidetracked those initial efforts at saving the

Thicket. By the mid 1960s, when Gunter and Fullingim were pushing for legislation, less than 400,000 acres of wilderness remained.

In 1967 U.S. Supreme Court Justice William O. Douglas published *Farewell to Texas, a Vanishing Wilderness*, in which he estimated that the Big Thicket contained only 300,000 acres, or about 10 percent of its original size, and was disappearing at the rate of 50 acres a day. Fullingim spoke with Douglas about strategies for getting congressional support for a national park.

Pete Gunter described the complicated bureaucratic underbrush the wilderness proposal had to negotiate. "It is no longer possible in the Thicket to find 5,000 contiguous acres of completely untouched land—the amount of primitive wilderness legally required to make a region into a national park . . ." To help with publicity, the *Observer* reviewed *Tales From The Big Thicket*, a collection of anecdotes told by old-timers in the Thicket area, including a chapter by Archer Fullingim.

By 1969 Fullingim thought "the Big Thicket will be lost forever if the people don't back Yarborough's Big Thicket bill." He linked the Thicket to the rising concern about the environment in general. "Scientists say that by the year 2000 there won't be enough oxygen left on earth for the world to survive . . ." because of deforestation and accumulated pollution, "but if we have the Big Thicket National Park with both pine and hardwood it may exude enough oxygen to keep . . . all the new babies born last year in Hardin Memorial Hospital alive . . ."

Lloyd Bentsen beat Senator Ralph Yarborough in the 1970 Democratic primary. Fullingim accused Bentsen, who would face Republican George Bush for the Senate race, of smearing Yarborough with vicious lies. "Bentsen is far to the right of Bush; so far, in fact, that Bush seems like a Democrat compared with Bentsen." Fullingim resented Yarborough's defeat. The Big Thicket had lost its most vocal legislative advocate.

The Printer wrote that he went to the Thicket one Sunday instead of to church, "and I assure you that no cathedral seemed as divine and exalting." He wanted to take George Bush there because "once Bush sees that he will see that that area must be the Big Thicket National Park, and don't ever get the idea that the real Thicket is impassable and impenetrable." Lack of access to the Thicket was among the arguments the Forestry Association used against the idea of a national park.

One such ad, in the *Observer*, was headlined: "Archer Fullingim Is Smartening Up—He Doesn't Want a National Park, Either." But the ad was quoting "the sagacious and scholarly editor from Kountze" out of context. Fullingim was arguing against even the changes park development would bring. "What we want is to save at least 100,000 acres . . . permitting only trails and primitive camping . . ." Fullingim felt certain the Thicket would attract many people, "especially in about ten years when people start running from each other to get away from the hordes smothering and surrounding them."

Trying to rally support for the Thicket wilderness, The Printer hosted members of ten conservation groups on the "first annual Big Thicket Pilgrimage." He ran lots of photographs and headlined one story "Pilgrimage Shouts Necessity of Saving Big Thicket." The Kountze News celebrated Earth Day, a nationally coordinated attempt to raise environmental issues in June 1971, with a full back page protesting littering and pollution in streams and forests. Fullingim would continue to run that page for years.

Fullingim had to acknowledge that "the most vocal enemies against saving the Big Thicket live in Southeast Texas . . . These people say that the reason they are against saving it is that it will take away their jobs and tax money . . ." But Fullingim thought that "what's really bugging them is their fear that saving the Thicket will take away . . . their most precious right, the hunting of deer and squirrels." For whatever reason, few local residents supported The Printer's campaign for a national park. The owners of Thicket land were absentee corporations headquartered in New York and Chicago. And Pete Gunter, president of the Big Thicket Association, lived in Denton, far from the area he sought to protect.

In August, Ronnie Dugger reported a phone call from Fullingim asking for help to save the Thicket. "'I'm *desperate,*' he said, in a tone of voice that was. 'Tell 'em I'll do anything with 'em. I'll lay down in front of the bulldozers with 'em—I'll climb up in the trees.'"

Pete Gunter detailed the ownership of Thicket land, including Southland Paper Mills of Lufkin. "The Dallas Morning News has close corporate ties with Southland . . ." The newspaper officially backed a 35,000-acre park. Another major landholder was Eastex, a subsidiary of Time, Inc., of New York. By 1973, Eastex had become the largest landowner in East Texas, with more than one million acres. Gunter suggested a boycott of Time publications, including *Time, Life,* and *Sports Illustrated* magazines. The Printer pointed "Both Barrels" at these distant boards of directors, telling them, "It's becoming increasingly difficult for me to sit idly by and watch your crews poison the hardwoods."

Time, Inc., acknowledged some pressure. In the middle of a *Life* article on "The Last Ivory Bill," with large, lush photographs of Thicket flora, the editors printed a boxed disclaimer: "Eastex International, a pulp and paper subsidiary of Time, Inc., is a major landholder in the Thicket area. Since 1957 Eastex has been actively engaged in a long-term program of reforestation." The editors did not explain that Eastex was planting pines to replace the hardwoods and undergrowth the company was destroying.

A year after he called Ronnie Dugger for help, Fullingim, now seventy, again threatened to stop the machinery of destruction with his own body. "So who will go with old Arch Fullingim to the Holy Ghost Thicket and lay down in front of the bulldozers? That's a call for volunteers." By 1973, The Printer's masthead quoted Crazy Horse: "One does not sell the earth upon which one walks." Fullingim gave his most eloquent description yet of the religious feeling that came over him sometimes in the East Texas forest: "In the Depths of the Holy Ghost Thicket, where slivers of sunlight pierce the leafy overstory, where the only sound is that of insects and birds and an alligator swishing in the water of Black Creek, where all of a sudden you feel the presence, you feel the exhilaration, you feel the bone shaking excitement, you shiver and the cold bumps come on your arms and neck, and the orange toadstools on the ground add to the ecstasy."

He wrote an open letter to Congressman Charles Wilson, addressing him as "Timber Charlie," to warn him against recreational development in the Thicket. "If we save the heart of the old bear thicket we must leave it as it is and carefully guard it." By early 1974, Fullingim was tired and ready to retire from publishing. But he traveled to Washington to help lobby for passage of the Big Thicket bill.

Fullingim printed his last issue of the *Kountze News* on February 28, 1974, though his editorial column would run one more year. The October issue of *National Geographic* featured a long article on the "Big Thicket of Texas." Including a full-page photograph of Fullingim, the article acknowledged his efforts to preserve the Thicket. On October 11, President Gerald Ford signed into law a bill creating a national Big Thicket Reserve of 84,500 acres in Southeast Texas. The Printer's battle of many years had finally borne fruit.

Fullingim figured this fight was the biggest of his life. Even his own death could not shut him up. Fullingim "got the last word at his funeral by authorizing his tombstone inscription: 'His favorite Kountze news story for 25 years was the Big Thicket.'" But when Roy Hamric asked Fullingim, who had just retired, what he was proudest of, The Printer said, "Well, before John Kennedy became

president, I was sort of a racist. . . . I don't know that I approved of
integration . . . But . . . I saw the light, and I thank God. . . . That,
and helping to save the Thicket . . . are the best things I've done."

The Uncivil War

Fullingim's claim that John Kennedy showed him the error of his
racist ways has an ironic ring. Elected to office by a slender margin,
Kennedy had no wish to alienate white southern Democrats. Reluctant to lead the cause of civil rights, Kennedy struggled to manage
the rising clamor for change. The 1954 U.S. Supreme Court *Brown*
decision desegregating American schools was one of many mile-
stones on the road to the full enfranchisement of blacks as citizens.

Black expectations had been rising since the Roosevelt administration and World War Two. Black soldiers returned from fighting
against fascism abroad to confront racism at home. Between 1930
and 1960, the southern rural population fell from 16.2 million to 5.9
million, sending many blacks into southern cities. From 1940 to
1960 more than 3 million blacks left the South for urban ghettos in
northern cities, where they began to accumulate political power.

Archer Fullingim saw the school integration decision as a cynical
Republican attempt to get the black vote away from the Democrats.
He claimed, "There are lots of colored people who are wary of deseg-
regation." Southern black schoolteachers were afraid they would
lose their jobs in integrated schools, in his view. Fullingim berated
Vice-President Nixon for claiming "honorary membership" in the
NAACP, then downplaying the affiliation during a stop in Houston.
"The hypocrisy of the Republicans was never better illustrated than
in Nixon's Houston boo-boo. They are not for colored people; they
are not for anybody except Money Bags."

In 1957 the Eisenhower administration passed the first civil rights
legislation since Reconstruction and sent federal troops to Little
Rock, Arkansas, to enforce school desegregation. Fullingim thought
that "Ike himself has violated the Constitution" by his actions
against the "heroic Governor Faubus" of Arkansas. The Printer decided to educate those of his readers who had "the misguided impression that Texas is more west than South . . ."

It would surprise many Texans to learn that Texas, bitter and
defiant to the end, was the last state to be readmitted to the
Union after Reconstruction . . . For seven years, Texas was the
most unreconstructed state in the South. . . . for seven long
years, a Supreme Court ruling allowed Union troops, most of

them negro, to rule Texas, robbing, pillaging, murdering, stealing, burning, threatening, while the Republican party in Washington gloated with revenge . . . [The current civil rights bill is]
the most wicked bill aimed at the South since Reconstruction.
Its goal is the same . . . to destroy the South's social order
through enforced integration and racial intermarriage . . . Oh,
what a black day that was when we southerners conspired with
the historic enemy to put another Reconstruction president in
the White House.

What angered Fullingim most was the Republican claim that white
southerners hated blacks. "That is a lie. We love the colored people."
He denied thinking "of the colored man as a second class citizen . . ."
but also denied that "integration is inevitable and eventual."
    The Printer tasted the consequences of his attitude at a local
Kountze cafe. A connoisseur of café cooking, Fullingim praised the
food at Ruby Lee Marshall's place in "the Quarters," the black section of town. "I'd eat down there more often . . . but when I do I get
dirty looks from the colored people whose looks seem to say, 'You
are always preaching segregation. Why don't you practice what you
preach?'"
    Fullingim despised the 1958 gubernatorial candidates Price Daniel
and W. Lee O'Daniel for calling each other "nigger lovers." "The term
is the essence of sinful hate . . . but its only effect on me is to make
me hold in contempt the person who uses the term." Fullingim reiterated his love for blacks, "and I despise any person who calls me a
'nigger lover' in an attempt to make me like them less . . . So let
them call me a 'nigger lover' for I'm proud that I don't hate the
Negro." The Printer's increasing empathy with blacks was apparently caused at least in part by his disgust with those who wanted to
keep them down.
    For the next four years, from 1958 to 1962, Archer Fullingim kept
silent about race relations in the Kountze News, a sign that he was
rethinking his position. By 1960 black activists by the thousands
were sitting in at restaurants and other public facilities throughout
the South to protest segregation. Freedom Riders forced integration
of public transportation. Both forms of protest met with violence.
The Kennedy administration, elected on a platform committed to
civil rights, used federal power to confront southern state officials
who refused to protect blacks seeking enfranchisement.
    The Printer made a tentative return to racial topics in June 1962
with a nostalgic remembrance of "Luther Tippin, a Negro who
worked as farm hand and handyman for my father" until Archer

Fullingim was fourteen. By October, he was ready to announce his secession from the Confederacy. "I fought the War between The States until 1952 . . . For 50 years I cussed the damyankees and the Republican party . . . I held the Republican party responsible for the War, the South's defeat and Reconstruction." But when southern Democrats turned out for Eisenhower in 1952, "I put away the stars and bars and admitted myself to the union." Repressing his rants against federal intervention at Little Rock in 1957, Fullingim said he knew it was time for the South to become part of the American democracy "regardless of race, creed or color, and I am reconciled to becoming an American rather than a Texan or a professional phony Confederate."

In April 1963, Martin Luther King led a campaign to stop segregation in Birmingham, Alabama. Local officials responded with brutality. The media, sensitized to the civil rights movement and to King's career, relayed images of Birmingham's violence to the world. Fullingim added his voice to those who found it "hard to believe this sickening oppression is taking place in the United States of America. Freedom? There is no freedom for the Negro in Birmingham." He thought official treatment of blacks rivaled "any tales of torture that have come out of a Communist police state." Alabama, Georgia, and Mississippi, by denying blacks the right to vote or to "parade and picket," were "defying the Constitution and flying in the face of Christianity."

President Lyndon Johnson prodded Congress to enact the Civil Rights Act in 1964 and the Voting Rights Act in 1965. Fullingim enthusiastically approved these new laws. But he stirred up racial controversy locally in 1966. The Kountze school board, which initially voted to integrate the public schools, decided to rescind the integration order. Fullingim approved the board's action on the grounds that most black teachers were not qualified to teach at white schools and would lose their jobs in an integrated system. But as The Printer reported in his next issue, teachers at Carver, the black high school, "were so up in arms about that article that they called me on the carpet and for an hour at the colored school raked me over the coals . . . There were no Uncle Toms in that room."

When a black teacher asked where The Printer got his information about the inferiority of black teachers to white, Fullingim had to admit it was hearsay among whites. "I learned some startling facts," Fullingim reported, that black schools lacked teachers and equipment.

Fullingim had progressed from unenlightened views about blacks but knew most of his readers had not. He tried to bring them along, to tell them "Martin Luther King . . . is no more of a Communist than you are. King wants only one thing: civil rights for his race." Fullingim was becoming disenchanted with Vietnam but not with those who fought and died there, a disproportionate number of whom were blacks and Hispanics.

"Negroes are Americans, same as whites. There are conservative, moderate and liberal Negroes. There are radicals among them, just as there are among whites . . . All whites are not Ku Kluxers. All Negroes are not Black Power advocates."

On April 4, 1968, Martin Luther King was assassinated in Memphis, stirring a deep empathy in Archer Fullingim:

"For two days I was a Negro . . . I was in the march in Memphis and marched behind the mules and wagon carrying the coffin in Atlanta. I repeat, I was a black man, and I was full of sorrow because of the death of Dr. King. I'm not going to tell you what I thought while I was a Negro, because you white people wouldn't want to hear it, but I want to tell you whiteys and honkeys something. You ought to be black for a couple of days just to see what it's like . . . It would do you good."

The assassination of Robert Kennedy in June caused Fullingim to note that, "In the last several years, it seems, we just assassinate Kennedys and Negroes." To those who "all of a sudden are worrying whether murder and assassinations haven't become a habit with us," Fullingim said "it's been a habit all along." He cited figures showing six thousand killed by guns each year, "13 in Texas over the weekend. Each of their lives is just as important as that of Bobby . . ." Medgar Evers' killer had never been caught and "nobody in the South has been convicted in the scores of assassinations and burnings in the last few years . . ."

By 1970 The Printer could look back and recall that "Twenty years ago I was a rank segregationist; I really thought the Negro race was inferior. Now I know that it isn't. I know that Negroes are Americans in every way, and . . . have just as much intelligence as the white man . . ." He noted he had also changed his views about the Vietnam War, but couldn't boast about his new views. He thought, "Events change our minds for us," though there were "still some miserable, frustrated souls" who could not accept change. "They are our pollutionists, our Big Thicket destroyers."

Strike No Glancing Blows

In February 1974, his final month as publisher of the *Kountze News*, Fullingim flew to Burbank, California, to tape the NBC "Tomorrow"

show with Tom Snyder. "This printer has been trying to figure out
why he did it, but he did . . . Probably ego had a lot to do with it." He
gave a blow-by-blow account of his visit to Los Angeles, though
he saw little of the city. The high point of his appearance on "Tomorrow" came when Fullingim yawned on camera. Tom Snyder,
amused, said, "Are we keeping you up, Arch?" Fullingim replied,
"I'm not going to help you carry this show."

Announcing the end of his career, Fullingim told his readers, "I
am 72 years old and rich, so why shouldn't I retire?" His paper sup-
plier had discontinued the size of newsprint Fullingim's old Linotype required. The Printer did not have the energy to retool his machinery. But though "the newsprint situation triggered our decision
to sell the paper . . . there were other compelling reasons."

"The News needs an editor who will attend every meeting of the
city council and the school board, and I'm not going to do it. I'm just
too tired to sit up half the night with the board or the council." Fullingim had spun out various retirement travel fantasies over the
years, but he had outlived the urge to travel. Instead, he planned "to
continue my 35-year search for the ivory-bill woodpecker. I will
have time now to go into the depths of my beloved Holy Ghost
Thicket."

He also nurtured a plan to "write the book that I have been writing
in my head for the last five years," one less than half the length of
"the 400 page novel I wrote in 1949 and never got printed . . . and
don't ask me about it, because if you do I may talk and a person can
talk a book to death . . . I have talked many books to death. I'm
damn sure not going to talk this one to death." There is no evidence
that Fullingim ever completed this novel. He may have talked it to
death after all. Or he may have wasted too much time watching television. The Printer was a confessed addict of the boob tube.

Fullingim had noticed early on—in 1954—"the technique the
Republicans have worked out in their appearances before the TV
cameras . . . It is a wedding of soap opera with the most advanced accomplishments of science . . . Now the speaker is both actor and
conversationalist." In 1958 he opined that "looking at Playhouse 90
on TV is worse than being on dope." The ambiguous endings of this
weekly dramatic series frustrated Fullingim, who complained that
"Playhouse 90 plays have no third acts like any other play. A third
act is supposed to tell you how everything turns out . . ." but this
show just stopped and forced viewers to guess. Fullingim swore
never to watch the show again but he did, every week. "I have got
the habit. It's like being on dope."

On New Year's Eve in 1959, The Printer resolved to "try and shake my TV habit," but he doubted he "could kick the habit if I wanted to." He noticed that he forgot a program as soon as it ended and another began. "We have almost, but not quite, got to the point where we regret to turn off the TV when company comes. And it is very bad when one would turn down association with human beings to see Gunsmoke or Perry Mason."

He admired the Pentecostal families who called the TV antenna "the devil's flagpole" and refused to permit television sets in their homes. "I feel their children are benefitting from the TV ban." Television was not primarily instructive, merely entertaining. "More than anything else, the American people are addicted to entertainment, and for some vague reason I know that is not good." He felt guilty giving up his entire leisure time to television. "I read about half as many books this year as I read last year." Fullingim admitted, "I've got the monkey on my back," and when his TV went on the blink for three months "we nearly had the delerium tremens until we got it fixed."

Interviewers who saw Fullingim in his last years mention his continuing addiction to TV. One would-be visitor was turned away. "When I knocked on the door, he opened it and fussed at me for being late then said I would have to come back in two hours because he was watching his soaps."

A Dallas newspaper columnist had heard that Fullingim never answered his phone while the soaps were on. Paying an unannounced visit to The Printer's house, the writer found the television "blasting" and The Printer shouting back, "cussing out some soap opera crook or adulteress . . ." Inside, "seated before the TV and shoving aside a half-eaten TV dinner was a striking figure. With wild white hair spraying, Fullingim resembled my notion of an Old Testament prophet."

Archer Fullingim was winding down and his body was wearing out. He was hospitalized more frequently in his final years for various ailments, including some related to his war injuries. He lost vision in one of his eyes. He suffered from severe gout and had to undergo surgery for hemorrhoids. As his columnist and friend Gordon Baxter remembered, Fullingim had "the sides cut out of his shoes so they wouldn't hurt. He hurt a lot after he passed eighty. Carried a red rag on his shoulder to ease the pain."

For a year after he quit publishing, he wrote a column in his former paper, renamed the *Kountze News-Visitor*. Mostly he commented on the Watergate scandal. President Nixon's resignation speech "infuriated" him because "it was the old Nixon, admitting nothing, not even admitting that he was resigning to keep from being impeached." By January 1975, Fullingim admitted "it gets harder and harder to write." His final column, February 27, dismissed Lloyd Bentsen as "a caretaker of the Texas oil industry and a person who takes advice from John Connally."

Toward the end of 1975 Fullingim, who was still talking about writing a book, discovered he had already written one. Selections of his writing from a quarter century at the *Kountze News* were gathered and pruned by Roy Hamric, who based his introduction on a long interview with The Printer. In 1976 the Texas Institute of Arts and Letters awarded Fullingim's selected works a prize for journalism. Fullingim told Hamric he was disappointed by most Texas weekly newspapers. They were all alike, their pages crammed with pictures of people.

"One longs for the days of Brann and *The Iconoclast* . . . after reading the milktoast editorials of most 'weaklies.'" Fullingim thought country journalism had become like city journalism. "Their main business is to make money. Their aim is to protect their status, to protect big business, big oil, to protect period, because they figure if they do, they'll make money."

In 1979, celebrating twenty-five years of publishing the current version of their magazine, *Texas Observer* editors asked Fullingim for an essay on the theme "making a difference in the next 25 years." Fullingim thought "being a liberal in the next 25 years is not going to be as easy as it was in the last 25." William Clements, the Republican governor elected the previous year, was a "rattlesnake" who had already harmed Texas more than the entire "notorious" Reconstruction era. "There are now more members of the Ku Klux Klan in Texas than there are in any other state in the union."

He charged the *Observer*, his "inspiration" for the past twenty-five years and "the guide and conscience for the liberals," with becoming too "placid and intellectual." He warned that the liberal press "must not strike glancing blows . . . The troops need inspiration as well as information—and not too long-winded either . . . we need to do what we have been doing, but put it down where the browns, blacks, and us poor white trash can understand it quickly."

Fullingim lived out his bachelor days to the age of eighty-two at Kountze, by the Big Thicket. On November 26, 1984, he died at Silsbee Doctors' Hospital after a two-week stay. Even his enemies treated his passing as front-page news.

5. A Freak from the Underground

Maybe that's why we're hated. We tell the truth; we've got nothing to lose. We do have something to gain, however. It's our self-respect. Yeah, we tell the truth. It's about time some newspaper did.

—*Stoney Burns*, Dallas Notes

In the fall of 1974, the campaign to "Free Stoney Burns" climaxed in Central Texas. Supporters of the controversial Dallas journalist sold T-shirts to raise money for his defense fund. They sent petitions with thousands of signatures asking the governor of Texas to grant him a pardon. Convicted of possessing a small amount of marijuana, Stoney Burns was about to start a ten-year prison term. His precise sentence was ten years and a day, the added "day" making him ineligible for the usual early release and parole for good behavior. He would have to serve the full ten years.

The spiteful sentence was only one of many signs that Texas authorities were not kindly disposed toward Stoney Burns. When Burns was arrested in March 1972, the Texas penalty for possessing less than an ounce of marijuana ranged from two years to life in prison, one of the harshest pot laws in the nation. It was too harsh for many Texas prosecutors, who had begun to drop charges against the growing number of young, middle-class first offenders rather than subject them to prison. But they did not drop the charges against Stoney.

Ten months after his arrest, under pressure from law enforcement officers, the Texas Legislature rewrote the marijuana laws, making possession of less than an ounce a misdemeanor. But Stoney had already been tried and convicted, rushed through the system, by his own account, ahead of hundreds of other pending cases. Designed to be retroactive, the new law enabled the release of hundreds of state prisoners. But Stoney was not released.

Since the day of his arrest, Stoney Burns had protested he had no knowledge of the marijuana Dallas police claimed to have found in the glove compartment of his car. Considering his many run-ins with the law and his awareness that he was under constant police surveillance, Stoney knew better than to risk carrying pot. As *Time* magazine put it that fall, "The law in Dallas, from all appearances, had been bent on getting Stoney Burns for years."

Stoney Burns in the *Iconoclast* office, 1972.
(Courtesy of Stoney Burns.)

Stoney Burns, ca. 1986. (Courtesy of Stoney Burns.)

Stoney's legal problems began shortly after he became an editor of *Notes From The Underground* in the spring of 1967. Mimeographed on the campus of Southern Methodist University, *Notes From The Underground* offered an irreverent alternative to the student newspaper, an alternative the SMU administration soon banned from campus. Stoney's first arrest was for violating a city ordinance against "selling merchandise without a permit." But as the rhetoric in Stoney's several publications became more heated and aimed at more prominent targets, the frequency and severity of his legal problems increased.

The Dallas police raided the *Notes* editorial offices on various occasions, with warrants authorizing searches for pornography or drugs or runaway teenage girls. They seized office equipment and held it for weeks. They searched or detained staff members and visitors coming or going from the newspaper premises. Though the police maintained a constant surveillance of the *Notes* offices, they did not apprehend the vandals who broke in and destroyed thousands of dollars of typewriters and other office equipment. In one four-month period in 1969, the *Notes* office was vandalized three times.

Notes From The Underground moved off campus in the fall of 1967, becoming simply *Dallas Notes*. Stoney resigned from *Notes* in October 1970 to escape his legal problems and his paralyzing notoriety. He went to Austin to help launch the *Lone Star Dispatch*. When that newspaper died after three issues, Stoney returned to Dallas and joined the staff of the new *Iconoclast*, where he worked until March 1973. His career as an "underground" journalist lasted only about six years.

During that six-year period police arrested Stoney Burns on charges ranging from trespassing to obscenity to contempt of court. Following an outbreak of violence in a Dallas park in 1970, he was arrested and tried for "interfering with a police officer during a civil disturbance." Burns was appealing his conviction on this charge, and his three-year prison sentence, when police arrested him for possessing marijuana.

Aside from his difficulties with the Dallas police, Stoney suffered other forms of harassment. As he recalled later, "My car got shot up several times . . . My house was broken into and vandalized. I got crank calls all the time, and the police would stop people leaving my house for stuff like not making a turn signal when they pulled away from the curb." In 1969 a young man told Stoney he had been hired to beat him up but decided against it. Later that summer several men jumped Stoney "and administered a thorough beating."

What was it about Stoney's journalism or his personality that antagonized the authorities and excited such violent hatred in the community? Just about everything. While Archer Fullingim criticized the political and social barbarities of the 1960s and 1970s from his safe rural distance, Stoney Burns lived and wrote in the center of the storm. Dallas was nowhere near the vanguard of radical change. The overt upheavals that marked the era—the race riots, antiwar demonstrations, and campus unrest—largely bypassed that city. But the merest whisper of such faraway threats to values and stability tormented the conservative heart of Dallas.

Stoney Burns publicly supported all those who thought justice should triumph over the rules. Powered by an anarchic energy and a highly developed sense of the absurd, Stoney personified everything official Dallas loathed. Long-haired and bearded, Stoney advocated liberal and joyful doses of sex, drugs, and rock and roll. Early on he declared himself "against any criminal laws in which there is *no victim*, such as laws against the use of harmless drugs, inhuman abortion laws and anti-homosexual laws."

His paper used scatological language in headlines and printed sexually explicit and antireligious cartoons. Stoney and his staff referred to the Dallas police as "pigs," detailed the hypocrisies of Dallas City Council members, and ridiculed local Congressman Joe Pool. Stoney photographed undercover narcotics officers and published their pictures, along with their names and addresses, in his paper. He helped organize love-ins in city parks.

Stoney Burns was one of hundreds of editors who began publishing so-called underground newspapers in the late 1960s. With varying degrees of political awareness and social commitment, this alternative press fashioned itself into a voice for the voiceless. These papers fought against unfair treatment of blacks, Mexicans, women, and homosexuals, against the irrational war in Vietnam, and against hypocritical officials greedy for power at the people's expense. They reported the "struggles" of students, workers, minorities, soldiers, and foreign peoples, pooling their information by means of the Liberation News Service and the Underground Press Syndicate.

As one journalist recently wrote, "Dallas, even in the age of Aquarius, was as psychologically short-haired and cold as the ninth level of hell." In such an atmosphere—and because, as another writer has suggested, "the counterculture element in Dallas was, well, pretty much under-the-counter"—the good-natured, almost apolitical, rebellion favored by Stoney Burns grievously affronted the Dallas establishment. Advocating freedom, Stoney became trapped by a celebrity that turned to martyrdom.

"I run a newspaper," he told an interviewer in 1970. "I like to report whatever is happening. Sometimes they force me into being a leader, but it's not a role I enjoy at all." But neither did he shrink from battle. With the help of the ACLU, Stoney took his challenge of the Texas obscenity laws to the U.S. Supreme Court. Less than three weeks after Stoney Burns entered the Texas Department of Corrections at Huntsville, Governor Dolph Briscoe commuted his sentence. Two days before Christmas in 1974 he was a free man. But the years of arrests, court fights, intimidation, and harassment had frightened him and worn him out. His iconoclastic press career was finished.

Growing Up Absurd

Stoney Burns was born Brent LaSalle Stein on December 4, 1942. The son of a middle-class Jewish couple, Roy and Esther Stein, Stoney grew up comfortably in Dallas, where he attended Hillcrest High School. In 1946 Roy Stein founded the Allied Printing Company, a business he built into the largest commercial printing concern in Dallas. The printing trade was apparently a family tradition. Stoney told an interviewer in 1983 that he traced his ancestry to Robert Estienne, official printer to the king of France until 1539. Stoney's grandfather immigrated to the United States to print gold on cigarette papers for the American Tobacco Company. In his own fashion, Stoney Burns would carry on the family trade.

Lawrence Wright, five years younger than Stoney, described the Dallas in which he came of age before the Kennedy assassination. "Its people dressed alike, talked alike, and thought alike," as did most middle-class citizens everywhere, but "the similarity had been carried too far in Dallas. America was a conformist society, perhaps, but conformity had been taken to extremes in Dallas." Roy Stein exhibited a mild resistance to this mold, revealing an antic sense of humor that would be at least part of his legacy to his son.

In 1954 Roy Stein started running funny little ads in the *Dallas Morning News* as a way to publicize his business. The ads featured small photographs of a bald-headed man with a pencil mustache— Roy Stein—touched up to catch a reader's attention. In one photo, Stein seemed to have a second pair of eyes on his bald head. In another shot he had an apple on his head and an arrow through his cheeks. Other photos showed him with devil's horns coming out of his bald head, or wearing funny ears, with the caption: "LOOK TWICE! Once for quality, once for price."

After the ads had been running for five years, the *News* rewarded Stein with a feature story. Stein was pleased at his success. "We do a million dollars worth of volume a year, and that's pretty good for a small printing company, isn't it?" Stein concocted the funny ads because "we want people to talk about it." Even Stein's apparently harmless humor generated "crank letters about his advertising, but he consigns those to the wastebasket and does not let it bother him." The article concluded by characterizing Stein in a way that might have described his son ten years later: "He's just an idea man who's gathered a bunch of idea men around him to build up a business."

As a student, Stoney fancied himself a good writer but he did not get much encouragement from teachers. "Miss Taylor taught me junior English in high school. She tried to teach me junior English, she'd say. I passed the course, but she advised me not to take senior English. I'd never pass, she said. I was stubborn though. I took senior English. I hated it more than I hated the subject my junior year. Mrs. Cox, the teacher, advised me not to go to college. Learn a trade, she said, trying to be as diplomatic as possible."

Stoney enrolled at the University of Oklahoma where he tested well enough to enter the honors English course. His first assignment was a five hundred-word essay on "How I Spent My Summer Vacation." He wrote about his job with Snowcrop, mailing refunds to customers who sent in lids of a new twelve-ounce orange juice container along with brief testimonies about why they liked the new size. He titled his essay with his favorite among these responses: "Because it mixes perfectly with one pint of vodka." He was proud to receive the only A in the class. "High school teaches you to write boring," Stoney thought. "I could never write boring." Of the many insults detractors later hurled at his writing, "boring" was not among them.

After two and a half years at Oklahoma, Stoney spent a summer at the University of Texas at Arlington. In 1964 he graduated from the University of Arizona. After school, Stoney came back to Dallas and went to work selling printing for his father. He also acted as an adviser for a fraternity on the campus of Southern Methodist University. He knew the three SMU students who, early in 1967, bored with the sterile offerings in the student newspaper, decided to start their own alternative paper. At the suggestion of a professor, they named their effort after a Dostoyevsky novel, *Notes From The Underground*.

Forerunners of a national alternative journalism had appeared in the previous decade. I. F. Stone began his four-page *Weekly* in Washington in 1953, exposing the official fraud and mismanagement he found buried in public documents almost no one read. The *Village*

Voice started in New York in 1955 as part of a cultural and intellectual reaction to the conformist era. But the clearest progenitor of the late 1960s underground newspaper explosion was Art Kunkin's *Los Angeles Free Press*, begun in 1964. Kunkin's paper served as a model for those that followed by eschewing the accepted formula of "objective journalism" in favor of a "truth" untold in mainstream media. He solicited the perspectives of minorities and the poor instead of the usual authorities.

Kunkin's *Free Press* struggled until the Free Speech Movement at Berkeley in the fall of 1964 gave him a cause to cover. When the black Los Angeles district of Watts burned in the summer of 1965, the *Free Press* got closer than any other paper to the reasons for the violence and to those who created it. The *Berkeley Barb* and New York's *East Village Other* began publication in the summer of 1965, followed in 1966 by the *San Francisco Oracle*. Also in 1966 the Underground Press Syndicate was formed to share stories among papers and, later, to help defend against the increasing legal assaults on the underground press. On October 10, 1966, the first issue of the *Rag* appeared in Austin and sold 1,500 copies.

In retrospect the underground press of the 1960s has become identified with its crusade against the U.S. war in Vietnam. Vietnam was a major preoccupation of these papers, but the original impetus for the new, rebellious media was broader and more amorphous and preceded the war. It had to do with a segment of bored and restless youth, more numerous and more affluent than any in history, and their revolt against the prosperous prison of middle-class America. Lawrence Wright recalls his adolescence in a wealthy Dallas suburb. "To grow up in this heaven was rather like living in a plastic bag. There was a suffocating sense of confinement and of breathing one's own air. Too much order, too little risk, made life anxious and trivial."

Growing up in Royal Oak, Michigan, Tom Hayden, future leader of Students for a Democratic Society (SDS), felt a similar alienation. "There seemed to be only one reality, one set of values: those of the comfortable middle class . . . It was the boring and prearranged nature of this existence that caused . . . [what] would grow to rebellion later." Many of these young escaped their confinement by means of movies and especially music.

Rock and roll invaded the country on long-playing records, car radios, and portable sets with raunchy rhythms celebrating freedom from any prearrangement. To beat radio censorship, rockers encoded their increasingly provocative messages about sex, and later drugs, in ways easily deciphered by youthful listeners but inscrutable to their parents. Nurtured to an unprecedented degree by mass media, the generation that ran the sixties underground press placed a great importance on media images. In September 1963, CBS Television Network doubled the length of its nightly television news broadcasts to thirty minutes and NBC quickly followed suit. It was fortuitous preparation to present an era of dramatic changes, one of the most dramatic being the way those changes were presented.

Much has already been written—and much more will be—about the elements that composed the upheavals of the 1960s and early 1970s: the struggle for civil rights, the war in Vietnam, birth control and sexual freedom, the rise of feminism, the level of affluence, the revolt against conformity, the availability of "recreational" mind-altering drugs such as marijuana and LSD, and the media technology that conveyed images of these elements and others instantaneously around the world. The major schism within the so-called counterculture, and among the publishers of underground newspapers, was between political radicals and the cultural radicals, whom the media dubbed "hippies."

The SDS was one among various political groups that styled themselves part of the New Left, as opposed to old-style Marxism. The New Left hoped to cause drastic changes in the hegemonic capitalist system, which rewarded the wealthy few while oppressing the poor majority. Serious, committed intellectuals, the New Left organized demonstrations and marches to rally support for its causes. Hippies thought the political "game," even the right-minded version played by the New Left, was a waste of time. Drugs helped them see through the illusion of modern civilization. Many dropped out of "straight" society, let their hair grow, and communed with their higher selves. Hippies thought if they could make enough people see the light the insane social system would collapse of its own weight.

Revelations in a Lava Lamp

Two of the SMU students who started *Notes From The Underground* in 1967 were members of the SDS. Doug Baker and J. D. Arnold typed up their information and made photocopies secretly on machines at Texas Instruments. Their distribution consisted of removing the official school newspapers from boxes on campus and replacing them with copies of *Notes*. When the editors decided to print one thousand copies instead of five hundred, they had to find a printer. But that proved challenging.

The April 27 issue, edited by Baker and Nancy Lynne Brown, detailed the paper's problems. Arnold had quit as editor, their election issue had failed to come out, and their printer had refused to print any more issues. None of the four printers they had hired agreed to print *Notes From The Underground* more than once after reading what was in it. The rest of the issue consisted of correspondence between a disgruntled former SMU professor and the university officials who denied him tenure.

The next issue, dated May 1, consisted partly of "I Goofed," an apology by Doug Baker for giving the former faculty member a platform for his grievances just because he donated money to the paper. On page 2 was a rant against "the remaining male editor" by his co-editor, Nancy Lynne Brown. " . . . I was totally against the waste of space, prostituting the title 'Notes to the Underground' [sic] for 12 pages of self-justification . . . So perhaps you saw it at the newsstands and read it. *If so, you were duped."*

This confused, amateurish attempt at underground journalism seemed about to expire for lack of resources, organization, and editorial harmony. But it was dramatically rescued and revitalized by an unlikely savior, who had just been "born" in Chicago—Stoney Burns.

In the spring of 1967, Brent Stein, salesman for Allied Printing, attended a print show in Chicago. He visited an old college roommate from Arizona, a former wild man who credited his newly mellowed state of mind to marijuana. When Stein's friend gave him marijuana he felt his "mind expand, watching the birth of the universe in a lava lamp." He thought "how great it would be if people worked from their convictions, instead of merely working for a wage." He wondered deeply about his own life, his own convictions. And that's when he became Stoney Burns.

Why "Stoney Burns"? In 1983 Stoney told an interviewer that "Stein means stone in German, and Brent literally means burnt." But Doug Baker recalls that Stoney "modeled his pen name after a TV character named Stoney Burk to take advantage of the similarity of the names ('Say, I've heard of you')." From that point on, everyone called him Stoney except "my parents and the police."

Stoney saw that Baker and Brown were trying to express their beliefs, but *Notes From The Underground* was "a sloppy product." He offered his services to the paper chiefly to improve the production values, an offer quickly and gratefully accepted. Stoney's professionalism immediately transformed the struggling paper, beginning with the May 27 issue. He designed an attractive masthead with flourishes of psychedelic art and laid out the copy in readable columns, with photographs and cartoons. He also started charging—ten cents a copy. Besides the graphic overhaul, Stoney's writing began to define some of the enduring themes of the Dallas counterculture.

"Cops Start Anti-Love Campaign!" This headline on Stoney's front-page story signaled an end to the tentative style of previous issues. Accompanied by a lyric from the rock group Buffalo Springfield ("There's something happening here. What it is ain't exactly clear . . .") and a photo of a grim-faced policeman, Stoney's article plunged Dallas into the sixties.

> Over a hundred Dallas hippies tried to have a love-in last Saturday, May 20. Unfortunately about twenty paranoid cops had a hate-in and, baby, they had the guns. It all started about one o'clock at Stone Plaza. The Dallas fuzz, unaccustomed to seeing so many people smiling and laughing and loving humanity, thought something illegal must be going on. Under the flimsy excuse that the happy hippies were drawing a crowd, the cops made the long-haired boys and mini-skirted girls disperse.
>
> After having their constitutional right to free assembly violated, the gentle youths decided to go down to Dealey Plaza where there would be less people to attract. Within five minutes the cops were there.

Calling Dallas "the city of instant paranoia," Stoney opined that "if Christ had come back to Earth with His long hair, sandals and robes, He probably would have been busted." This identification of Christ with the despised, nonconforming hippies was a favorite theme of sixties radicals, a sentiment calculated to outrage pious churchgoers.

Stoney Burns was listed as "Cyclops Image Maker" in this issue, along with Doug Baker ("Pluto") and Nancy Lynne Brown ("Persephone"). An article by Jerry Farber entitled "The Student as Nigger" explained "the Auschwitz approach to education" in American universities. A cartoon, "In Sepia Dallas," showed a reporter listening to three faceless figures labeled "A high official," "A usually reliable source," and "Persons in a position to know." The caption explained that these three figures were the main sources "for the phoney stories that generally appear in the daily press . . . generally they come as facts until you read into the story about two paragraphs . . . so read carefully . . . cause then you'll discover . . . that some crimes are NOT committed by a Negro."

The reputable Dallas journalist and author A. C. Greene wrote to congratulate the editors on their brash and daring new enterprise. "Most good newspapermen were, at one time or at all times, in trouble with their school administration as undergrads . . ." Greene assured them. "I was kicked out of a church school for printing some unpalatable truths." The following issue, the biggest yet at twenty pages, came out a week late due to an "overabundance of news" and an "overworked and undermanned" staff. With the school year over, most of the student staff had quit for the summer, but the editors decided to keep publishing.

"*Notes From The Underground* is growing like wild marijuana. It's all we can do to stay ahead. We need more workers. Also two of our editors were married since the last issue." Pluto and Persephone had patched up their feud and joined together in matrimony. *Notes*, now a member of the Underground Press Syndicate (UPS), reprinted an article from the *Rag* asking readers not to go to San Francisco's Haight-Ashbury that summer (to counter a popular song inviting everyone to join a summer of love there "with flowers in your hair"), and a long manifesto about "Social Change in America" from *New Left Notes*, the official SDS organ.

Stoney started a column called "Undercurrents," criticizing a local radio station manager for banning "suggestive" rock songs and attacking the state for spending $5.5 million for San Antonio's Hemisfair while more than half that city's people lived in poverty. He congratulated the *Dallas Times Herald* for a "well-written and unbiased article on LSD usage by our generation. It really surprised us by its frankness and truthfulness. We may even live to see the day when a Negro appears in 'Big D Beauty Shopping.'" Elated by their rapid rise, the editors announced that two news dealers had agreed to sell the paper, which now cost fifteen cents.

Still riding high and running behind schedule, the July issue of *Notes From The Underground* was the most outrageous yet, starting with the cover promise of "FREE POT DETAILS INSIDE." The free pot offer turned out to be a rumor of "a virtual Ponderosa of Marijuana" growing wild in Fort Worth. *Notes* offered semiprecise directions to this bonanza and a free lifetime subscription to anyone who "finds the grass and proves it to us by bringing us a pound or so . . ."

The "Free Pot" issue featured a long interview with Sonny Barger, president of the Hell's Angels Motorcycle Club, who detailed some of the illegal and obscene activities he enjoyed. Two other apparently innocuous items contained portents of future trouble, including Stoney's review of a rock concert, in which he reported "a brief hassle with the bellicose cop at the stage-door entrance," and Doug Baker's attempt to sell *Notes From The Underground* on the SMU campus before being stopped by campus police.

"'NOTES' BUSTED FOR SELLING AT STONE MALL" was the cover story in early August. Police had arrested Stoney and another *Notes* staff member, who were peddling newspapers at Stone Mall Plaza, for violating a city ordinance against selling merchandise without a permit. The story called it "the latest in a series of crackdowns to force the flower children and the fundamentalist preachers from meeting there."

The two men went to court with an American Civil Liberties Union lawyer, but the arresting officers failed to show up. Charges were dropped. *Notes* ran an obituary: "In Memoriam. Press, Freedom of. Died July 8, 1967 at Stone Mall Plaza in Dallas, Texas of an overdose of police harassment." The back cover was a full-page wanted poster for "Jesus of Nasareth, Alias The Prince of Peace; practices medicine without a license, loiters around synagogues, has 'visions' (probably hallucinatory caused by drugs), anti-war demonstrator, typical hippie attire—long hair, robes, sandals . . ."

Notes From The Underground also carried an exclusive story about Dallas Congressman Joe Pool. On another visit to Chicago, Stoney read about Pool's arrest for drunk driving. He realized the Dallas press had decided to forego all mention of the incident. He called Baker, wrote a story based on several sources, including wire reports and the Chicago newspapers, and sent it to Dallas in time for the early August issue.

The *Notes* story, "Joe Pool Arrested . . . 'Drunk' Says Cop," told how Pool spent five hours in the Arlington County, Virginia, jail after ramming his car into the rear of another at 2:45 A.M. Pool kept insisting that he had congressional immunity from prosecution. But the local judge cited him for reckless driving and failure to produce his automobile registration.

Bashing Joe Pool became a habit at *Notes From The Underground*, which posed the question: "How can a city as 'image conscious' as Dallas keep electing a clown like Joe Pool to make Dallas the Laughing-stock of Washington?" Stoney Burns warned: "McCarthyism is not dead. Our own congressman Joe Pool is head of the House Un-American Activities Committee and is never at a loss for words when it comes to calling somebody a 'Communist.'" He noted that Pool had introduced a constitutional amendment that would permit Congress to revoke the American citizenship of "'those who would undermine the foundation of our natural respect for law and justice.'" Burns rebuked the reasoning in Pool's newsletter explaining his proposed amendment to his constituents. "Oh, well, Pool will still keep sending out his red, white and blue bullshit newsletters, and when election time comes around again, we'll see . . ."

Notes From The Underground had ordained its own destiny in the first few months of its existence. By ridiculing Joe Pool and his backers, thumbing their noses at the local media, and flaunting their lack of respect for majoritarian values, the *Notes* staff shocked the community and infuriated local authorities. Stoney's early arrest, though minor, indicated how those authorities planned to exact their revenge.

Keeping Cool with Pool

Citizens of Dallas did not need to read *Notes From The Underground* to know something was wrong in America. Ted Dealey's *Dallas Morning News* kept taking the country's temperature and diagnosing fever. A September 1967 Associated Press poll found "Americans Concerned about Vietnam, Racial Unrest," high prices, and "turbulence" among the young.

A survey of Texans showed that only 47 percent approved the job President Lyndon Johnson was doing, down from 84 percent in 1964. And that was 7 percent above the national figure. Only 36 percent of Texans approved the way war was being waged in Vietnam while 51 percent disapproved, almost the exact reverse of responses a year earlier. The handling of racial problems met with similar sentiment (33 percent approved; 56 percent disapproved). This feeling was understandable since, as another AP story indicated, "urban rioting triggered by racial hatred has caused more than $100 million in property damage in 1967—with the grim returns still trickling in . . ." The story did not mention the loss of life.

With such massive chaos so close at hand, the *Dallas Morning News* elected to fortify the trenches. Instead of sending readers off to harvest wild marijuana, the *News* warned against a "North African power strain" of the weed that "reportedly produces withdrawal symptoms." The *News* saw Stone Mall Plaza not as the grave of free expression but as "a gathering spot for sidewalk preachers and beatnik groups." Rather than dismiss Joe Pool as a "clown," the *News* supported his efforts to uphold American values.

When a draft information center opened near the SMU campus to counsel males eligible for military conscription, Pool was upset. He saw the center as part of "a plot to disrupt the Selective Service" and introduced a bill to prevent it. To help inform his HUAC colleagues about the situation, Pool said "The Committee will be provided with copies of a publication, 'Notes From The Underground . . .' The publication attacks the draft and the war in Vietnam." The *News* editorialized that "as usual, Pool and the Committee are justified in making investigations like these."

Joe Pool's face made the cover of *Notes From The Underground* in October with the phrase "Keep Cool with Pool!" A long story centered on how, "in cooperation with the Dallas dailies, Pool is misinforming the public so that he can get himself re-elected." *Notes* charged that "Pool has illegally arranged for the termination of the lease held by the Dallas Draft Information Center which is operating legally. At the same time he has done nothing about the Draft Resistance (with aid from SDS and SNCC) which may use illegal means."

Doug Baker and Stoney Burns confronted Pool with his garbled facts at a press conference October 6. As Stoney wrote, "I asked about his sources. 'I don't have to reveal them,' he said. I told him NOTES wasn't the unofficial voice of SDS. He said it was . . . This conversation didn't last long."

Pool ended the conference on an emotional note, saying, "I am a graduate of SMU and I resent these people who would destroy our very security by undermining our armed forces and are using my alma mater for this organized sabotage." Burns and Baker judged these sentiments to be "garbage from A. Cess Pool . . ." And while "SMU is hardly a center for organized sabotage (not counting our football team) . . . HUAC is a political pork barrel where greedy politicians feed on publicity created by people's passions, fears and emotions."

The *Dallas Morning News* editorial writers had a busy October. They condemned Martin Luther King's "'non-violent movement'" as "the father of violence," responsible for "riot, murder and mayhem." The editors criticized all those who favored reducing penalties against the use of pot, including Dr. James Goddard, member of a presidential commission to study the drug laws. The *Morning News* saw the nationally organized March on Washington against the Vietnam War as "coercive protest," not "peaceable assembly," and thought the government should "act against those responsible."

On October 22, soldiers were driving peace marchers back from the Pentagon. Eighteen men went on trial in Meridian, Mississippi, for the 1964 murder of three civil rights workers. Vietnam War protests were reported in Paris, Munich, Tokyo, and London. The *Morning News* editorial attacked *Notes From The Underground*. "Filth by any name is still smut. Such a concoction is 'Notes From The Underground' . . ." The *News* protested "attempts" to peddle *Notes* to Dallas high school students. After seeing this "pernicious parasite . . . the reader realizes that he doesn't have to visit the city dump regularly to know what trash is."

Two days after this editorial appeared, Dr. Willis M. Tate, president of SMU, banned *Notes* from campus. "SMU maintains a free press and responsible publications for open discussion of controversial issues," Tate's statement read. But after looking at *Notes From The Underground*, Tate concluded it was "detrimental to the best interest of the University and contrary to its purposes."

A story in the *Morning News* entitled "HUAC Losing Out as Powerful Force" noted that two bills proposed by committee members had stalled on their way to a vote. As if to counter the trend, Joe Pool spoke at Yale University the next day, calling the underground press "Communist-inspired." "A nationwide underground press syndicate has been formed by 'traitors' to oppose the war in Vietnam, Rep. Joe Pool charged Monday night in a speech at the Yale campus here . . ." Pool said the underground papers were obscene by design, "to attract the irresponsible readers whom they want to enlist in their crusade to destroy the country . . ." Reviewing and approving Pool's speech, *Morning News* editors reminded readers that Pool "has a ringside seat on subversion . . . Thus, when he charges that there is organized treason in a nationwide syndicate of smutty newspapers, the charge cannot be taken lightly."

Marshall Bloom reported the Pool speech for the Liberation News Service (LNS), carried by *Notes From The Underground*. Bloom and Raymond Mungo had founded LNS during the national October Vietnam protest as a way of supplying packets of news to subscribing papers nationwide. Their merger meeting with the UPS two weeks before Pool's speech had attracted more than three hundred newspaper representatives. Bloom thought that meeting might have ignited Pool's conspiracy fears. He ridiculed Pool's allegations.

"Reviving a charge made against Socrates, Pool said that the underground newspapers 'capitalize on the innocence and confusion of the very young . . .' Several times in his speech, Pool blamed the right of free speech as the cause of these newspapers."

J. D. Arnold, SMU senior, cochairman of the local SDS chapter, and columnist for *Notes From The Underground*, defied the campus ban on selling the paper. On November 20 he was suspended from school. *Notes* quoted U.S. Supreme Court decisions to argue against SMU's right to suspend Arnold. Eventually a U.S. district judge ordered the school to let Arnold take his final exams for the fall term, on the condition he never reapply for admission. President Willis Tate reiterated his ban of *Notes* from campus, provoking an editorial against his decision from the school paper, the *SMU Campus*.

Also in November, Doug Baker resigned. As he wrote later, "Offered a deal I couldn't refuse by SMU and my parents, I sold *Notes* to Stoney . . ." Baker's resignation left Stoney Burns alone at the top of the masthead. In his column, acknowledging the change, Stoney expressed his admiration for Baker's persistence. "God knows we've had enough outside criticism and harassment. Doug kept on with this paper in spite of the outside opposition. In fact, he kept on with *Notes* BECAUSE of the outside opposition." Stoney thought Baker had continued the paper, despite the lack of money and help and the alienation of friends, "just because he had to breathe and create and live . . ."

By the end of 1967, the alternative college newspaper at SMU had been thrown off campus and was no longer permitted to sell papers there. All the original editors had quit. No printer in the Dallas– Fort Worth area would touch *Notes From The Underground*, even on a cash-advance basis. The staff had to drive the copy to Waco, nearly one hundred miles away, where William Foster, publisher of the *Waco Citizen*, printed their paper until 1971. Enduring the harassment of its sales force, opposition of the daily newspapers, and vilification by the local congressman, *Notes From The Underground* had become its own biggest story.

Apocalypse Now

In March 1968, Stoney Burns celebrated an unlikely anniversary. "NOTES is a year old. A lot of people didn't think we'd ever make it. A lot more people *hoped* we wouldn't . . . Some of us (alas, even us) thought we'd never last . . ." Only recently had the staff begun to sell subscriptions for a full year instead of six months. In the previous issue, Stoney had shortened the name of the paper to *Dallas Notes*. Now he used the anniversary to preach defiance to his enemies.

> Joe Pool calls us "subversives," The Morning News calls us "filth," The Times Herald calls us "hippies," the City Council calls us "radical college students," and SMU, which spawned us, refuses to recognize our existence at all . . .
>
> We gave up the idea of changing people's minds because of a lack of material with which to work. Let the zombies go through life accepting as inevitable that which is not. At least we know better and this helps us keep a foot in reality . . .
>
> So Johnson declares a news blackout on rising American deaths in Vietnam. Westmoreland asks for and will probably get another 200,000 troops; blacks live and die with no chance to be accepted as citizens; cops harass persons who won't conform to a mindless standard; and NOTES celebrates its first anniversary. Congratulations. Big deal.

In the same issue, a *Notes* editorial condemned the way "the news is managed in Dallas . . . Everybody doesn't subscribe to the *New York Times* so they can get the 60% of the news that never reaches Dallas except for the national news telecasts." The editorial urged readers to watch CBS or NBC nightly news and compare the coverage to the Dallas papers. Citing three examples of locally unreported news "critical of the Dallas Oligarchy," the editorial promised that *Notes* would try to take up some of the slack.

Despite Stoney's swagger, *Dallas Notes* continued to struggle for survival. To help stop the constant turnover at the chronically understaffed paper, Stoney eventually paid employees about forty dollars a week. He did not pay himself, but lived day to day on commissions from ad sales or by hawking the paper. Most sellers paid twenty-five cents for two copies, then sold them for twenty-five cents each. When Stoney needed breakfast money he would grab a stack of papers and sell them, keeping the full amount. If subscription money arrived in the mail, he would eat a ninety-nine-cent breakfast at a drugstore near the post office. For a while he was partially supported by a waitress at Steak and Ale.

Notes also had trouble getting advertising, forcing Stoney to devise unorthodox sales tactics. None of the movie theaters or chains would advertise. Finally one prospect told Stoney, "If you get the Interstate chain"—the largest one—"all the others will follow." Stoney clipped an Interstate ad from another paper, reprinted it in *Notes*, and showed the paper to other theater chain owners, who then bought space. Eventually Interstate itself bought ad space in *Notes*.

Besides financial worries, *Notes* suffered constant harassment from various quarters. Much of the mail arrived opened and signed "opened by mistake by U.S. Marshall's office." *Notes* never got mail on Mondays. Stoney figured whoever was going through their mail at the post office did not work on Sundays. Some of the mail contained threats, such as a letter promising Stoney "corporeal" harm if he continued "mentioning or referring to SMU in any way in your smut sheet. [Signed] ALUMNI, STUDENTS AND FRIENDS OF SMU."

"*Notes* advertisers and retailers also received threats of consumer boycotts if they interacted with *Notes* in any way whatsoever." *Notes* paid some convenience stores to display issues, but many newsstand owners in Dallas were successfully intimidated and would not sell it. Some were afraid if they sold *Notes*, the police would arrest them for selling *Playboy* or on some other trumped-up offense.

Police "rousted" distributors and sellers for "inciting to litter." "Recalls Stoney Burns, 'If you sold a newspaper to someone, that could be considered inciting to litter because they just might throw it on the ground . . . It was selective enforcement.'" Perhaps in this climate it was understandable that some *Notes* staff members preferred to adopt pseudonyms. Bylines increasingly featured names such as "Medusa," "Largo," "Clarke Kent," or "The Hickory Kid."

In January 1968, the Tet Offensive brought the Vietnam War into Saigon, and into American living rooms on TV. The gruesome battle scenes belied optimistic government predictions that the fighting would soon end. The day after Lyndon Johnson resigned the presidency in late March, he addressed the National Association of Broadcasters, blaming them for his political defeat.

On April 4, Martin Luther King's assassination in Memphis touched off riots in eighty American cities. A *Notes* eulogy reckoned that "Dallas as a whole probably felt intense relief that the crime did not happen here. The local establishment press ran stories with themes such as 'Now Memphis Knows How Dallas Felt.'" *Notes* thought the Dallas newspapers were trying to say that "sick communities are not responsible for crimes committed in the name of sickness."

The same issue carried "Scum Resurrected," yet another version of Christ as a hippie, written in the standard news story formula. "Jesus Christ, of no fixed address, was brought before Magistrate Pontius Pilate and bound over for trial. He was arrested in the company of several suspected homosexuals while loitering in an olive grove near Jerusalem . . ." *Notes* gave extensive coverage to the April student takeover of the administration building at Columbia University in New York.

When Robert Kennedy was assassinated in Los Angeles June 5, Stoney Burns again attacked local media coverage. "The niggers and the college students have killed Kennedy. I read about it in an editorial on the front page of the Dallas Times Herald . . ." He quoted the *Times Herald*'s condemnation of "civil disobedience, however wrapped in sanctity . . . on the college campus" or "clothed protectingly in nonviolence . . ." Stoney summed up the message with sledgehammer irony. "A society that tolerates liquor stores that do a big business in guns is not to blame. Only the people who do not agree with the society are to blame. It's the American Way . . . the gospel according to the *Times Herald*." A brief Liberation News story on the same page described the bust of *Kaleidoscope*, an underground Milwaukee paper, for printing obscene matter.

Through the spring and summer of 1968, *Dallas Notes* continued its attack on favorite local targets while keeping readers apprised of national "revolutionary" trends via UPS and LNS stories. The paper celebrated the joys of marijuana smoking and the perils of getting busted. When a Dallas theater was shut down for showing pornography, Stoney opined that "personally, I'd rather kids watch stag films rather than some of violence shown on both the movie screens and the boob tube. Sex isn't pornographic but killing is."

When Joe Pool refused to testify in a Chicago case challenging the constitutionality of HUAC, *Notes* highlighted the hypocrisy of "Dallas' favorite son-of-a-Birch . . . He never hesitates to label as 'unAmerican' anyone who refuses to testify before his star-chamber committee . . . yet he is now dodging his own duty to testify— smacks of unAmericanism by his own definition, doesn't it?" *Notes* ran extensive coverage of events in Chicago during the Democratic National Convention in August, when police and demonstrators clashed as "the whole world was watching."

The October 16 issue carried an article by Roy Stamps entitled "Dallas Nudie Movie Capital." As Stoney recalled, "We published a story on the making of exploitation movies in Dallas, and printed a movie still on the cover, of an orgy scene, but everybody's wearing underwear." On the night of October 30, the ideological struggle between *Dallas Notes* and the city authorities turned into open warfare. Police raided the *Notes* offices at 3117 Live Oak with a pornography warrant that barely covered their rage. *Notes* provided its readers with a detailed account.

Detectives from the Vice Squad of the Dallas Pig Department raided the NOTES office on Wednesday night, October 30, with a search warrant allowing them to seize "pornography." The pigs carted off two tons of alleged pornography . . . all the back issues of NOTES and all other underground papers in our office . . . in two flat-bed trucks brought for that purpose.

Booked for "Possession of Pornography" were Publisher Stoney Burns, Editor Rodd Delaney, and Circulation Manager Donna Delaney, Rodd's wife . . . Besides the back issues of NOTES and other UPS papers, the pigs took three typewriters, cameras, lenses and other darkroom photographic equipment, graphic arts equipment, over $100 in checks, approximately $30 in cash, bookkeeping records, subscription lists, and all other material which might be used to publish a newspaper. They also seized many political books and posters (Is Chairman Mao pornographic?).

The pigs had a field day wallowing in the filth they made by breaking bottles, ripping up posters and unopened letters (both incoming and outgoing), tearing loose the refrigerator control dial, ripping out lamp wiring and crushing jewelry.

The pigs also seized pills ("Investigation of State Narcotics Law") which later proved to be baby vitamins, birth control pills and asthma medicine. The narcotics charges have been dropped but the asthma medicine is being held for investigation.

At the station, Stoney Burns admitted the kidnapping of the Lindbergh baby but an officer told him he was wanted for more important offenses. The officer then admitted that it was a "Political Bust." (Was there every really any doubt?)

Channel 8 News had a ball. They called it "the biggest smut haul ever in Dallas." The three alleged pornographers, having watched TV, knew how to act and shielded their faces from the camera just like the big-time criminals.

The pigs also arranged to have Burns' phone service disconnected and Kathleen McDonald-Balling, Women's Editor, lost her job over the incident—a misdemeanor charged to other people.

. . . this issue was printed with borrowed equipment . . . citizens from all walks of life have rallied to the defense of the accused persons.

Notes apologized to subscribers for not being able to mail their copies. "We have taken steps toward the release of our business records and subscription lists, which were seized as 'pornographic' during the recent raid." Two days after the raid, the *Dallas Morning News* editorialized that since student rebels claim they "can't trust anyone over thirty years old . . . Perhaps a change of scenery would be in order." The *News* recommended such rebels be deported to the "Hippie Paradise" of Upper Volta, where the female life expectancy was thirty-one, or Gabon, where the male life expectancy was twenty-five.

On November 15 the Dallas police raided the *Notes* offices again, this time on a warrant for marijuana. They "broke down the back door to the *Notes* office and barged in without warning . . ." Again the police found no illegal drugs, but again they confiscated everything in sight including copies of *Notes*, rented typewriters, and desks. They pulled the telephones out of the wall. The second police raid caused *Notes* some publishing delays.

Stoney enjoyed the chance to describe the brutish behavior of the police on a radio talk show. But as usual he found fault with the *Times Herald*'s coverage of the second raid, quoting their lead: " 'Two men and three teenage girls have been charged with possession of obscene literature as a result of a narcotics raid . . . etc.' In one sentence they got all the things that sell newspapers: sex, dope, teenage girls and older men." It did not matter to the *Times Herald* that the other male was also a teenager, and that only Stoney was over twenty. "Never mind that no narcotics were found (We NEVER hold). Never mind that NOTES is *not* pornographic. And they accuse *us* of yellow journalism."

Moat City Mayhem

The American Civil Liberties Union agreed to represent Stoney Burns and *Dallas Notes* in the obscenity cases. On January 14, 1969, the ACLU filed suit against the Dallas Police Department and District Attorney Henry Wade, charging them with "suppression of freedom of the press and suppression of political dissent." The lawsuit contended that the two police raids violated six different amendments to the Constitution.

"Members of the Dallas Police have demonstrated over a period of time increasing hostility to the existence of Dallas NOTES and to the persons responsible for its publication," in the words of the ACLU suit. According to a *Notes* article, "Besides the two illegal raids pigs have illegally detained Editor Burns and searched his car without justifiable cause, used unlawful surveillance of the NOTES office and succeeded in scaring off several staffers." By late January police had still not returned the property seized in the two raids.

The ACLU suit alleged that "the conduct on the part of the Dallas Police is part of a conspiracy having as its object prohibiting the expression of ideas that are alien to the defendants, and having as its ultimate goal the abolition of Dallas NOTES."

Though Stoney's ACLU attorney, David Richards, cautioned against overconfidence and advised silence, Stoney could not foresee any problems, "so why not freak out the press and the pigs? Maybe we can get our message across and prove to a few Dallasites how stupid the pigs really are." Stoney figured he had been misrepresented in the Dallas newspapers because "Establishment journalists seldom give both sides of a story for fear of losing a good 'source of information,' in this case, the pigs. Long live freedom of the press."

At the end of January, *Notes* received most of its equipment back from police but did not have long to make use of it. "The Dallas Pig Department returned a sizable quantity of property seized from Dallas NOTES on Thursday, Jan. 30, but the next day vandals broke into the office and smashed four typewriters which had been returned." The *Notes* story speculated that since few persons had known of the property's return, perhaps "the pigs had broken into the office . . ." or "tipped off some friends who did so . . . Staffers were amazed that the vandalism was allowed to occur under the watchful eyes of Dallas' finest, who watch . . . the newspaper office almost constantly."

A week after the break-in, on February 7, "NOTES editor Stoney Burns' automobile was found riddled with bullet holes . . ." Stoney had come out of a bar at midnight the previous night to find his tires slashed. He got a ride home with friends and returned the next day to find the car "shot fulla holes." According to the *Notes* story, "This was the third time Burns' car had been shot while parked in the same neighborhood." The first shooting occurred the previous Thanksgiving, the second two weeks later.

"Burns has not gone to the pig department with a complaint because he knows they're notoriously inefficient—especially when it comes to investigating charges brought by freaks or radicals." Instead of the police, Stoney turned the case over to "the White Panthers, an organization which specializes in handling matters of this nature."

Dallas Notes continued to star in its own headlines. On February 27, the newspaper staff went to court and got a postponement on the pornography charges. "When editor Stoney Burns returned to the offices at 4:30 P.M. on that day he found the back door open . . . Typewriters and equipment totalling $400 were destroyed or left inoperable." This time Stoney did inform the police, but "No detective has contacted the paper, so it is assumed the incident will go uninvestigated."

Stoney likened the intimidation of the *Notes* staff by police to that of the bullying U.S. foreign policy in Vietnam and elsewhere. But the young *Notes* workers were middle class and "not used to being treated like niggers. They had no intention of rolling over and playing dead. Also, these kids were smart and educated. They knew how to use the system and where to go to find help—as at the Dallas Legal Services."

The *Notes* writers also knew the soft spots at which to aim their blows. Since 1937 Dallas had been run by the Citizens Charter Association, which picked political candidates and determined their policies. When a *Notes* headline asked, "Who Controls Dallas?" the story named names. Stoney's paper continued to berate the local media, with a special scorn for the *Dallas Times Herald*, which ran self-promotional fillers saying, "Watch out changing world . . . the Times Herald will report you." To aggravate the *Times Herald* and the paper's publisher, Felix McKnight, *Notes* ran satirical fillers saying, "Watch out Times Herald . . . Dallas Notes will scoop you."

A *Notes* story quoted a *Times Herald* reporter, "who shall remain nameless since his hang-up is a steady salary," as he did his job, "taking words and sentences out of context" at an interview. "The reporter admitted that the truth cannot be reported in the Dallas Times Herald because the publisher belongs to the Dallas Country Club and drinks liquor with the heads of TI, LTV, etc." Under these circumstances, the *Times Herald* could not let "the truth come out," and its own reporters knew it. "But the name of the game is 'exploitation' or maybe 'advertising'—certainly not 'journalism.'"

On April 16, Stoney Burns was arrested for trespassing on the SMU campus. On his way into an auditorium to see a rock concert, Stoney paused to hawk copies of *Notes*. When campus security officers ordered him to stop, Stoney refused. Though Stoney had press tickets to the concert, the University Park police booked him for trespassing, then released him on a twenty-dollar bond. He was found guilty of misdemeanor trespassing on May 24 and fined twenty-five dollars.

On April 25 a three-judge federal panel met to consider the constitutionality of the Texas pornography statutes. A U.S. circuit court judge and two U.S. district judges heard arguments from ACLU lawyer David Richards on behalf of Stoney Burns and *Dallas Notes*. A second lawyer represented four Grand Prairie news dealers facing the same charges.

According to the *Notes* report of the hearing, lawyers for the attorney general and the Dallas district attorney "admitted that parts of the Texas law are indeed unconstitutional but that should not make the whole statute bad." Noting that "county judges have kept postponing the trials of staff members arrested in the two raids," *Notes* concluded, "the whole mess has become a political football with no judge willing to let 'that radical newspaper' go free."

On May 18, Stoney Burns covered a Ku Klux Klan rally in downtown Dallas "four blocks from the assassination site." As the longhaired, bearded editor joined the small crowd, he was spotted by the speaker, "Granny Hate," who "spewed out her usual tirade against 'niggers, jews and com'nists' but immediately switched to 'dirty hippies' when she saw me . . ." Stoney saw a reporter there from the *Dallas Morning News*, who said he doubted he would file a story.

He didn't mention the fact that both daily papers and their TV subsidiaries have blackouts on news which may tend to be 'harmful' to the city's image. The rest of the nation knows that Dallas is the Hate Capitol of the Nation . . . but most local citizens are blissfully unaware of the fact. At least they never read about it in the local press. (Watch out Times Herald . . . the world is changing and you don't even know it.) This selective reporting is what is known as "Ostrich Journalism"—hide your head in the sand and the problem disappears.

On May 27, for the third time in four months, vandals broke into the *Notes* office. They destroyed a typewriter and a typesetting machine worth a total of $1,450. According to the *Notes* account, "There is a definite pattern to the three vandalisms, and there is circumstantial evidence to suggest that the police have been responsible." Reviewing the three incidents, the *Notes* story emphasized the lack of police cooperation.

"Someone is trying to shut NOTES down by destroying its equipment. The person isn't interested in stealing the equipment . . . So far he has destroyed 8 typewriters . . ." The newspaper was succeeding as a capitalist enterprise, but the capitalist system would not offer the paper its protection, despite constant police surveillance of the office.

Stoney offered a warning to Dallas elected officials: "Your sons and daughters are watching your duplicity and double standards. Unless you fulfill your obligations to protect *all* your citizens you may be the ones needing the protection. But please realize this is not a threat—it is only a statement of fact."

The underground press was embattled all over the country, partly because of its success. "By July 1969 the *Los Angeles Free Press* sold 95,000 copies a week, the *Berkeley Barb* 85,000, *The East Village Other* 65,000—all up from 5,000 or fewer in 1965." But hundreds of other papers had come to life in far less likely places, such as *Kudzu*, in Jackson, Mississippi, *Grinding Stone* in Terre Haute, Indiana, and *Inquisition* in Charlotte, North Carolina. Perhaps the most truly "underground" were the "sixty or so" antiwar papers published "on or near military bases here and abroad." Some of the earliest and best-known of these GI papers were Texas publications: *Gigline* of El Paso and *Fatigue Press* of Killeen, among others.

By the late 1960s the underground press had become a target of the FBI counterintelligence program (COINTELPRO), directed against suspected subversion in the New Left, civil rights, and antiwar movements. On July 5, 1968, J. Edgar Hoover sent a memo to his Albany, New York, office outlining a twelve-point program to deal with the New Left. The program included manipulation of both mainstream and underground media. The memo suggested that since the use of "marijuana and other narcotics" was common among young political leftists, agents urge local authorities to arrest activists on drug charges.

On November 5, 1968, the day Richard Nixon was elected president, Hoover sent a memo to FBI offices asking for detailed analysis of underground publications "being printed and circulated in your territory on a regular basis," including personal information about editors and staff. The FBI went so far as to create its own mock underground newspapers, *Armageddon News*, in Bloomington, Indiana, and *Longhorn Tales*, in Austin, Texas. The widespread harassment of underground papers—by the FBI, the CIA, and other government agencies—is thoroughly documented in several books, most notably, *Unamerican Activities: The Campaign against the Underground Press*, by Geoffrey Rips.

The struggles of Stoney Burns with the Dallas authorities were no less intense for being part of a larger pattern of harassment. Across the country in the late 1960s and early 1970s, editors of underground newspapers suffered physical beatings, false arrests, destruction of property, and repeated violations of their civil liberties—especially their right to free speech. Most of the crimes against these journalists were committed by, or with the approval of, the police. Chroniclers of this officially sanctioned repression cite the tactics used against Stoney Burns as among the harshest and least justified anywhere. Stoney's persecution by Dallas authorities had begun to attract national attention. But the increasing notoriety only served to intensify, rather than inhibit, the official hostility.

Massacre in Lee Park

On June 18, 1969, a panel of three federal judges ruled the Texas obscenity law was "too vague" and ordered it overturned. *Notes* savored its victory in a story entitled "Pornography Law Fucked." "Criminal charges of possession of pornography against seven NOTES staffers will have to be dropped . . . District Attorney Henry Wade was pissed off and said he will appeal the court's decision . . ." The ruling also stopped obscenity prosecutions against four news dealers in Grand Prairie and one in Dallas. Stoney became an underground hero who had faced down the forces of repression. But other stories in the same issue about arrests of the *Notes* staff showed the decision to be only one battle in a ongoing war.

In July the *Wall Street Journal* ran a long, front-page story about Stoney Burns titled "Stopping the Presses." The article reviewed the two police raids on the *Notes* office and noted Stoney's charge that his right to free speech had been violated. "Dozens of his counterparts in the flourishing underground press—now numbering 200 or more papers in the U.S. and Canada—testify to similar incidents of what they call 'harassment' by the police, courts and the general public."

The *Journal* quoted Lieutenant Truman Snider, "the Dallas police officer who led the search of Mr. Stein's office last October," who denied any harassment. The most dramatic statement in the article was made by another journalist.

"'I think the underground press is an irresponsible press that really doesn't deserve support from the American daily press,' says Felix McKnight, co-publisher of the Dallas Times Herald. 'We're not interested in furthering the life of a publication that we think is detrimental to the best interests of the community, especially the young.'" *Notes* reprinted the *Journal* article, making Felix McKnight's interpretation of the First Amendment available to a different readership.

Others besides McKnight thought *Notes* "detrimental to the best interests of the community." According to Doug Baker, "Some one hired a bad-ass black man from Fort Worth to come by the *Notes* house and knock some sense into Stoney." Seeing posters of black "revolutionary" leaders he admired, "like Huey Newton, Eldridge Cleaver and Bobby Seale he . . . split after informing Stoney that, indeed, someone was out to get him." Later that summer, three less politically fastidious black men "jumped" Stoney "and administered a thorough beating that left his face red and blue and black and puffy . . . Having let his hair grow out, he looked like a wounded lion."

Notes reported that the offices of *Space City*, an underground newspaper in Houston, were firebombed. The editors of *Fatigue Press*, in Killeen, were convicted of marijuana possession and sent to Leavenworth prison. In September *Notes* accused Dallas police of beating and arresting staff member Jim Smith without any reason. In October the University of Texas at Arlington obtained an injunction to prohibit the sale of *Notes* on its campus.

Dallas Police Chief Charles Batchelor and District Attorney Henry Wade appealed the federal obscenity ruling to the U.S. Supreme Court. In December the Supreme Court agreed to hear the case. In their brief, Batchelor, Wade, and the other appellants appeared to equate freedom with trouble. "Today, the people of our society have never been so free . . . And also today, never have there been so much discontent, unhappiness, turmoil and actual violence."

While conceding that "individual rights are good and desirable . . ." the officials thought that "at the present time, some consideration must be given to the curbing and curtailing of this right." Minority voices could threaten the social order. "Where the exercise of free expression of ideas threatens the existence of the society (which guarantees free speech), free speech may and should be proscribed."

Stoney's reaction was obscene. "Those guys that want to shut down NOTES are full of shit. NOTES isn't dirty. They're just jealous because their pricks have turned to marshmallow and their cunts feel like dried fish . . . We won't be fucked with."

In January 1970, Dallas police perpetrated what Stoney Burns later called his "favorite bust." A comic strip drawn by Charlie Oldham, featuring a character named Vaseline Pete McSlippery, ended with Vaseline Pete performing oral intercourse with a woman. District Attorney Henry Wade and City Attorney Alex Bickley filed a complaint. Judge Dee Brown Walker of the 162nd Judicial District Court ordered page 8—containing the offending cartoon panel—removed from all unsold issues of the January 21 *Dallas Notes*.

While Sheriff C. Lum Lewis and three deputies ripped the pages from the papers, two Dallas television stations broadcast the action, "including close-ups of the 'offensive' page to thousands of viewers. Neither station has been busted yet," *Notes* reported. Unable to resist a chance to make the authorities look foolish, Stoney ran the offending comic panel on the cover of the next issue, but with the crucial section blanked out and covered with dots. The cover said: "Hey Kids! Just connect the dots and you too can be arrested."

Inside, *Notes* ran an "approved alternate ending" to the comic strip. In this version Vaseline Pete is stabbing the woman and snipping off her toes, muttering, "I'm gonna cut ya t'bits . . ." The woman replies: "Oh, is *that* all? I thought maybe you wuz gonna perform an *unnatural sex act* on me!!" Beneath the strip *Notes* ran a comment: "Children can be corrupted by sex, but violence is as Amerikan as apple pie and imperialism, right, Mr. D.A.?"

Notes ridiculed Felix McKnight for writing editorials against miniskirts while carrying ads featuring miniskirted models. Responding to a March 15 *Times Herald* editorial calling *Notes'* "delight in obscenity almost grade-schoolish," the *Notes* response said, "But words are not obscene. Pictures of people fucking are not obscene. What is obscene, Felix, are crimes with *victims:* murdering people, like the genocide against the Vietnamese . . ."

On March 31, five undercover Dallas police officers arrived at the *Notes* office with a warrant to search for marijuana and LSD. According to Doug Baker, "While the police searched the house, the staff artist ate 10 hits of speed and eight joints with a little help from production." As police raids at *Notes* offices became more frequent, bust veterans would simply keep working as the police searched, while new staff members cowered in terror. Stoney confessed to his own sense of fear "when the cops busted in, guns drawn," but was determined not to show it, "not to give them any satisfaction."

Sunday, April 12, 1970, "was the first really fine day of spring. Several thousand people gathered in Lee Park. It was such a fine day that several people went swimming in that open cesspool, Turtle Creek. They were arrested." On those few facts, summed up by Doug Baker, everyone agreed. But the events that followed the arrest of the Turtle Creek swimmers would be disputed for years in Dallas courtrooms and newspaper columns, and become known as the Lee Park Massacre.

The April 13 *Morning News* reported the "Bottle-Throwing Melee" that took place as the crowd gathered to protest the arrests and the police called for reinforcements. Estimating the crowd at about three thousand and the number of police at two hundred, the article noted fifteen arrests and six officers treated for injuries. The following day, the *Morning News* reported that Brent LaSalle Stein had been charged with "interfering with police officers during a civil disturbance," a felony punishable by two to ten years in prison. "Police said Stein, alias Stoney Burns, was arrested after he urged a crowd to 'Come on, let's go get the pigs,' pointing to a group of police officers." *Notes* reporter Jay Gaulding wrote a different account.

> Stoney Burns and I were standing in the crowd along the roadway when a pig in a white hat began pushing and cussing at the ones standing in the gutter. Everyone was chanting, "Pigs go, Pigs go." In exasperation the white hat picked up a metal pop can and threw it directly at us. A barrage of bottles arched out into the boulevard landing indiscriminately on the patrol cars and tourist vehicles . . .
>
> At this point Stoney and I were standing about forty feet from the pigline on a grassy knoll sort of overlooking the confrontation. One of the motherfuckers pointed directly at Stoney and yelled, "There's the one we want, right there!" Four of them charged up the hill towards us. "Run, godamnit," one NOTES staffer yelled, "We've got an issue to put out this weekend." "No," Stoney replied. "They know where I live and would just come after me anyway. I've got bond money and I'll just go peace-

fully." All he had time to do before the four cops jumped him was throw both hands in the air and shout, "I'll go peacefully!" They knocked him to the ground and beat the holy shit out of him. They dragged him down the hill to the concrete and then, joined by a fifth crony, carried him to a nearby pigmobile. A bottle sailed through the air and busted the window out of the car he was being forced into. He admitted later the support sure made him feel good. They transferred him to the back of a piggy-wagon and drove off.

Stoney discussed the charge against him, which "has never been used. No one even knows what 'interfering with a police officer' means. In my case it seems to mean that I was there acting like a newsman, that's all. I didn't off a pig, or throw a bottle or slash a tire." He appealed for witnesses and for money to help fund his defense.

In June, *Notes* reported what happened when "Editor Stoney Burns decided to go down to the Dallas City Council Chambers to defend Freedom of the Press against the Decency onslaught. The Citizens for Decent Dallas and the Citizens for Decent Literature, two Birch-brained organizations . . ." wanted the Council to ban the sale of *Notes* to minors. Stoney made a pitch for the First Amendment and tried to convince officials that controversy only improved his sales. The council voted to "shut Burns up. There were no rebuttals. Councilman Ted Holland said Burns could 'go back to the gutter.' Stoney Burns said, 'Thank you, Your Honor, for your "proper channels." '"

Stoney told an interviewer from his own paper, "I'd like to see NOTES as a large weekly newspaper—accepted by the community for what it is . . . and make it into a really first-class newspaper." Instead of his usual defiance, Stoney showed signs of battle fatigue. "I'd like to get away from the city, frankly. But right now, I'm hung up here."

He was feeling the pressure of his upcoming October 19 trial for the Lee Park disturbance. At a pretrial hearing only one of Stoney's witnesses was permitted to speak. But several police officers testified that Stoney had been leading an assault force at Lee Park. "They've got me and there's no way they're going to let go," Stoney told a *Times Herald* reporter in September. Stoney, described as "a frail-looking hippie who wears long frizzy hair," again claimed that all efforts to stop the underground movement would only make it grow. " 'Notes' grew from 500 circulation to a legitimate 12,000 in three years,' he said. 'And a now there's five other (underground) papers in town.'" About a month before his scheduled trial date, Stoney Burns resigned as editor of *Dallas Notes*. When the trial was postponed until February, Stoney got out of Dallas.

Trials and Tribulations

Dallas had experienced a sudden proliferation of underground publications. Newspapers such as *Dallas Liberation Front Digest, Lee Park Free, Panther,* and *Thorn* (aimed at high school students) were active in late 1970. Doug Baker, an original editor of *Notes,* had returned to Dallas from California and come to work for Stoney. The two friends disagreed about editorial policies. Baker left to publish *Dallas News.* The first issue of *News* appeared in August 1970, timed to appear biweekly in the weeks *Dallas Notes* did not publish.

J. R. Compton suceeded Stoney at *Notes.* But Stoney and Doug Baker did not care for Compton's product, and "sold their 998 shares to the White Panther Party of Fort Worth." The Panthers crashed the *Notes* staff meetings and tried to restore some of the paper's lost "radical flair." Two competing versions of *Notes* appeared briefly in January. To stop the confusion, Compton renamed his paper *Hooka.* The Panther Party paper, *Outlaw Times,* appeared in February. *Dallas Notes* no longer existed.

Stoney Burns helped launch another newspaper venture in Austin, with some alumni of *Space City* and the *Rag.* The first issue of *Lone Star Dispatch* appeared in late November. Named so that its initials would be those of the hallucinogenic drug, the *Dispatch* proclaimed itself the "Official Publication of the Central Committee of the Provisional Government of the Democratic Republic of Texas." The paper exhibited classic countercultural uncertainty about whether political or cultural revolution should predominate.

"It is the responsibility of the revolutionary peoples of Texas to recapture the vision symbolized by the Lone Star . . . the founders of the Lone Star Dispatch offer a new symbol for Texas . . . the bright red star of socialist internationalism." Stoney did not find this style of rhetoric congenial. "I was just trying to simplify my life" by doing only layout and graphics, he said later. "But nobody on the staff knew anything about journalism, though everyone had an ideological ax to grind." The differences between Stoney and his coeditors were fundamental. "They thought that freedom was in everybody having a job, and I thought it was in not having a job." After three issues of *LSD,* Stoney took his drafting table and went home.

"Stoney Burns, controversial Dallas newsman, has been deselected from the Lone Star Dispatch because of his elitism, sexism and racism," according to reports in the Dallas underground papers. The *LSD* staff "found his politics of 'Rock and Roll, Dope, and Fucking in the Streets' immature. Stoney has no 'concept of raising revolutionary consciousness—the main objective of a newspaper,'" said the collective." An *LSD* "spokeswoman" said it would be "unhealthy" if Stoney started a rival paper, "Because we plan to put out LSD, not a Hippy-Dippy LSD." But a fourth issue of the paper never appeared.

While Stoney was in Austin the U.S. Supreme Court reheard arguments in the two-year-old Texas obscenity case against him and *Dallas Notes*. Assistant Attorney General Lonny Zweiner admitted *Notes* was "pretty tame" compared to hard-core pornography. The *Notes* story featured optimistic rumors that "in the first hearing before the court last summer, Justice Black was reported to be dumbfounded" about some of the items seized in the raids. "Justice Potter Stewart took an even dimmer view" and "called the smash-and-grab tactics of the Dallas Police Department 'outrageous.'"

Back in Dallas in January 1971, Stoney went to work as an investigator for Fred Time, the lawyer who was representing him at his Lee Park Massacre trial. In late February, as Stoney's Lee Park case came to trial, he got some bad news from Washington. The U.S. Supreme Court ruled eight to one that the three-judge panel in Dallas "should not have held the law unconstitutional in 1969 because there was no evidence of 'irreparable injury' to the publisher, Brent Stein." Justice William O. Douglas wrote a "vigorous dissent," condemning Dallas police for their "search and destroy raid" at the *Notes* office. A *Times Herald* editorial praised the high court decision.

Stoney's trial for "interfering with a police officer during a civil disturbance" began February 22. Forty Dallas police officers were sworn in as prosecution witnesses. Only ten testified and only one, Alfred M. Cessna, swore that Stoney had interfered with police officers. "Cessna testified that Stoney led 30–50 people towards him while he pointed at the officer and said, 'Kill the pig bastard.'"

During the trial the prosecuting attorney, Assistant District Attorney John Stauffer, several times compared Stoney to a messianic cult guru. When Stoney testified that he feared a police beating after his arrest, Stauffer said, "It's too bad they didn't kill you." Stoney's lawyer moved for a mistrial on the basis of Stauffer's remark, but the judge denied the motion. After seven hours of deliberation, the jury declared it was deadlocked. Stauffer offered to drop the felony charge if Stoney would plead guilty to a misdemeanor charge of inciting to riot, which carried a maximum sentence of one year in jail and a thousand-dollar fine. Stoney refused. Judge R. T. Scales declared a mistrial and ordered a retrial in May.

Between trials Stoney Burns returned to journalism as art director and sports editor for the *Dallas News*. By May the *News* had become a weekly. Because of its name, much of the paper's mail was sent first to the *Dallas Morning News*, causing delays and confusion. Stoney lobbied for a name change.

On May 24 Stoney returned to court for the second Lee Park trial. As the *News* reported, Stauffer seemed to be trying to create a mistrial this time. He called Stoney a "guru," a "messiah," and a "führer." He handed a document to a defense attorney, then jumped up and grabbed it away, shouting it was not for him but for the jury to read. Judge Scales found Stauffer in contempt of court and fined him ten dollars.

Stauffer asked Cessna if Stoney looked different "than he does here today with a business suit and tie on?" Cessna said yes. "'He had a long beard that seemed somewhat shaggy; had considerably longer hair.'" Describing his arrest of Stoney, Cessna said, "'I grabbed him by the hair of the head, of which he had a substantial amount. It was pretty hard to grab anywhere without grabbing hair.'"

On the second day of this trial, the district attorney's office offered Stoney a two-year probated sentence in exchange for a guilty plea. Stoney refused the deal. The jury, discounting most of the testimony but upset at the reported obscenities and "jumping up and down," found Stoney Burns guilty. On June 11, Judge Scales sentenced Stoney to three years in prison. Stoney vowed to appeal. At the sentencing, Roy Stein "wrestled" a young photographer "to the courthouse floor and broke a camera lens valued at $2,000." Stoney's father had been trying to block the young man from filming his son leaving the courtroom. He was fined $100.

Stoney had been estranged from his parents for several years. Though Stoney had changed his name to protect his father's reputation, *Notes From The Underground* had deeply offended Roy Stein. The intensity of his father's revulsion had surprised Stoney. As a boy he had watched his parents' reaction to the televised Army-McCarthy hearings and figured they were liberals, that they would understand. But the long-haired credo of sex, drugs, and rock and roll had appalled the elder Stein. He had fired his son from Allied Printing.

Now, trying to show his support, Roy Stein had succumbed to emotion. He did not know that the young filmmaker, Michael Grant, was an SMU graduate student sympathetic to his son. Grant would exhibit his documentary about Stoney's plight—a film titled "Stoney's Greatest Hit"—to help generate public support for the "peaceful and courageous" journalist.

The last issue of *Dallas News* appeared July 16. On July 23 the editors announced that "DALLAS NEWS is now the ICONOCLAST." A letter from Gilbert Shelton, artist and author of "The Fabulous Furry Freak Brothers" comic strip, may have inspired the choice of name. "Are you hip to William C. Brann and his Iconoclast magazine that he published in the late 1800's? He was shot by an irate reader . . ." The editors relayed the dictionary definition of *iconoclast* as "a breaker or destroyer of images that are regarded as ridiculous, superstitious or erroneous. Those established ideas, images, and institutions whose time has passed will be attacked by the ICONOCLAST."

Looking back at the underground papers of recent years, the editors promised a new level of professionalism, to follow the energy and courage of William Cowper Brann. "The ICONOCLAST is an old Texan newspaper with a great tradition." They recalled Brann's attacks on "the Baptists who controlled much of the finances in Texas," and his scorn for "the daily newspapers which he mostly trusted to tell lies and cover up the conventional crookedness of established businesses." They mentioned the feud with Baylor and the shooting that ended Brann's life. "With Brann's death the Waco ICONOCLAST died. As the Weathermen say, 'It's new morning, changing weather.' The ICONOCLAST lives!"

The Iconoclast Lives

Stoney Burns tried to declare himself a pauper in August. He wanted to prove he lacked enough money to appeal his conviction in the Lee Park Massacre case. Judge Scales, who had sentenced Stoney to three years in prison, denied the request. Weighing heavily against Stoney was his own testimony that "he voluntarily left a $100-per-week job at a legal office here because his court trial had left him 'disillusioned with the whole legal system.'"

Stoney was living on the commissions for advertising he sold for the *Iconoclast*. By his own estimate, he sold 80 to 90 percent of the paper's ad space. With Stoney, Doug Baker, and J. D. Arnold running the *Iconoclast*, the originators of Dallas underground journalism had begun again, battle-scarred but irrepressible. The *Iconoclast* still ran wacky drug stories. In October the *Iconoclast* claimed seven U.S. presidents had smoked pot, including Washington and

Jefferson. A UPS story in December claimed that "marijuana causes immortality" and quoted a bogus medical expert who said that "no marijuana smoker has died in the last 1600 years."

But the paper had begun to notice ecological issues. The *Iconoclast* published large photos of the Big Thicket. *Moat City Monitor*, a calendar of musical and cultural events around town begun that fall, increasingly defined the paper's concerns. Imitated immediately by underground rivals, the events calendar would eventually spawn similar sections in the two major Dallas dailies. SMU lifted its ban against underground papers, allowing the *Iconoclast* to be sold on campus. Another sign of the paper's increased influence was the extent to which other media followed its lead on stories.

In 1971 KERA-TV in Dallas produced "Newsroom" five nights a week. Funded by the Ford Foundation, the idea was to simulate the sort of discussion that took place in editorial conferences at newspapers. News professionals would discuss primarily local issues among themselves, for the interested citizen viewer. "Newsroom" was organized and run by a former *Dallas Morning News* reporter, Jim Lehrer, later a national news anchor on public television. When an *Iconoclast* reporter asked him "why Newsroom doesn't give credit to ICONOCLAST when it breaks a news story first and Newsroom borrows it, Lehrer assured this reporter that this was merely a subconscious oversight" with no relation to politics. But another "Newsroom" veteran said the program constantly used unacknowledged tips and ideas from Stoney Burns.

Some *Iconoclast* stories had teeth, charging narcotics officers with brutality, pointing out racist language in the *Dallas Morning News*, and explaining that the chairman and the president of the powerful Dallas Citizens Council, Tom Thumb owners Charles and Robert Cullum, did not even reside in Dallas. Stoney tried to keep his personal profile low—at first. He wrote a gossip column as the "Meanderings of Bellicose Bullfeather." This contrivance allowed him to discuss himself in the third person. "One of the jurors who voted to convict Stoney Burns of his felony charge . . . has also smoked dope with an ex-ICONOCLAST staffer. Where's *his* head at?"

Surrounded by his old friends, protected by a second alias, Stoney regained his sense of humor. "The not-for-profit corporation that publishes ICONOCLAST is now known as Reliable Sources, Inc. . . . Now ICONOCLAST staphers can say with impunity, 'Reliable sources said today that . . .'" In February 1972, convicted felon Stoney Burns, still on bail pending his appeal of a three-year prison sentence, announced his candidacy for sheriff of Dallas County.

He promised a campaign based on the concept of "'law and

order—justice and mercy. We need to return to the principles of the colorful lawmen of yesteryear, such as Wyatt Earp . . . and the Lone Ranger.'" Stoney told the *Iconoclast* that "His first act as sheriff would be to reform the Dallas County Jail . . ." If he were elected, "Dallas County would be 'relatively safe' for marijuana users since his deputies would make their first mission the enforcement of the law in the area of 'crimes with definite victims.'"

"Patsi Aucoin writing in the *Richardson Daily News* found Stoney 'the most convincing candidate among the six Democrats and one Republican challenging Sheriff Clarence Jones . . .'" She reported that the district attorney was investigating Stoney's eligibility in view of his Lee Park conviction, and quoted Stoney's satisfied assessment. "That means they take me seriously."

On Friday, March 3, Dallas police arrested Stoney Burns for possession of marijuana. The precise details of the arrest and the amount of marijuana found varied in different media. After leaving a bar with two friends about 11 P.M., Stoney started to drive away in his van when police stopped him. Sergeant Wayne Fowler told Stoney "he had received confidential information from a source 'who's never been wrong before' that marijuana was in Stein's van."

Whether or not Stoney agreed to let police search the van remained a point of contention. The *Iconoclast* reported that one of the police officers "allegedly found a 35 mm. film tin half full of marijuana stems, leaves and seeds in the glove compartment of the van, after he had searched the rest of the truck thoroughly." The *Morning News* quoted police who said the film can "contained about 25 grains of marijuana, enough to make five to eight cigarettes."

According to the *Morning News*, "When [Officer] Walden tried to show the substance to [Sergeant] Fowler, Stein allegedly attacked the officers, trying to knock the container from Walden's hand. Fowler grappled with Stein and managed to subdue and handcuff him." Stoney spent the night in jail but went free on a writ bond the next day. Police confiscated his van. "Stein says he has no knowledge of how the grass may have gotten there and is willing to take a lie detector test to prove his innocence," the *Iconoclast* reported. "Stein declined to comment on the effect this might have on his campaign for sheriff."

Bullfeather was especially bellicose. He opined that "Brent 'Stoney Burns' Stein was not busted for grass because he is running for sheriff, but because the newspaper has recently been revealing the secret identities of various local, state, and federal narcotics agents and informers . . ." But the columnist gave notice that police intimidation would not work. "If someone who stays as clean as

Stoney can get busted, it can happen to anyone. But it won't stop this paper from exposing narcs." He then gave physical descriptions of several suspected undercover narcotics officers.

Stoney continued to make good on Bullfeathers' pledge. On April 6 a phone caller told the *Iconoclast* that undercover Texas Department of Public Safety narcotics officer Bob Hardin was at the county courthouse to testify at a trial. Hardin had a reputation for brutality. Several drug suspects had alleged that Hardin beat them while they were in custody. Stoney and J. D. Arnold hurried over to the courthouse. When Hardin walked into a corridor outside the courtroom during a recess, Stoney took his photograph. Police tried to stop Stoney and grab his camera. Arnold protested. Bailiffs arrested Arnold and District Judge Ed Gossett sentenced him to three days in jail and fined him one hundred dollars. Stoney was later arrested but not immediately charged. The *Iconoclast* published a special issue the next day with Hardin's photograph on the front page.

Burns and Arnold were charged with contempt of court and ordered to trial on April 21. At the end of the five-hour proceeding Judge Gossett pronounced the two men guilty and sentenced them to six months in the Dallas County jail. Released on five thousand dollars bond, the journalists filed an appeal. Despite his two convictions and his upcoming trial for possession of marijuana, Stoney, and the *Iconoclast*, continued to taunt Dallas police and expose undercover narcotics officers.

Bullfeather criticized the inflated estimates of drugs seized in police raids, "but that is how narcs pat themselves on the back, overestimating the importance of their jobs—and by busting high school students." Quoting state legislature statistics, Bullfeather informed readers that "Dallas and Harris counties supply over half the marijuana inmates to Texas prisons. 29.23% of the marijuana prisoners come from Dallas county alone . . ."

These figures were much on Stoney's mind as the date of his marijuana trial approached. The *Iconoclast* featured Stoney on their cover in October, captioned: "Stoney Burns Tells: 'Why I Won't Get a Fair Trial.'" Stoney confessed to his mounting sense of dread. "Every time I have a trial, and this is my third jury trial, I start getting more uptight until I'm a nervous wreck by the time the thing starts. This time it's worse than usual . . ." He gave his version of the arrest, describing the search of his van as coercive and the evidence as a police plant. His lawyers, Ed Polk and Jim Mattox, made a motion to suppress the evidence but Stoney was pessimistic.

"Probation seems as unlikely in my case as the prospect of acquittal . . ." Noting the inequities of the drug laws in different states, Stoney accused the district attorney's office of "ramrodding my case through, ahead of similar cases that have been on dockets for much longer" because of his "unpopular political philosophy." He thought authorities wanted "a conviction before public opinion swings toward the position that pot is just not the threat to society that people once thought it was," a trend he saw as imminent.

The *Iconoclast* reported that "Judge R. T. Scales took only three seconds to issue a decision Monday, after five hours of conflicting testimony, denying Stoney Burns' motion to throw out the indictment against him due to improper search procedures." The writer thought the police testimony "bordered on the incredible" and quoted a "veteran courthouse observer" as saying police had "the sorriest grounds for probable search and seizure ever seen."

Stoney's trial did not last long. He later described how prospective jurors were asked "how many would be reluctant to give a life sentence. Burns said 85 per cent raised their hands. Those jurors were excused, he said, and the others chosen from among the remainder." When Judge Scales asked Stoney how he pleaded, he said, "Not only am I not guilty of this, but no one is so guilty of possession of a harmless non-addictive herb that he should have to spend even the minimum of two years away from friends, family and loved ones." His lawyers claimed "the search was illegal, wiretapping was used against the underground newspaper editor and that witnesses have been harassed by Dallas police officers."

The jury took five hours to find Stoney guilty. Though not surprising, the verdict was still a shock. The *Dallas Times Herald* reported Stoney's reaction: " 'I beg you. Please don't send me to jail,' Stein told the jury . . . Tearfully he told the jury he is a 'gentle' man who has never owned a knife or gun. Stein's attorney, Jim Mattox, asked the jury the 'relevance'" of sending Stoney to the penitentiary for " 'some seeds and stems.'" Mattox also argued against the validity of the marijuana laws. But the jury took only two and a half hours to sentence Stoney to ten years and a day in prison. The *Iconoclast* explained that "a day" added to the ten-year sentence gave Stoney no chance of parole. Stoney's bail was raised to ten thousand dollars.

Bullfeather said, "That ten year sentence handed down to Stoney Burns on a simple possession rap has sent waves of shock and disbelief through the hip and radical community. It reminds them that we still live in a barbaric and backward state." Stoney kept up humorous banter, political criticism, and revelations about undercover narcotics agents. He gave out the names and home addresses of two

agents in his December "Bullfeather" column. When the city of
Dallas asked the state legislature for new laws giving "extra powers
and protections to the city government," Bullfeather said such laws
would "make sure more ordinary citizens wind up in jails. A police
state, you say? Ah, yes, but it is laughable and frightening . . . that
these proposals came from . . . City Attorney Alex Bickley," who
Stoney thought should know better "than to ask for these patently
unconstitutional measures."

After the Fall

"Some people have criticized Bullfeather for blatant plagiarism and
to this I must plead guilty . . . For example, this paragraph you're
reading now was copped verbatim from the *San Diego Door* . . ."
Stoney received more national publicity when *Playboy* magazine reported on his marijuana sentence in its February issue. Bullfeather
reported further plots against him. "DPS narc Bob Hardin (photo),
known for his brutality and for lying under oath, offered to drop
charges against an acid-dealing friend of Bullfeather's if he would
help bust Stoney Burns, J. D. Arnold . . ." and others.

On March 2, 1973, Bullfeather announced that Stoney Burns had
resigned as *Iconoclast* art director. "Stoney has been 'unemployed'
before, however, and he always seems to end up back in the alternative press business eventually." In fact, Stoney already had plans
to start another publication. But first he had another date in court.
The Texas Court of Criminal Appeals had agreed to consider revers-
ing Stoney's Lee Park conviction, based on the behavior of the prosecuting attorney.

On April 11, the appeals court reversed Stoney's conviction for
"interfering with a police officer during a civil disturbance" at Lee
Park. The court agreed with ACLU attorney Fred Time that pros-
ecutor John Stauffer had argued his case improperly, calling Stoney
"hippie," "guru," "messiah," "crud," and "Buffalo Bill." He had
asked a witness if Stoney's companions looked "like Mennonites or
Amish people" and said the testimony of defense witnesses turned
his stomach.

Judge Truman Roberts wrote that Stauffer "left little room for reasonable minds to differ as to whether his actions could be labeled
harmless." ACLU lawyer Fred Time, happy about the verdict, la-
mented the waste of money to try and re-try the case. Stauffer had
another conviction reversed that spring. On Flag Day in 1970, David
Renn had flown an American flag with the fifty stars replaced by a

peace symbol, which resulted in his arrest and trial. During final arguments, Stauffer held up an American flag and used his fingers as symbolic scissors to re-create Renn's act. "Snip, snip, there goes Rhode Island. Snip, snip, there goes Pennsylvania . . ." Stauffer also called Renn a hippie, a communist, and "the anti-Christ." For years after the reversal, Stauffer entertained statewide meetings of prosecutors by repeating his star-cutting performance.

By leaving the *Iconoclast*, Stoney had realized his "lifelong desire to retire before age 30." Now he embarked on a project that would unite his various interests—photography, music, the gossip column—with good graphics and production values. He wanted a publication that would not compete with the *Iconoclast*. Doug Baker was changing the *Iconoclast* to attract a wider audience and more advertising. Jack Anderson's column began to appear, followed by those of Ralph Nader and Paul Krassner. Baker hired a new editor with mainstream media experience to replace Stoney and chart a new direction.

Stoney's creation was *Buddy*, "Texas' first pop music magazine," named for "Texas' first rock and roll star," Buddy Holly. Announcing the new venture, Stoney said "*Buddy* (the magazine) will have record and film reviews as well as a news section, a gossip column, and an events column" and interviews with pop stars who came to play in Dallas. *Buddy* was free at record stores, sustained by large ads from record companies and local clubs. The first issue appeared in July 1973.

Bellicose Bullfeather no longer attacked narcotics enforcement or the political power structure. His *Buddy* column, "BlahBlah," consisted mostly of gossip from the world of rock and roll music. But if Stoney had settled into a less contentious posture regarding the authorities, he still had unfinished business to settle with the law.

In January 1974, the Texas Court of Criminal Appeals again came to Stoney's rescue. The court voted three to two to dismiss contempt of court charges against Stoney Burns and J. D. Arnold. Since the incident involving the undercover officer "did not occur in the courtroom" and did not in any way prejudice that trial, there was insufficient evidence to support the charge. Nor did the court find any proof that the two journalists had physically restrained Officer Robert Hardin in order to take his photograph, as Hardin claimed. Stoney said, "Obviously I'm very pleased. But more important than the decision is to me personally it shows that even a corrupt Dallas judge cannot trample on the First Amendment."

Stoney had avoided serving six months in jail for contempt of court and three years in prison for interfering with a police officer during a civil disturbance. But there was still the matter of the marijuana conviction. Stoney had some grounds for optimism. In August 1973, the Texas marijuana law had been changed, making possession of small amounts by first offenders subject to a maximum six-month misdemeanor sentence. The legislature had intended the new law to apply retroactively, but the Texas Court of Criminal Appeals found the retroactive provisions of the new law unconstitutional.

That decision was bad news for the more than seven hundred persons in Texas jails on marijuana possession charges in 1973. "The average sentence was 9½ years. Thirteen were serving life sentences." It was also bad news for Stoney. In October 1974, the court of appeals upheld his conviction. With no legal recourse remaining, Stoney began an intensive public relations effort, in the hope of attracting a pardon from Governor Dolph Briscoe. Earlier in the year Briscoe had announced "Project Star," to review the sentences of first-offenders convicted for possessing four ounces or less of marijuana.

In an interview with the *Daily Texan*, Stoney presented his predicament as political. "My charge was possession of marijuana, but my crime was publishing an underground newspaper." He said he did not know how "the ⅟₁₈ of an ounce of stems and seeds" got into his van. "But I do know that I advocated the end of the war, was for lighter marijuana penalties and was for legalizing abortion. Now all of that is fashionable. But then, you were a Communist." The *Texan* agreed that Stoney was now paying for being "a liberal-radical in a conservative-reactionary city."

As a last-ditch stall, Stoney filed a second appeal, a motion to have his case reheard. The maneuver kept him free but not for long. On November 22, a Dallas district court upheld Stoney's sentence and ordered him to report to jail. He appealed to Governor Briscoe. Briscoe's press secretary said the governor was aware of the case but had to wait for a formal recommendation from the Board of Pardons and Paroles. With help from the National Organization for the Reform of Marijuana Laws (NORML), Stoney's supporters organized a campaign to send letters, telegrams, and petitions to the governor on his behalf.

After twelve days in the Dallas County jail, Stoney was transferred to Huntsville state prison unit on December 4, his thirty-second birthday. State Representative Ronnie Earle of Austin, who initiated Project Star, let reporters know he thought Stoney would be pardoned. Earle's assistant said Briscoe had already pardoned more than 245 people convicted under the old pot law. "Burns is the last of the marijuana desperados." College groups ran "a t-shirt and petition drive to free Brent Stein, better known as Stoney Burns, from state prison before Christmas."

Stoney was assigned to work in the prison hospital, "which he says is run mostly by marijuana prisoners—'They're the ones with enough intelligence to know what they're doing.'" He enjoyed the fact that prison officials made drug offenders the prisoners with easiest access to syringes and pharmaceutical supplies. On December 19, Governor Briscoe commuted Stoney's sentence. He left the Huntsville prison as one of 120 prisoners released in time for Christmas.

In Theodore White's adjusted chronology, the decade of the 1960s really began with the assassination of President Kennedy in November 1963. Following White's logic, we could say that the sixties really ended with the resignation of Richard Nixon, in August 1974. But Stoney Burns did not emerge from the sixties until the day he left prison a free man, with one hundred dollars in his pocket for a ticket home. He resumed editing *Buddy*, which was kept alive by friends while Stoney was in jail.

But in some ways Stoney Burns still lingers in the afterglow of the 1960s. A Dallas reporter visiting Stoney on the occasion of his fortieth birthday found him parrying with the IRS about back taxes. *Buddy*, ten years old, enjoyed a free distribution of 100,000 copies in Dallas and Houston. He still visited rock clubs, for business and pleasure. "Stoney is now a Dallas celebrity of sorts. Policemen who once arrested him now approach him at clubs and parties smiling and saying, 'Hey, Stoney, remember me?'"

Stoney has developed a certain repertoire of anecdotes, ripostes, and one-liners to deal with the inevitable questions about his radical past. "Personally, I hope they never legalize pot. If they did, you wouldn't be able to buy it on Sundays." Stoney tosses the remark off casually, like a hip Will Rogers. But the comment is part of a well-honed routine. He has said it to at least three interviewers in the last six years, and probably many more. He has a number of these verbal gems to please and deflect the curious. But there is another, more serious, purpose.

Revising and interpreting the 1960s became a growth industry in the 1980s. Historians, sociologists, and memoirists sift and resift the compressed, confusing data of the period in search of causes and effects. As the sixties recede from us, verifiable facts become as elusive as motivations and meanings. And no one has a greater proprietary interest in those facts than activists such as Stoney Burns, who made their reputations then and depend upon them now.

There are those who dispute Stoney's interpretation of bygone events. Brad Bailey's 1988 article about the history of the Dallas underground press drew an angry response from J. R. Compton. He said "many of the 'facts'" in Bailey's story were "patently untrue." Compton, who succeeded Stoney as *Dallas Notes* editor and then published *Hooka*, called the *Iconoclast* a "mediocre pretender." Of course, Compton has his own version of history, his own identity to protect.

Doug Baker continued publishing the *Iconoclast* with a series of short-term editors until 1977. Though the two major Dallas dailies left plenty of room on the left for a nonradical alternative newspaper, the *Iconoclast* never achieved sufficient circulation to attract advertisers and stay healthy. The current seventy-eight thousand circulation of the *Dallas Observer* attests to the viability of the idea the *Iconoclast* began. Doug Baker now lives in San Francisco and works for the Bank of America. J. D. Arnold is now the "operator of a tour bus in New Mexico." And Nancy Lynne Brown, who married and divorced Doug Baker, became Nancy Smith, society columnist for the *Dallas Times Herald.*

Stoney still lives in Dallas, publishes *Buddy*, and jokes amiably, vaguely, about the crazy old days when everything seemed to be happening very fast. His hair is gray. His attitude has mellowed. But every now and then he shows flashes of his old self, as he did in a 1986 column.

> Freedom of the press has been under attack recently from all sides. The Southland Corporation in Dallas made news by banning *Playboy* and *Penthouse* from its 7–11 shelves. Their decision was made only after a policy of keeping those magazines behind the counter (where they didn't sell too well anyway) instead of on the regular magazine racks . . . Oh, thank heaven, it's reassuring to be able to look to 7–11 for moral guidance. (We'll have to remember to call them for their positions on abortion and capital punishment).
>
> More recently we've been defending the *Dallas Observer* regarding a full page ad . . . for a prominent gay bar . . . The message was that teenagers, 18 and 19 years old, will be welcome in the club . . . We believe . . . that if an advertiser pays for the space, he can put anything he wants within his border. That's true Freedom of the Press. And although it's not protected by the Constitution, we'll also defend gay boys' rights to put their weenies wherever they want, as long as it doesn't abridge the

rights of others. The legal age of consent is 17 in Texas, by the way.

That such remarks may sound mild, and even quaint, is a measure of the distance we have come since Stoney Burns and his underground colleagues around the country first challenged the respectable limits of journalism.

6. Writing Wrongs

Issues seem to reappear in Texas politics, and conflicts in public values are not
finally resolved but only advance and recede in prominence.

—*Norman D. Brown*

Writing in the *Texas Spectator* in the late 1940s, Hubert Mewhinney criticized the timidity—and inadequacy—of the objective approach to writing the news. "If Jimmy Allred says it's raining, and W. Lee O'Daniel says it isn't raining, Texas newspapermen quote them both, and don't look out the window to see which is lying, and to tell the readers what the truth is at the moment."

Mewhinney's description remains pertinent. Too many journalists cover events in packs, writing formula stories based on official press releases, with rebuttals from familiar, sanctioned opposition spokespersons. None of the Texas independents would be surprised that large chains and the corporate mentality have increased their domination of American mass media. But the accelerated rate at which newspaper competition has vanished, ownership has consolidated into fewer hands, and news content and style have been standardized in all media would shock the iconoclasts.

Alexander Cockburn, acerbic columnist for the *Nation,* has expressed disdain for what he calls "the first law of all journalism, which is to confirm existing prejudice, rather than contradict it." The Texas independents shared Cockburn's view. Disgust with the mainstream and special-interest publications of their times was part of what motivated the iconoclasts to go into independent journalism. Antipathy toward existing media was the single clearest value they held in common.

Independent journalists share several traits with preachers. Both harbor an urge to guide and instruct. Both assume clear moral choices. The iconoclasts urged readers to recognize and fight injustice, to honor their highest instincts, to do the right thing. Their independence from doctrine made them sensitive to doctrinal abuses. Because Protestant denominations—especially Baptist and Methodist—have long exerted profound influence on social and political life in Texas, conflict between the iconoclasts and the churches was inevitable.

With deadly precision, William Brann indicted the incongruous values of piety and profit that Waco Baptists tried to reconcile. Don Biggers confronted religious hypocrisy in the person of J. Frank Norris. He found Norris' campaigns against rum, Romanism, and the teaching of evolution abuses of the pulpit.

Several of the Texas iconoclasts set up a radical, personal vision of Christianity in opposition to religious institutions and spokespersons. John Granbery espoused his belief in Christ as a reformer and an advocate for the dispossessed. Stoney Burns and company, with their romantic characterization of Christ as a hippie, belittled the prejudices of the power structure with one of its own shining examples. The independent journalists could identify with the role of Jesus as prophet without honor in his own land.

Archer Fullingim developed his own secular vision of heaven and hell. He came to see Dallas as the Infernal City, incubating the hate and intolerance that poisoned modern life. Paradise lay closer at hand, in the threatened sanctuary of the Big Thicket, a natural chapel where he found the Holy Ghost feeling.

Battles over the precise location of the border between church and state rage on in Texas and elsewhere. A 1989 Houston newspaper headline defined one front of that battle: "Issue of evolution in textbooks sparks furor at board hearing. Creationists warn of God's wrath if proposal approved." Texas is the second-largest bulk purchaser of textbooks in the nation. Publishers adapt national textbook content to Texas guidelines.

A 1987 poll by Texas A&M University "found that 70 percent of state residents want creationism taught in school along with evolution." But the Texas attorney general and the State Board of Education threw out a state rule requiring that creationism and evolutionary theory both be included in biology texts. William Brann and John Granbery—sons of ministers—would be appalled that the content of human knowledge was being argued and controlled by preachers and politicians.

The teaching of evolution, the right to abortion, and state funding of religious education are a few of the issues based on religion that continue to preoccupy Texas and the country. Religious political figures such as Jerry Falwell and Pat Robertson have risen to national prominence by means of television. The influence of these men and others indicates a resurgence of fundamentalist faith wed to a superpatriotic capitalism. The Texas iconoclasts would find the phenomenon familiar.

Nor would current racial conflicts surprise them. In August 1989, *Time* magazine ran an article entitled "Texas Time Machine," about the efforts of minorities to secure adequate representation on the Dallas City Council. The article said: "The civil rights movement that swept the South a generation ago somehow bypassed Dallas." Stoney Burns, who criticized racism in Dallas a generation ago, would concur. The divergent views of the writers in this book bear chronological witness to the shifting attitudes of Texans toward different races, and to an understanding of racism itself.

Quick to condemn other forms of intolerance, Brann took the inferiority of blacks for granted. Biggers remained silent about blacks, but did protest the exploitation of Mexico by U.S. corporations and praised the populist Mexican revolutionary Pancho Villa. Granbery based his arguments for equality—of both sexes, all races, and all nations—on Christian principles, often preaching to unsympathetic ears. He served on commissions for racial equality in housing, education, and criminal justice, embracing allies wherever he found them, including the Communist party.

Fullingim referred to himself often as "poor white trash" to indicate his awareness that the majority of whites were also oppressed by the white Texas powerholders. By enlarging his self-concept to include blacks, Hispanics, and the rebellious youth culture of the 1960s, Fullingim recognized racism as part of the strategy of disenfranchisement that served the ruling class. He came to see what Granbery had long been preaching, that racial divisiveness was a mainstay in the structure of the status quo.

Stoney Burns took this knowledge for granted. Stoney's generation of iconoclasts also saw racism at work in the economic exploitation of Third World peoples, most aggressively in the Vietnam War. John Granbery would have endorsed that analysis.

Racial integration arrived late in Texas, and then only through enforced decisions of the U.S. Supreme Court. When Heman Sweatt applied to the University of Texas law school in 1946, his rejection began a four-year legal battle. In June 1950, the U.S. Supreme Court ruled in *Sweatt* v. *Painter* that the "educational opportunities offered white and Negro law students by the state of Texas were not substantially equal," and required Sweatt's admission. The University of Texas did not graduate a black student until 1959, nor hire a black professor until 1964.

Sweatt v. *Painter* helped prepare for the more sweeping *Brown* v. *Board of Education* ruling in 1954, which outlawed racial segregation in schools. The *Brown* decision led to the showdown in Little Rock and racial confrontations in the 1960s in schools, restaurants, and voting registries. But advocates of racial equality know that laws do not change attitudes. Racial inequities and violence continue today in Texas and nationally. The laws themselves require surveillance to maintain their powers. In June 1989, a federal appeals court declared that the Topeka Board of Education, defendant in the *Brown* case, had "failed to carry out fully the Supreme Court's mandate" of thirty-five years earlier. In Louisiana, in 1989, David Duke, a former member of the Ku Klux Klan, was elected to the state legislature.

Racism is part of an Americanism the Klan sees threatened by ethnic and religious diversity. Klan attacks on blacks, Catholics, Jews, and foreigners were carried out in the name of patriotism. Klan members marched with their faces hidden, holding American flags. But the Klan is only one example of what Richard Hofstadter calls the "paranoid style in American politics." All the iconoclasts confronted it.

Hofstadter defines the paranoid style as "overheated, oversuspicious, overaggressive, grandiose and apocalyptic in expression." Unlike the clinical paranoiac, the political version sees hostile conspiracies directed not toward him personally but "against a nation, a culture, a way of life" and views his own role with patriotic "righteousness and moral indignation." Hofstadter cites the 1950s rhetoric of Senator Joseph McCarthy as an example.

John Granbery and Archer Fullingim took on McCarthy and his red-baiting followers in Texas. For decades Granbery warned of the baser impulses hidden beneath the lofty and deceitful language of the superpatriots. Fullingim bellowed his sense of personal insult at the narrow, paranoid definition of American patriotism, which branded uncongenial ideas as communist-inspired.

Well before the elevation of communism to an almost satanic status, the paranoid political style took other forms. William Brann dismissed most politicians as fools draped in the flag, but took severe affront at the Catholic-hating American Protective Association. Like the Klan, the APA warned of a plot by the pope to undermine American institutions. Brann pointed to the support of the APA by J. B. Cranfill and other respectable Christians, who found the APA message congenial if not one they could publicly endorse.

Texas has provided fertile soil for paranoid politics. Martin Dies expanded the genre as chairman of the House Un-American Activities Committee. The careers of Richard Nixon and Joseph McCarthy, founded on accusation and innuendo, were part of the Dies legacy, to the disgust of Granbery and Fullingim. Stoney Burns provoked Dallas HUAC member Joe Pool into launching investigations of left-wing student groups, antidraft organizations, and Stoney's own paper. FBI Director J. Edgar Hoover, perhaps the most powerful paranoid of all, initiated a full-scale surveillance and subversion of American alternative newspapers.

In some instances, the rhetoric of the independent journalists reached the "overheated, grandiose and apocalyptic" level of their targets. Brann was especially susceptible to writing self-intoxicating prose. Stoney Burns' papers indulged in provocative stories and headlines, and the use of terms such as *pigs* for police. But John Stauffer, the assistant district attorney who prosecuted Stoney for his part in the Lee Park melee, returned the favor in court. His insults caused Stoney's conviction to be overturned.

Stauffer's courtroom dramatics also forfeited the 1970 conviction of a young man who flew an American flag with a peace symbol in place of the stars. At the 1984 Republican national convention in Dallas, another young man, who burned an American flag outside the convention hall, was arrested and convicted of desecrating the flag. In 1989 the U.S. Supreme Court reversed the verdict, ruling that burning an American flag was an act of free speech, protected by the Constitution. The decision ignited overheated rhetoric in editorial columns, on television talk shows, and in front of microphones at the highest levels of government.

Why Did They Do It?

Describing the psychopathology of journalism, Alexander Cockburn sees journalists as gossipmongers. Their primal desire to tell all is blunted by environments hostile to that desire. To maintain their network of sources and their standing in the community, journalists must dilute their information and pull their punches, compromises that lead to despair. The psychopathology of iconoclastic journalism is far more intense, pushing its practitioners beyond normal limits.

The Texas independents in this book defied their hostile environments and refused the compromises that might have increased their status and their safety. Driven by a missionary urge to write the truth as they perceived it, the iconoclasts disdained the journalism they saw around them, determined to claim a higher ground. But what fueled the fires within them differed as radically as their personalities.

William Brann was an angry man. His mother died when he was two and his father sent him off to be raised by others. Denied an education, Brann ran away from his foster home at thirteen. He found refuge from the lonely, brutish world in books and libraries. His own gift for language saved him from the streets but not from his emotional pain. Was he trying to show his father he would have been worth keeping, worth educating? Maybe he thought writing well was the best revenge.

Brann turned his anger on the rich who squandered advantages he had never had, on the pompous and powerful who seemed almost proud of their ignorance. Brann's rigid Victorian attitude toward women tainted his love for his daughter. When she took poison and Brann "knew that he had killed her," his anger must have intensified. Some of it must have been directed against himself. Was Brann's fight for Antonia Texeira a roundabout redemption for causing his daughter to kill herself? Was his refusal to leave Waco after two beatings his own kind of suicide? No amount of psychologizing can explain Brann's talent, but we may wonder where Brann's courage ended and his uncontrolled rage began. With savage skill, he harnessed his anger to a ferocious wit that drove his enemies to violence and ultimately destroyed him.

Don Biggers discovered pathos on the disappearing frontier. His anger surfaced when he understood how speculators and politicians exploited the Texas plains he loved. He admired the courage of those who settled and worked that rough territory, but hated their ignorance, which allowed them to be cheated of their reward. These values impelled Biggers into farming and politics, but mostly into crusades against the abuses of land speculation, commodity trading, and public trust.

Like Brann, Biggers employed humor as a weapon—in jokes, puns, and cartoons. But his wit lacked Brann's eloquence and focus. Sometimes Biggers seemed to confuse his sarcastic jokes with his true feelings, like an actor who lapses into his role. Biggers directed his rage constructively—against oil stock swindlers, corrupt politicians, and the prison system—but ultimately his anger overwhelmed his humor and embittered his old age.

Archer Fullingim grew up close to the land as Biggers had. His enduring affection for the natural environment led to his crusade to save the Big Thicket. But his family's hard struggle for marginal survival in hard times drove him to escape. Not until he had traveled widely and worked many years as a journeyman journalist did Fullingim venture to enunciate a worldview.

Maybe Fullingim's rather late start on his interior odyssey heightened his passion. Years of keeping all but conventional and mildly humorous sentiments out of his newspaper writing—perhaps reserving his deeper feelings for the fiction he planned but did not write—gave him a sense of urgency. As he grew older and his body

failed, Fullingim declared several times his impatience with anything but the truth. Like Brann and Biggers, Fullingim was probably
most distressed at the apparent inability of individuals and entire
classes of people to learn from history or to profit from their
mistakes.

Growing up in the airless conformity of 1950s Dallas, Stoney
Burns inherited an irreverent sense of humor and a subdued liberalism from his parents. Though as Jews the Steins were outsiders in
a Protestant world, they assimilated and prospered. Stoney followed
their example and might have continued his father's business had
his own vague discontent not made him susceptible to the wildly
changing times.

Stoney's arrival in journalism had an offhand, accidental quality.
His postadolescent middle-class irreverence graduated to radical social criticism partly based on the immoderate reaction of official
Dallas to any criticism at all. Stoney joined a generation of youthful
upstarts who pointed out discrepancies between the mouthed ideals
and the actual practices of those in power. His ability to make his
enemies look ridiculous gave his views a sting and made his persecution as inevitable as Brann's.

Protesting injustice and proposing alternatives were already John
Granbery's methods before he became a journalist. With his thorough knowledge of history, comparative cultures, and economics,
Granbery understood how society's manipulators gained their ends
at the expense of others. He considered the fight against them his
mission. But Granbery knew better than to adopt the tactics of his
enemies. He realized, as Biggers did not, that the real enemy was
despair.

Like the other independent journalists, Grandbery read widely in
periodicals from Texas and beyond. None of the Texas iconoclasts
trusted local media to report all the news. Part of their self-appointed function was to supply that expurgated information from
other sources, or to force better coverage. All five editors liked to reprint material from obscure or distant sources in their own periodicals, as they in turn were reprinted elsewhere. Such newspapers
and magazines provided the Texas writers with spiritual nourish-
ment, a sense of community so important to writers who often felt
isolated or opposed by their immediate environments.

For whom did the Texas independents write? For themselves, for
fellow iconoclasts, and for the iconoclast in each of us. Their journalism indicted the causes of quiet desperation and proclaimed
them unnecessary. Their writing appealed to values apart from
those operative in corrupt social and political institutions. The as-

sumption of such values reveals an underlying hopefulness, even idealism, among the iconoclasts. Their attacks on the unwholesome aspects of the way things are sounded a call to explore more worthwhile alternatives.

Iconoclasm in Texas Today

The writers in this book are but a few of the many independent voices in Texas journalism during the past one hundred and fifty years. Such voices have not been rare, only too rarely remembered. Celebrating their individuality, the Texas independents preserved the tradition of speaking one's mind on issues of all sorts, however unfashionably. Some Texas journalists continue in the cause.

The *Texas Observer*, declaring itself "A Journal of Free Voices," remains a dependable source of information and opinion not otherwise available in the Texas press. The *Observer*'s modern incarnation began in 1953 when Granbery's contemporary, Paul Holcomb, sold his interest in the *State Observer* to a group headed by Texas Democratic women. They combined Holcomb's magazine with the *East Texas Democrat* to produce the *Texas Observer*. Published by Mrs. R. D. Randolph, the new weekly's editor was Ronnie Dugger, former editor of the *Daily Texan*.

Dugger and his associate, William Brammer, were followed by a succession of editors dedicated to getting at the truth about Texas and Texas politics, including Willie Morris, Greg Olds, Kaye Northcott, Molly Ivins, Jim Hightower, and Geoffrey Rips. Morris, who confronted university censorship as editor of the *Daily Texan*, drew his inspiration from H. L. Mencken, Lincoln Steffens, "Brann the Iconoclast," and previous *Observer* editors such as Ronnie Dugger, among others.

The record of *Observer* alumni proves the importance of the *Observer* as an institution that has nurtured independent voices for nearly four decades. Morris became an editor at *Harper's*. Dugger wrote books about academic freedom at the University of Texas and the problems of the Reagan presidency. Until 1990, Jim Hightower headed the Texas Department of Agriculture with a Populist agenda designed to protect small farmers and ensure safe food. Geoffrey Rips exposed the federal effort to suppress the underground press of the 1960s and 1970s. Kaye Northcott writes for the *Fort Worth Star-Telegram*. Molly Ivins writes a syndicated column on Texas politics for the *Dallas Times Herald* and another for the *Progressive*.

Ivins is well known nationally for her commentaries broadcast on National Public Radio and the Public Broadcasting System. Her political analyses are as funny as they are merciless. As a longtime observer of the Texas Legislature, Ivins echoes the sentiments of previous Texas iconoclasts. Explaining to her readers why the Texas Legislature—or the "Lege"—is not competent to enact abortion legislation, Ivins wrote that "After covering them for 20 years . . . I'm still convinced that you can go into any community in this state, take the first 181 people to cross the main street, and you'd come out with a higher average caliber than you get in the Lege."

Ivins noted that in the course of her recent reporting she had referred to Texas legislators "as airheads, pinheads, droolers, mean-spirited, gutless, a public disgrace, ludicrous, nasty, ignorant," and other unflattering terms. Ivins can be counted on to reveal the improprieties and the stupidities perpetrated by Texas legislators. Her disgust with politicians rivals that of Granbery or Brann.

Ray Reece is a different sort of muckraker. A contemporary of Stoney Burns, Reece abandoned his doctoral work in literature at the University of Texas in 1967 to help wage war against the war in Vietnam. He wrote for the *National Guardian*—later the *Guardian*—an independent radical weekly in New York. Returning to Austin in 1973, he found what he called a "desecration" of the natural environment in progress. As an associate editor of *Texas Architect* magazine for three years, Reece began to investigate energy power and politics.

During a brief stint at the *Texas Observer* in 1976, Reece interested the editor at the time, Jim Hightower, in a series of articles about the politics of solar energy. In 1979 Reece published *The Sun Betrayed*, "a report on the corporate seizure of U.S. solar energy development" linking local, state, and national energy politics. The crisis spawned by the Iraqi invasion of Kuwait in 1990 demonstrated the ongoing pertinence of his analysis. Reece became active in Austin politics, helping spearhead opposition in 1981 to the city's investment in a nuclear power plant to supply future energy. Under city contract, in 1983 Reece wrote an energy management master plan for Austin.

In 1984–85, Reece worked for the preservation of a greenbelt along Austin's Town Lake. He cochaired the Town Lake Park Alliance, opposing lakefront development, and edited the *Town Lake Monitor* to publicize the Alliance campaign. In 1986 Reece began to write editorials for the *West Austin News*, a small independent weekly. He writes mostly about local issues, many involving politics and the environment, opposing big-money developments he finds beneficial to a few investors but harmful to the community.

Reece has been especially critical of the *Austin American-States-*

man, the city's only daily paper, for its favorable treatment of ecologically harmful developments and for its silence on various critical issues. Reece has pointed out that Roger Kintzel, *American-Statesman* publisher, has applied for exceptions to the local park ordinances to expand the plant of his newspaper, which has not reported Kintzel's activity.

In 1989, when the *West Austin News* won an award for general excellence from the Texas Community Newspaper Association, Reece spelled out his journalism values. "We are committed not only to the *people* in our community . . . but to the *idea* of community. We are old-fashioned in this regard and proudly so. We are committed to local autonomy and self-reliance, to local ownership of businesses and land, to mutual aid and voluntarism, to vigilant protection of community resources, including our hammered and seriously deteriorating natural environment."

A younger activist and writer, Daryl Slusher was born October 13, 1953, in Roanoke, Virginia. Slusher came to Austin in 1976, graduating from the University of Texas in 1979. He became active in local politics when he decided that "the races need to be united against the oligarchy." He helped run city and state campaigns of Hispanic candidates running for public office in the early and mid 1980s. Like Reece, Slusher worked with the Town Lake Park Alliance.

In 1985, Slusher and another Daryl, whose last name is Janes, started their own bimonthly publication, the *Daryl Herald*, "keeping an eye on city government." After two and a half years, the Daryls stopped publishing together. Slusher began the *Austin Mirror*, again trying to move into the vacuum left by the *American-Statesman*, which Slusher says "does not cover local events unless they have an interest in them." Slusher began calling it the *Austin American Real Estatesman*, to indicate the paper's boosterish attitude toward developers whose advertising it craves.

Since the *Mirror* ceased publication at the end of 1988, Slusher has become a columnist for the *Austin Chronicle*, a weekly with a circulation of about fifty thousand. Slusher's "Council Watch" keeps the heat on local politicians, exposing their incompetence and moral lapses with a wit and fervor akin to Molly Ivins' coverage of the state legislature. Slusher advised his readers in 1990 that "the city council is shrouded in a thick fog of non-reality, a fog of legal technicalities, technical jargon, political opportunism and hypocritical rhetoric. The fog often prevents city leaders from recognizing brutal realities" such as the threats to local neighborhoods and the environment from land developers.

Alpine, a tiny town in the Big Bend area of West Texas, is home to independent journalist Jack D. McNamara and his *Nimby News*. A former press officer for the Marine Corps in Washington, D.C., McNamara holds a doctorate in journalism from the University of Texas at Austin. He moved back to Alpine, where he grew up, to build a home and retire. In 1987, Brewster County commissioners announced their decision to build a federal prison near Alpine, without consulting voters. McNamara joined a group opposed to the "flawed" procedure of the decision. When he saw that the prison and other local issues were not getting media coverage, he started his own paper. *Nimby* is an acronym for "not in my back yard."

Beginning in January 1988, the *Nimby News* appeared as a bimonthly newsletter produced on a personal computer. McNamara quickly took up local criminal justice issues, especially dubious drug enforcement policies and operations. McNamara has used the Open Records Act to find and expose the uses and abuses of public funds. When a local sheriff refused to comply with a records request from McNamara, the editor filed a petition for mandamus with the Eighty-third District Court to release them. The district attorney informed the Texas attorney general that the confidential records had been destroyed. In spite of such setbacks and the threatening phone calls he gets "all the time," McNamara noted in June 1990: "We gave ourselves an attitude check the other day and the indicator was pointing more toward amused than outraged."

The *Nimby News* has changed to a tabloid format and a more professional layout. The December 1990 issue featured advertising for the first time. McNamara previously refused ads because he feared retaliation against advertisers would make his paper vulnerable to financial pressure. With the help of his wife, Bonnie, and his daughter, Kathleen, McNamara hopes to keep the *Nimby News* alive and thriving. "We see much rich material ahead. We expect many strange sights as the rocks are turned over and the sunlight hits the creatures underneath."

In Pasadena, near Houston, Samuel and Diana Jackson publish the weekly *Gazette Express*. Diana was already running a successful weekly in Pasadena, the *City Gazette*, when she met Samuel in 1983. They married two years later. Building on Diana's advertising base, the Jacksons started the *Gazette Express* to oppose local political corruption, which they saw as rampant. Samuel Jackson's weekly column may discuss alcohol addiction, television morality, or child abuse, but the major focus is local politics. In 1987 both Jacksons campaigned for city council, but neither was elected.

Besides Samuel Jackson's column, the *Gazette Express* carries editorial cartoons drawn by "Chaz" and labeled "prepaid by cartoonist." The cartoons portray Pasadena Mayor John Ray Harrison as a drunken philanderer and petty tyrant, and city government as corrupt. Harrison has claimed he does not read the paper. But with a circulation of eighty thousand in Harris, Brazoria, and Galveston counties—including Houston and Galveston—the *Gazette Express* reaches many readers in Southeast Texas.

Samuel Jackson has accused Harrison of acting like a "czar" who favors friends and destroys enemies with little regard for the law, "a criminal that just hasn't been caught yet." He has also accused Harrison and Harrison's friends of framing Sherwood Cryer for attempted murder. Cryer, a longtime critic of Harrison, was a partner of singer Mickey Gilley in the lucrative Gilley's Nightclub. Samuel Jackson continues to dig into the lawsuit in which Cryer lost seventeen million dollars in 1988 to Mickey Gilley.

On April 30, 1988, Samuel decided to investigate claims of police brutality by contriving to get himself arrested. Diana drove him to the Pasadena police station and told a police officer her husband was drunk. What happened next is disputed. According to the *Pasadena Citizen*, "As the officer and the woman were talking, Samuel Jackson got out of the car, unzipped his pants and began urinating on the ground, police said." Samuel accused the *Citizen* of "dreaming up a wild story that should never have been printed."

Though Samuel Jackson encountered no police brutality while in jail, he was shocked by his arrest for disorderly conduct. He saw his arrest as political. "I found that if an officer writes a report for political reasons he can be given a desk job and promoted." He also resented the police news leaks and the mayor's claim not to know of his newspaper. Jackson felt fortunate that the Houston media took up his case. "Many people came forth claiming police brutality in the Pasadena jail after my story broke in the papers."

In February 1989, the first issue of the *Hays County Guardian* appeared in San Marcos. "Some of you may be asking yourselves why we started this paper," said the premiere editorial. "After all, San Marcos already has a daily and a weekly paper . . . However, these papers can get a little one-sided." The *Guardian* pledged to be "alive with ideas, news stories and other information which may often be controversial." Environmental issues—local, state, national, and international—were the main focus of this and subsequent issues of the *Guardian*. But one front-page story, "University Gags Free Speech," protested Southwest Texas State University's (SWT) restriction of free speech to specified times and places on campus. First Amendment rights were eventually the basis of a lawsuit by the *Guardian* against the university.

Most of the *Guardian* staff had some relation to Southwest Texas, as alumni, students, or former students. They made use of the school's computer system to produce their paper. In their earliest issues, the staff pasted in ads from other papers to attract paid advertising. Using Greenpeace facilities to locate and reprint national and international stories, the *Guardian* pursued a policy of aggressive investigative reporting on local issues.

When General Electric and Rohr Industries announced plans to locate in San Marcos, the *Guardian* warned of the environmental impact. *Guardian* reporters found hazardous wastes improperly stored on city property, gas leaks at the city maintenance barn, and asbestos in SWT dormitories. The paper awarded booby prizes in their "worst road" contest and ran photos of the "winners" on their front page. The *Guardian* worried most often about water supply and the quality of local rivers. When the city of San Marcos hoped to attract the Houston Oiler football team for practice, the *Guardian* revealed that the field, less than two hundred yards from the San Marcos River, was sprayed with mesamate, or MSMA, a highly toxic chemical.

By June 1989, the *Guardian* noted that the paper "is obviously upsetting a few people in the area." Three complaints alleged that the paper's location violated zoning laws. But the three complaints had "the same wrong address. Actually they did not even get the right neighborhood." *Guardian* advertisers also reported pressure from their landlords to withdraw from the paper. But the *Guardian* continued, with such memorable headlines as "Drug War Over, Drugs Win." It was Southwest Texas State that gave the paper pause.

In October and November, SWT officials warned the *Guardian* that the paper could not be distributed anywhere on campus. They threatened legal action. Since the SWT community represented a large percentage of *Guardian* readers, the lack of campus access meant a dramatic decrease in advertising directed to SWT readers. The nineteenth issue appeared a week late. Then the paper stopped publishing.

The Society of Professional Journalists protested the denial of campus access to SWT President Jerome Supple. Society officials pointed out that the *University Star*, the school newspaper, is distributed freely about the campus. Supple replied in October 1990 that the *University Star* was a "special case." "I appreciate the First Amendment watch-dog efforts of the Society of Professional Journalists," Supple wrote. "We agree in spirit if not in procedure." The *Hays County Guardian* staff filed a suit in the 201st District Court against Supple and other SWT officials for "an unreasonable interference with and infringement upon" their rights of free speech. The case went to court in December 1990, and the District Court ruled in favor of the university. As of October 1991, the *Guardian's* appeal was pending and the staff was planning to resume publication if the appeal was successful.

It is difficult to say whether these examples point to a resurgence of independent journalism in contemporary Texas. My search for independents during the last century of Texas history was a winnowing of various candidates, a process of elimination based on a criterion of independence. Finding current iconoclasts is not as easy. Daryl Slusher thinks most journalists now are more cautious, too concerned with their own comfort, unwilling to take risks. But that has probably always been true of the majority.

Environmental concerns appear to be among the strongest motivations for current independent journalists. In August 1990, the first issue of *Texas Environment*, projected as a quarterly magazine, appeared in Austin. The editor, Susanna MacKenzie, sees her publication as "a vehicle for empowering citizens to take action to protect their right to a clean, healthful environment."

There are also signs of iconoclasm in the electronic media in Texas. Since 1978, Frank Morrow has produced "Alternative Views" on the public access channel of the Austin cable system. The program reviews news from the alternative and foreign press and looks in depth at topics not covered or inadequately covered in the mainstream media. Also featured are critics of current issues and policies who do not appear on network television. More than sixty cable systems nationally now broadcast "Alternative Views." The use of public access channels and increasingly inexpensive technology may auger an eventual iconoclastic video revolution. A similar availability of ever-cheaper printing and graphics processes may also serve to empower independent writers. As Jack McNamara sees it, "We expect everyone with a computer and a copy machine will soon be publishing his or her own newspaper, thereby fulfilling A. J. Liebling's maxim: Freedom of the press belongs to those who own one."

A "senior White House official," explaining why President Bush likes having abrasive, overbearing advisers around him, quoted Thoreau as saying that "all progress depends on unreasonable men." The tough language and radical positions taken by such aides allow the president to appear judicious and conciliatory by comparison, when he finally makes a decision. In analogous fashion, the independents are Thoreau's "unreasonable men" of journalism.

Taking radical stands on issues, the independent journalists widened the scope of debate. Public opinion sometimes followed their lead but often did not. Sometimes popular sentiment settled midway on the spectrum between the extreme views of the iconoclasts and the received wisdom of the orthodoxy they questioned. At their best, these writers challenged the automatic assumptions and the attitudes of business as usual that permit the exploitation of the majority by the powerful few.

Opposition to the status quo put Texas iconoclasts at odds with the chief emissary of things as they are, the mainstream press. Media criticism is currently fashionable. Since Watergate, media critics seem almost as numerous as the journalists they observe. The Texas independent journalists helped pioneer the awareness that the press, even the apparently objective, factual dailies, have definite points of view.

The independents went after stories that otherwise eluded the press spotlight and therefore public scrutiny. In this sense also they enlarged the scope and substance of public discourse. None of the Texas iconoclasts believed the truth was available from the mainstream media. To the degree that we share this conviction, we have more reason to hope that independent journalism is not merely historical but ongoing.

Notes

Abbreviations Used in Source Notes

AA	*Austin American*
AA-S	*Austin American-Statesman*
ADS	*Austin Daily Statesman*
AusIcon	*Austin Iconoclast*
BEnt	*Beaumont Enterprise*
Billy Goat	*Billy Goat Always Buttin' In*
BR-C	*Blanco Record-Courier*, Johnson City
BrIcon	*Brann's Iconoclast*, Waco
BTHC	Barker Texas History Center, The University of Texas at Austin
DalObs	*Dallas Observer*
DMN	*Dallas Morning News*
DNews	*Dallas News*
DNotes	*Dallas Notes*
DT	*Daily Texan*, Austin
DTH	*Dallas Times Herald*
Eman	*Emanicipator*, Georgetown and San Antonio
FWR	*Fort Worth Record*
HC	*Houston Chronicle*
HP	*Houston Post*
HRHRC	Harry Ransom Humanities Research Center, The University of Texas at Austin

Icon	*Iconoclast*, Dallas
KN	*Kountze News*
NFTU	*Notes From The Underground*, Dallas
OBN	*Oil Belt News*, Eastland
PDN	*Pampa Daily News*
SAEx	*San Antonio Express*
SAL	*San Antonio Light*
StArch	State of Texas Archives, Austin
StObs	*State Observer*, Austin
SWC	Southwest Collection, Texas Tech University, Lubbock
TxBay	Texas Collection, Baylor University, Waco
TxDal	Texas Collection, Dallas Public Library
TxIcon	*Texas Iconoclast*, Austin
TxMon	*Texas Monthly*, Austin
TxObs	*Texas Observer*, Austin
UTAus	University of Texas at Austin

Introduction

xii "a struggle between": Taylor Branch, talk at Lyndon B. Johnson Library, UTAus, November 14, 1990.

xii The first paper printed: Marilyn McAdams Sibley, *Lone Stars and State Gazettes*, p. 28.

1. The Apostle of the Devil

3 "laid down his life": Walter Hurt, "The Texas Tragedy," in *The Gatling Gun*, June 1898.

3 "The deplorable tragedy": *HP*, April 3, 1898.

3 "a giant intellect": *SAEx*, April 6, 1898.

3 "extraordinary writing genius": *AA-S*, August 14, 1927.

4 "the most gorgeous": William Marion Reedy, quoted in *BrIcon*, May 1898.

4 "brave as Bayard": Hurt, *Gatling Gun*.

4 "Brann was idolized": Rupert Hughes, in Hurt, *Gatling Gun*.

4 "in all his gaiety": unidentified newsclip, TxBay.

4 "Too many men": C. G. Gillespie, in Joseph Martin Dawson, "Image-

Breaker Brann, Six Decades After," *Southwest Review*, Spring 1958, p. 152.

4 "I am only a fad": Brann to Reedy in Hurt, *Gatling Gun*.
5 "Instead of being fed": *BrIcon*, June 1896.
5 "The base-ball season": *TxIcon*, April 21, 1892.
6 "the greatest evil": *BrIcon*, November 1895.
6 "protests to the paper": John W. Randolph, "The Apostle of the Devil," p. 9.
6 "Alliance of Plebians": *BrIcon*, November 1895.
6 "We know full well": *BrIcon*, July 1896.
7 "While editing": *BrIcon*, October 1895.
7 "for the usual reason": Randolph, "Apostle," p. 12.
7 "one of her own age": W. C. Brann, *Complete Works*, vol. 12, p. 87; original suicide note at HRHRC.
7 In an editorial: *HP*, August 18, 1891.
7 And Brann "knew that he had killed her": Brann, *Complete Works*, vol. 12, p. 87.
8 "Mr. Brann has": Shaw, *BrIcon*, May 1898.
8 In 1891 Texas had: John R. Whitaker, "W. C. Brann: His Life and Influence in Texas," p. 13.
8 "simply an independent": *BrIcon*, February 1895.
8 "controlled freight rates": Alwyn Barr, *Reconstruction to Reform*, p. 96.
10 "Make a good sized portion": *ADS*, July 29, 1891.
10 "about the sourest": quoted in *HP*, August 11, 1891.
10–11 "While a number": quoted in *ADS*, August 17, 1891.
11 "The Negro": *HP*, August 18, 1891.
11 "putrid matter": *HP*, August 21–22, 1891.
11 "In nearly every": *ADS*, August 30, 1891.
11 "A contemporary critic says": *TxIcon*, March 31, 1892.
11 "worth reading": *AusIcon*, October 1891.
12 "Instead of hounding": *TxIcon*, April 21, 1892.
12 "Our boasted progress": *AusIcon*, October 1891.
13 "the Apostle of the Devil": Randolph, "Apostle," pp. 23–24.
13 "I get letters": *TxIcon*, April 21, 1892.
13 "brief survey": Brann in Whitaker, "W. C. Brann," p. 26.
14 "as editor": quoted in ibid., p. 30.
14 "battering away": *ADS*, April 25, 1893.
14 "I was in the habit": W. C. Brann, *Brann the Iconoclast*, vol. 2, pp. 132–133.
15 Porter published: Frank Luther Mott, *History of American Magazines*, p. 665.
15 "The aristocracy of intellect": Brann, *Brann the Iconoclast*, vol. 1, pp. 87–107.
16 "the largest . . . ever": *SAEx*, August 10, 1894.
16–17 Information about Waco from Susan Nelle Gregg, "Waco's Apostle," pp. 12–14; Tony E. Duty, "Waco at the Turn of the Century,"

Waco Heritage, Summer 1972; and Margaret Davis, "Harlots and Hymnals: An Historical Confrontation of Vice and Virtue in Waco, Texas," *Waco Times Herald*, August 10, 1917.

16   "Waco, we would have": *BrIcon*, February 1897.
17   By the mid-1890s: Rufus Jefferson Banks, "Brann vs. Baylor," manuscript, 45 pages, 1956, TxBay.
17   "Well supplied": *BrIcon*, February 1897.
18   "a corps of editors": Donald Grant, *The Anti-Lynching Movement*, pp. 9, viii, and 76–77.
18   Between 1882 and 1927: Walter White, *Rope and Faggot*, p. 234.
18   "The Tyler *Telegraph*": *BrIcon*, February 1897.
19   "The Apostle's Biography": *BrIcon*, March 1897.
19   "what lies heaviest": *BrIcon*, March 1895.
20   "not because I am the friend": *BrIcon*, April 1895.
20   "two-by-four fanatics": *BrIcon*, June 1895.
20   "Waco has entirely": *BrIcon*, September 1895.
20–21 Accounts of the Slattery affair in Charles Carver, *Brann and the Iconoclast*; *Waco Morning News*, April 25–27 and May 2, 1895; *BrIcon*, April and June 1895.
21   "Brann was": J. B. Cranfill, "Shaw: Free Thinker and Biographer of Brann," undated typescript, TxBay; "power for evil" in letter quoted in Whitaker, "W. C. Brann," p. 101. B. G. McKie describes meeting Cranfill in a typed statement at BTHC.
21   Teixeira accused Morris: *Waco Morning News*, June 16, 17, and 18, 1895.
22   "Instead of being": *BrIcon*, July 1895.
22   Rufus C. Burleson, "The Brazilian Girl and Baylor University," typescript, 4 pp., August 20, 1895, TxBay.
24   "the editor of the Houston *Post*": *BrIcon*, May 1895.
24   "Having grown grizzly": *BrIcon*, March 1897.
24   "a brake on the wheels": *Brann the Iconoclast*, vol. 2, pp. 259–265.
25   "shameless and rapacious": *BrIcon*, February 1898.
25   "about the size": *BrIcon*, August 1895.
25–26 "Journalism is no esoteric": *BrIcon*, November 1895.
26   "was probably cooped": *BrIcon*, February 1896.
26   "furnish forth more hidebound": *BrIcon*, September 1895.
26–27 "That's a difficult problem": *BrIcon*, May 1896.
27   "The dreadful scandal": *BrIcon*, July 1895.
27–28 "Waco is so pious": *BrIcon*, October 1896.
28   A subsequent study: Banks, "Brann vs. Baylor," TxBay.
28   "I note with unfeigned": *BrIcon*, October 1897.
28–29 Charles Carver said: Carver, *Brann*, pp. 144–148.
29   "The Baylor boys": D. K. Martin, letter, May 17, 1961, TxBay.
29   Brann told the *Dallas News*: *DMN*, October 3, 1897.
29   "It was not the students": in Carver, *Brann*, p. 151.
30   "the mobbing of Mr. Brann": J. D. Shaw, *Independent Pulpit*, vol. 15, no. 8.

31   "as a liar, a coward": G. B. Gerald, "To the Public," handbill, October 21, 1897, in Carver, *Brann*, pp. 160–164.

31   "I . . . begged him": B. G. McKie, typescript, BTHC.

31   "To the kindly offers": *BrIcon*, December 1897.

32   Fuller Williamson: Typed statement, February 9, 1934, TxBay. Contemporary accounts of the Brann-Davis shootings in *Galveston News*, *AA-S*, *HP*, and *Waco Weekly Tribune*, April 2–4, 1898.

33   "the pack of journalistic jackals": G. B. Gerald, *BrIcon*, May and July 1898.

33   "the most brilliant": Michael Monahan, in Mott, *Magazines*, p. 448.

2. The Lone Coyote

34   "There is no place": Don Hampton Biggers, *Billy Goat Always Buttin' In*, August 1908.

37   "He is one of those": Tom Arnold, *Life's ABC's*, January 1922.

37–38   "Town didn't amount": Biggers, letter, April 2, 1953, SWC.

38   "The school term": Biggers, letters, December 30, 1953, and December 26, 1944, in Seymour V. Connor, ed., *A Biggers Chronicle*, pp. 25–26. Connor's book consists of a reprint of Biggers' *History That Will Never Be Repeated* and a biographical sketch of Don Biggers (pp. 87–128). Connor interviewed Biggers' family and friends and collected correspondence, scarce publications, and family scrapbooks. All are now at the Southwest Collection at Texas Tech University, Lubbock. What Connor wrote and what he collected but did not write about have been invaluable in the writing of this chapter. Biggers' writings are from SWC unless otherwise noted.

38   "It was 175 miles": Biggers, *History That Will*, pp. 8–9.

38   "I took my first": Biggers, *The Josher*, August 1902.

38   "I was just a cub": Biggers, letter, n.d., BTHC.

38   "Don Biggers, as a young man": *Baird Star*, February 21, 1920.

38   "I used to work": Biggers, *Josher*, August 1902.

39   "The most labored": Biggers, *A Handbook of Reference*, p. 6, StArch.

39   "Cut my eye teeth": Biggers, letter to Boyce House, April 2, 1953, SWC.

39   "I worked mostly": Biggers, letter, April 2, 1953, SWC.

39   He established: Connor, ed., *Chronicle*, pp. 92–93.

39–40   "Biggers and a group": John Lee Smith to Connor, July 14, 1961, SWC.

40   He "made an extended": Connor, ed., *Chronicle*, pp. 92–93.

40   "I propose to": Biggers, *Colorado Spokesman*, December 7, 1900, BTHC.

41   "A sheet that" and following quotes: Biggers, *Texas Cleaver*, September 1, 1902.

42   "deprived them" and "blaze of glory": Biggers, *From Cattle Range to Cotton Patch*, pp. 10 and 56.

42   "A medium the chief": Biggers, *Lone Coyote*, April 1, 1908.

43 the Biggers' son Clyde: Clyde Biggers to Connor, August 16, 1960, SWC.

43 "Poor Old Mexico!" *The Farmer's Journal*, March 8, 1911.

43 "Don't waste a good man": Connor, ed., *Chronicle*, p. 107.

43 House Bill 28: Texas Legislature, *House Journal*, 34th Legislature, Regular Session, pp. 118 and 355, StArch.

44 "Representative Biggers": *AA*, May 20, 1915.

44 "Biggers was a small": Smith to Connor; Judge J. E. Vickers to Connor, July 19, 1961; and Clyde Biggers to Connor, SWC.

45 "one of the greatest": Biggers, *OBN*, October 11, 1918, StArch.

45 "The legislature is nothing": *OBN*, October 11, 1918.

45 "the fake oil scheme": *OBN*, January 24, 1919.

45 "We turned down": *OBN*, July 18, 1919.

46 "The state penitentiary": Biggers, *FWR*, December 10, 1919.

46 "the greatest crime": Biggers, *FWR*, December 13, 1919.

46 "I am not an aspirate": Biggers, unidentified clip, SWC.

46 "Politics has purified": Hugh Nugent Fitzgerald, *FWR*, in *Olden Advance*, March 27, 1920.

46 "truthful, honorable gentleman": Biggers, *Olden Advance*, May 15, 1920.

47 *Temple Mirror, Denison Herald, Austin American,* and other undated clips, Biggers scrapbook, SWC.

47 "plenty of trouble": Clyde Biggers to Connor, SWC.

47 "exposed a total": Biggers, "An Open Letter to Blue Sky Administrators," broadside, n.d., Shettles Papers, BTHC.

48 "the three main issues": Norman D. Brown, *Hood, Bonnet, and Little Brown Jug*, p. 3.

48 "Having sold the oil": Biggers, letter, April 2, 1953, SWC.

48 Biggers declared his aim: *Life's ABC's*, January 1922.

48–49 "socialism is a fantasy": *Biggers' Magazine*, March 1922.

49 "But Barnum was right": Biggers, *The Record*, July 4, 1930.

49 Clyde Biggers remembered: Biggers to Connor, SWC.

50 "No higher class": Biggers, *German Pioneers in Texas*, p. 49.

50 "Only great people": Biggers, *German Pioneers*, pp. 57–72.

50 "It was strictly": Biggers, *Our Sacred Monkeys*, p. 65.

50 "To a discerning": Biggers, *Sacred Monkeys*, p. 66. Ferguson highway scandal in Brown, *Hood, Bonnet*, pp. 278–296.

50 "Contracts were awarded": Brown, *Hood, Bonnet*, pp. 281–282.

51 "Have been, and shall": Biggers, letter, August 19, 1925, Kemp Papers, BTHC.

51 "An odd situation": quoted in Brown, *Hood, Bonnet*, p. 287.

51 "We don't know": Biggers, *BR-C*, September 25, 1925.

52 "some fifteen persons": Biggers, *Limelight*, May 18, 1926.

52 "attempted to convert": Connor, ed., *Chronicle*, pp. 117–118.

52 "as my experience": Oscar B. Colquitt, letter, December 31, 1925.

52 "today every daily": Biggers, *BR-C*, November 27, 1925.

53   "Long after the highway": Biggers, quoted in *Hamilton Record-Herald*, April 30, 1926, SWC.
53   "no one person": Biggers, *Limelight*, June 18, 1926.
54   "J. Frank Norris": *Haldeman-Julius Monthly*, March 1926.
54   In September 1927: clips from *San Saba Star, Palmer Rustler, Rockdale Reporter*, and others, September 29, 1927, SWC.
55   "Ferguson didn't support": Biggers, *Sacred Monkeys*, p. 78.
55   Biggers "was the one": Biggers, *Sacred Monkeys*, pp. 78–79.
55   "The obvious assumption": Tom Connally, *My Name Is Tom Connally*, p. 128.
55   John Lee Smith later recalled: Smith to Connor, SWC.
55   Connally told Clyde Biggers: Biggers to Connor, SWC.
56   "But there were other": Biggers, *Sacred Monkeys*, p. 79.
56   "we Democrats who": Biggers, broadside, October 4, 1928.
56   J. Frank Norris: Brown, *Hood, Bonnet*, pp. 410–411.
56   Biggers got into a fist-fight: Smith to Connor, SWC.
57   "There was plenty": Biggers, *Sacred Monkeys*, p. 84.
57   "We had to let": George Norris Green, *The Establishment in Texas Politics*, p. 18.
57–58   "We Are All": Biggers, *Record*, February 27, 1930. Other quotes from *Record*, vol. 1, through August 1930, SWC.
58   "It is not our dream": Biggers, *Bombardier*, March 1933.
59   "Come, folks": Biggers, *Sacred Monkeys*, p. 5.
59   "Jim is our greatest": Biggers, *Sacred Monkeys*, p. 103.
60   "Our Twelve Billion": Connor, ed., *Chronicle*, p. 121.
60   "I have just two words": Biggers, broadside, 1936, BTHC.
61   "I am a constant sufferer": Biggers, letter, December 27, 1939.
61   "Dad always had an itchy foot": Biggers to Connor, SWC.
61   "I know the west": Biggers, letter, April 2, 1953.
61   "the most pusillanimous": Biggers, letter, July 28, 1940.
62   "O'Donkey": Biggers, letter, August 2, 1939.
62   "If you have any other": Drew Pearson to Biggers, November 2, 1939.
62   "The Pigtown Purifier": broadside, HRHRC.
62–63   "any organization that": Biggers letters to and from Tom Connally, August 5, 26, and 31, SWC.
63   "Oliver Goldsmith": Biggers-Dobie letters at HRHRC.

3. A Rational Radical

65   "To only a very": John C. Granbery, *Eman*, September 1938.
67   "the emphasis was": *Eman*, December 1948.
67   "because we believe": *Eman*, November 1941.
67–68   "My favorite explanation": *Eman*, April 1940.
68   "extremes of Left and Right": *Eman*, April 1940.
69   "We are distressed": *Eman*, July 1948.
69   "our primary problem": *Eman*, March 1952.

69   "I haven't known": J. Frank Dobie in *Eman*, June 1953.

69   "Dr. Granbery's life": quoted in *Eman*, June 1953.

69   "the most modest": *Eman*, June 1949.

70   Fifty years later: *Eman*, November 1940.

70   "At about the age of 16": *Eman*, September 1947.

70   Granbery later described: *Eman*, September 1947.

70   "during the first year": *Eman*, June 1949.

71   "By confining my studies": *Eman*, September 1947.

71   "Suppose we undertake": *Eman*, October 1947.

72   "so searching and direct": May C. Granbery, *Eman*, February 1944.

72   In 1912: Takako Sudo-Shimamura, "John C. Granbery," p. 14.

72   "prestige" and "influence": *Eman*, June 1949.

72–73   Founded by the Methodists: Ralph Wood Jones, "A History of Southwestern University," pp. 459–478.

73   "The Church and Social Service": *Eman*, October 1942.

73   "so revolutionary are his views": John H. Griffith, letter, in Jones, "Southwestern," p. 491.

74   "with the Greek Army": May C. Granbery, *Eman*, February 1944.

74   "J. C. Granbery": *HP*, January 23, 1921.

74   At the State Democratic: Norman D. Brown, *Hood, Bonnet, and Little Brown Jug*, pp. 119–120.

75   "Threatened with a tarring": May C. Granbery, *Eman*, February 1944.

75   "probably never get over": Granbery, letter, in Sudo-Shimamura, "Granbery," p. 29.

75   "most willfully": *Taylor Daily Democrat*, November 7, 1924.

75   "despiritualizing influence": *SAEx*, April 23, 1923.

76   Granbery quickly organized: Merton L. Dillon, "Religion in Lubbock," pp. 474–479.

76   "Movements for social": John C. Granbery, W. C. Holden, and H. B. Carson, *Introduction to the History of Civilization*, p. i.

76   At one such meeting: Dillon, "Religion in Lubbock," pp. 476–477.

76   Campbell preached: *Lubbock Morning Avalanche*, February 9–13, 1932.

77   "studying, lecturing": *Eman*, December 1940.

78   "Orators Damn War": Paul Crume, *DT*, April 23, 1936.

78   Nazi swastika "emblazoned": *AA-S*, May 22, 1938.

79   "The groups did not": *Eman*, November 1944.

79   "all his speeches": Green, *Establishment*, pp. 22–24.

80   "I stand for": *Eman*, September 1938.

80   "If one believes": *Eman*, October 1938.

81   "Friends have been generous": *Eman*, August 1939.

81   "a depth of learning": letter, *Eman*, May 1939.

81   "Our home is": *Eman*, December 1946; June 1939.

81   "when Latin-American": *Eman*, April 1942.

82   "Yes, we are 'pro,'": *Eman*, January 1942.

82   "When the British": *Eman*, January 1940.

82   "We have spent hours": *Eman*, September 1941.

82–83   "masses of the unemployed": *Eman,* September 1938.

83   J. Frank Norris: Green, *Establishment,* p. 24.

83   "Now there's no denying": *Eman,* February 1939.

83   "courteously but emphatically": *Eman,* October 1939.

83   "O'Daniel in the Lions' Den": *Eman,* November 1939.

84   "Even the Boy Scouts": August Raymond Ogden, *The Dies Committee,* p. 43.

84   "too sensitive to reveal": Robert Griffith, *The Politics of Fear,* pp. 31–33.

84   He called it "cancerous": *Eman,* January 1939.

84   "a certain definite": Ronnie Dugger, *Our Invaded Universities,* p. 41.

85   "epidemic of Texas purges": *Eman,* March 1939.

85   "the only free-lance": *Eman,* February 1943.

85   Dobie reviewed: Dobie, *Eman,* August 1943.

85–86   "I have been watching": *Eman,* March 1944.

86   "Having academic freedom": Dobie, *Eman,* March 1945.

86   "The report is premature": *Eman,* April 1945.

86–87   "who betrayed the educational": *Eman,* March 1947.

87   "striking at the heart": *Eman,* April 1951.

87   "The Houston School Board": *Eman,* January 1950.

88   "during the first half": *Eman,* September 1951.

88   "the U.S. Communist Party": Hoover in Taylor Branch, *Parting the Waters,* p. 564.

88   "There's so much to do": *Eman,* January 1944.

88   "I am weary": *Eman,* June 1944.

89   "I once thought": *Eman,* July 1944.

89   "The vote for the writer": *Eman,* July 1944.

89   "in the United States": *Eman,* June 1946.

89   "It was our unpleasant duty": *Eman,* August 1948.

89   "We prefer an honest": *Eman,* November 1948.

90   "The editor is proud": *Eman,* April 1950.

90   "demagogues and peanut politicians": *Eman,* March 1949.

90   "they are Big Business": *Eman,* March 1948.

90   "People who are exposed": *Eman,* September 1943.

90   "What a lie!": *Eman,* August 1944.

90   "Personal journalism yielded": *Eman,* September 1944.

91   "It seems strange": *Eman,* May 1952.

91   "a fine educational service": *Eman,* March 1944.

91   He urged editors: *Eman,* April 1947.

91   "especially to avoid": *Eman,* December 1946.

91   He accused: *Eman,* January 1949.

91   "White Supremacy": *Eman,* August 1944.

92   "APATHY": *Eman,* November 1950.

92   "not on account": April 1951.

92   "a group of laymen": Don E. Carleton, *Red Scare,* pp. 101–134.

93   "Here by innuendo": *Eman,* October 1952.

93   "Methodism's Pink Fringe": Carleton, *Red Scare,* p. 106.

94   "the most reactionary": *Eman*, February 1952.
94–95 "The most astounding aspect": *Eman*, February 1952.
95   "Is This Perjury?": *Eman*, November 1952.
96   In 1951 the Minute Women: Carleton, *Red Scare*, pp. 111–129.
96   "there is no overhead": *Eman*, December 1945.
96   "I have been connected": *Eman*, June 1949.
96   "It is not easy": *Eman*, February 1940.
97   "Do you need help?": *Eman*, September 1941.
97   "we must confess": *Eman*, August 1949.
97   "there was perhaps not one": *Eman*, December 1943.
97   "If our democracy": *Eman*, March 1947.
98   "Dean of Texas Liberals": Paul Sparks et al., letter, BTHC.
98   "we had got into": May Granbery, *Eman*, November 1950.
98   "Often I wish": *Eman*, December 1945.
98   "Just a few months ago": *Eman*, October 1949.
98   "World Government": *Eman*, November 1949.
99   "our contribution": *Eman*, July–August 1950.
99   "high cost of segregation": *Eman*, November 1948.
99   "in such fields as education": *Eman*, June 1950.
99   "low methods": *Eman*, December 1950.
99   "surprised and disappointed": *Eman*, October 1952.
99   "General Eisenhower is": *Eman*, November 1952.
100   "a patriotic city": *Eman*, March 1953.
100   "fear is the most": *Eman*, July 1945.
100   "Opera Bouffe": *Eman*, June 1945.
100   "It's Time for a Change": *Eman*, October 1952.

4. The Printer Who Fired Both Barrels

101   "I guess Archer": Ronnie Dugger, *TxObs*, September 24, 1971.
101   "but I read": J. Frank Dobie, *HP*, June 1, 1958.
101   "one of the most": *DMN*, February 16, 1973.
101   In 1975 a book: *Archer Fullingim: A Country Editor's View of Life*, ed.
      Roy Hamric. The book won the Stanley Walker award from The Texas
      Institute of Letters. I relied on original *Kountze News* issues, except
      when they were missing from the two collections I consulted, where I
      use Hamric's selections. Hamric based his "Introduction" on an inter-
      view with Fullingim.
101   "Let me assure you": *KN*, July 5, 1961.
103   "and Lyndon Johnson": Gordon Baxter, *Kountze News-Visitor*, De-
      cember 6, 1984.
103   "charitable to his mania": *KN*, September 18, 1952.
103   "Archer Fullingim has retired": *Beaumont Enterprise*, November 27,
      1984.
104–105 "perhaps the most fascinating": Ivins, *TxObs*, December 12,
      1975.
105   "at a place called": *KN*, May 11, 1967.

105   "We lived on a hill": *KN*, February 18, 1961.

105–106 "about 1910": *KN*, February 15, 1973.

106   "All I remember": *KN*, November 10, 1960.

106   "in a carriage": *KN*, August 17, 1961.

106   "to Cottle County": *KN*, June 22, 1961.

106   "During the drouth": *KN*, May 21, 1961.

106   "I never did finish": *KN*, August 30, 1973.

107   "we'd be picking cotton": *KN*, November 16, 1967.

107   "the oldest junior college": *KN*, November 11, 1971.

107   "In 1921–22": *KN*, December 7, 1972.

107   "because we lived 180 miles": *KN*, December 9, 1965.

107–108 "when I told my father": *KN*, August 24, 1967.

108   "'I used to charge 'em'": Willie Morris, *TxObs*, August 29, 1958.

108   "I made a mistake": *KN*, August 11, 1966.

108   He hopped freight trains: Hamric, "Introduction," *Country Editor*, pp. 3–4.

108   "Travelling was almost": *KN*, August 8, 1957.

108   "'I told the owner'": Morris, *TxObs*, August 29, 1958.

109   "When I lived in Galveston": *KN*, July 13, 1967.

109   "I worked on": *KN*, October 5, 1972.

109   "That intense football period": *KN*, September 7, 1961.

109   "the president of the University": *PDN*, January 6, 1939.

109–110 "When I was 30": *KN*, July 6, 1967.

110   "Join the navy": *PDN*, July 30, 1942.

110   "I can out-walk anybody": *PDN*, August 13, 1942.

110   "I didn't go to Pampa": *KN*, September 8, 1966.

110   "Uncle Bunch": *KN*, May 21, 1964.

110   "My favorite of all": *KN*, August 8, 1957.

110   "But I did not go to sick bay": *KN*, June 8, 1967.

110–111 "A lot of people might": *TxObs*, August 29, 1958.

111   "Normangee had": *KN*, April 12, 1973.

111   In 1958 he showed: Morris, *TxObs*, August 29, 1958.

111   "what you might call authentic": *KN*, October 19, 1961.

111   "that book has been": *KN*, July 6, 1961.

112   "Blue Streak Model 31": *KN*, January 11, 1951.

112   "That takes confidence": Leon Hale, *HC*, April 11, 1985.

112   "I Heard: Continued": *KN*, August 30, 1951.

113   "the spirit of FCC": *KN*, June 12, 1952.

113   "Neil, you may be": *KN*, July 24, 1952.

113   "that if this printer": *KN*, August 7, 1952.

113   "The big daily press": *KN*, September 10, 1953.

113   "Big Lies Printed Only": *KN*, September 18, 1952.

114   "the strange fluid decade": Theodore H. White, *In Search of History*, p. 486.

114   "perjury" and "political lynchings": *KN*, January 1, 1953.

115   "ominous and daringly false": *KN*, July 23, 1953.

115   "the Texas metropolitan press": *KN*, December 3, 1953.

115 "doubly repulsive": *KN*, April 22, 1954.
116 At Amarillo: George Norris Green, *The Establishment in Texas Politics*, pp. 135–146.
116 "a great man": *KN*, July 31, 1952.
116 "a DED": *KN*, September 11, 1952.
116 "old Allan ripped his britches": *KN*, October 9, 1952.
116 "a dictator": *KN*, June 24, 1954.
116–117 "the dear, dear friend": *KN*, January 5, 1956.
117 "the closest Governor's race": *KN*, August 30, 1956.
117 "News Has Followed Crowd": *KN*, September 20, 1956.
117 "a brazen bucket": *KN*, February 16, 1956.
117 "against P. Daniel": *KN*, February 23, 1956.
118 "So what do we have": Fullingim, *TxObs*, September 5, 1956.
118 "a latter-day": *TxObs*, January 31, 1958.
118 "Under the corporations": *KN*, June 11, 1959.
118 "to destroy the public": Fullingim, *TxObs*, May 14, 1965.
118 "the most useless": *KN*, August 29, 1963.
118 "at least he admits": Fullingim, *TxObs*, July 22, 1966.
118–119 "If you have an eediot": *KN*, July 9, 1964.
119 "Dear Arch": *KN*, May 31, 1956.
119 "I've had enough": *KN*, August 28, 1958.
119 "there are a lot": *KN*, April 30, 1959.
119 "I felt kind of sorry": *KN*, April 11, 1968.
119–120 "distinct relief": *KN*, November 14, 1968.
120 "Nixon hasn't changed": *KN*, February 15, 1973.
120 "probably the worst": *KN*, May 17, 1973.
120 "debauchery": *KN*, June 21, 1973.
120 My Lai massacre: *KN*, April 8, 1971.
120 "This sickness": *KN*, June 14, 1962.
120 "You are not afraid": Dobie, letter, May 10, 1958, HRHRC.
120 "I would have": Dobie, letter, June 1, 1958, HRHRC.
120 "The bitterest enemies": *KN*, July 30, 1959.
120–121 "only one of 125": *KN*, June 7, 1962.
121 "for this blanket endorsement": *KN*, May 31, 1962.
121 "the professional Texans": *KN*, May 18, 1961.
121 "whose stilted editorials": *KN*, January 17, 1963.
121 "No Beaumont newspaper": *KN*, December 14, 1961.
121 "that prostitution": *KN*, January 12, 1961.
121 "jokingly referred": *KN*, July 11, 1963.
121 "the good people": *KN*, June 27, 1968.
121 "the real aim": *KN*, February 23, 1961.
122 "Dallas is the mecca": *KN*, September 22, 1966.
122 "the conscienceless": *KN*, June 26, 1969.
122 "Ted Dealy was a red-baiter": Peter Elkind, *TxMon*, July 1986.
122 "made an ass out of himself": *KN*, November 9, 1961.
122 "The John Birch-loving": *KN*, October 31, 1963.

123 "Welcome Mr. Kennedy": Elkind, *TxMon*, July 1986; Lawrence Wright, *In the New World*, pp. 36–47.
123 "personally, I regard": *KN*, August 29, 1963.
123 "a city now universally": *KN*, November 28, 1963.
123 "because by hating": *KN*, December 5, 1963.
123 "because like Lincoln": *KN*, January 2, 1964.
123 "The nurses' assassin": *KN*, August 18, 1966.
123 Hinckley graduated: Wright, *New World*, pp. 295–297.
124 "I am addicted": *KN*, November 9, 1967.
124 "weekly tantrum": Frank Tolbert, *DMN*, November 16, 1967.
124 "long haired youth": *KN*, July 16, 1970.
124 "Editorial writers": editorial, *DMN*, February 11, 1973.
125 "It scares me": *KN*, February 22, 1973.
125 "The forests are dependent": *KN*, September 25, 1959.
125 "The way the governor": *KN*, September 28, 1961.
126 "was suggested at this time": *KN*, March 8, 1962.
126 "it would be an extension": *KN*, March 29, 1962.
126 "would kill the very thing": *KN*, March 1, 1962.
126 "Now that the eventual": *KN*, June 27, 1963.
126 "First of all": *KN*, July 18, 1963.
126 Gunter pointed out: *TxObs*, August 23, 1963.
127 "It is no longer possible": *TxObs*, September 15, 1967.
127 "the Big Thicket will be lost": *KN*, November 6, 1969.
127 "Scientists say": *KN*, January 1, 1970.
127 "Bentsen is far to the right": *KN*, July 23, 1970.
127 "and I assure you": *KN*, July 30, 1970.
127 "Archer Fullingim Is Smartening": *TxObs*, January 8, 1971.
128 "What we want": Fullingim, *TxObs*, December 25, 1970.
128 "Pilgrimage Shouts": *KN*, September 24, 1970.
128 "the most vocal enemies": *KN*, June 17, 1971.
128 " 'I'm *desperate*': Dugger, *TxObs*, October 22, 1972.
128 "The Dallas Morning News": *TxObs*, August 27, 1971.
128 "It's becoming increasingly": *KN*, December 16, 1971.
129 "Eastex International": *Life*, April 7, 1972.
129 "So who will go": *KN*, August 29, 1972.
129 "in the Depths": *KN*, January 11, 1973.
129 "If we save": *KN*, February 8, 1973.
129 "got the last word": *HC*, April 5, 1987.
129–130 "Well, before John": Hamric, "Introduction," *Country Editor*, p. 17.
130 Reluctant to lead: Branch, *Parting the Waters*.
130 From 1940 to 1960: in Allen J. Matusow, *The Unraveling of America*, pp. 60–62.
130 "There are lots": *KN*, June 9, 1955.
130 "The hypocrisy of the Republicans": *KN*, October 4, 1956.
130 "Ike himself has": *KN*, October 3, 1957.

130–131   "It would surprise many Texans": *KN*, July 25, 1957.
131   "That is a lie": *KN*, October 10, 1957.
131   "I'd eat down there": *KN*, November 7, 1957.
131   "The term is the essence": *KN*, May 15, 1958.
131   "Luther Tippin": *KN*, June 21, 1962.
132   "I fought the war": *KN*, October 18, 1962.
132   "hard to believe": *KN*, May 9, 1963.
132   "were so up in arms": *KN*, February 17, 1966.
133   "Martin Luther King": *KN*, July 7, 1966.
133   "Negroes are Americans": *KN*, October 13, 1966.
133   "For two days": *KN*, April 18, 1968.
133   "In the last several years": *KN*, June 13, 1968.
133   "Twenty years ago": *KN*, July 2, 1970.
134   "This printer has": *KN*, February 21, 1974.
134   "the technique the Republicans": *KN*, May 13, 1954.
134   "looking at Playhouse 90": *KN*, March 12, 1959.
134–135   "try and shake my TV habit": *KN*, December 31, 1959.
135   "When I knocked": Buddy Moore, *The Kountze News-Visitor*, December 6, 1984.
135   television "blasting": Kent Biffle, "Editor Proved Pen Is Mightier than Buzzsaw," *DMN*, November 25, 1984.
135   Gordon Baxter: Obituary, *Kountze News-Visitor*, December 6, 1984.
135–136   "it was the old Nixon": Fullingim, *Country Editor*, p. 427.
136   "it gets harder": Fullingim, *Country Editor*, pp. 429–430.
136   "a caretaker": Fullingim, *Country Editor*, p. 4.
136   "One longs": Fullingim, *Country Editor*, p. 11.
136   "being a liberal": Fullingim, *TxObs*, December 28, 1979.

5. A Freak from the Underground

139   "My car got shot": in Brad Bailey, "The Pen and the Sword," *DalObs*, December 8, 1988.
140   "against any criminal laws": Stoney Burns, *NFTU*, August 15, 1967.
140   "Dallas, even": Billy Porterfield, *AA-S*, March 27, 1989.
140   "the counterculture": Lee Ballard, *Dallas*, April 1986.
140–141   "I run a newspaper": Burns, *DNotes*, June 17, 1970.
141   Stoney told an interviewer: *Dallas Life*, January 2, 1983.
141   "Its people dressed alike": Lawrence Wright, *In the New World*, p. 7.
141–142   "We do a million": *DMN*, May 3, 1959.
142   "Miss Taylor": Burns, *NFTU*, September 16, 1967.
142   "High school teaches": Burns, interview, March 4, 1987.
143   Kunkin's paper: Abe Peck, *Uncovering the Sixties*, pp. 19–30.
143   "To grow up in this heaven": Wright, *New World*, p. 115.
143   "There seemed to be": Tom Hayden, *Reunion*, p. 14.
145   He felt his "mind expand": Burns, interview.
145   In 1983 Stoney told: *Dallas Life*, January 2, 1983.
145   "modeled his pen name": Doug Baker, *Icon*, December 6, 1974.

146–147 "Most good newspapermen": A. C. Greene, *NFTU*, June 17, 1967.
147 Stoney started a column: *NFTU*, June 17, 1967.
148 "Joe Pool Arrested": *NFTU*, August 1, 1967.
148 "How can a city": *NFTU*, September 1, 1967.
148 "McCarthyism is not dead": Burns, *NFTU*, September 16, 1967.
149 A survey of Texans: *DMN*, September 21, 1967.
149 "urban rioting": *DMN*, October 8, 1967.
149 "North African power strain": *DMN*, September 22, 1967.
149 "a plot to disrupt": *DMN*, September 28, 1967.
150 "Keep Cool with Pool!": *NFTU*, October 17, 1967.
150 "the father of violence": *DMN*, October 11, 1967.
150 "coercive protest": *DMN*, October 21, 1967.
150 "Filth by any name": *DMN*, October 22, 1967.
150–151 "SMU maintains": *NFTU*, November 1967.
151 "HUAC Losing Out": *DMN*, November 5, 1967.
151 Joe Pool spoke at Yale: *DMN*, November 7, 1967.
151 "has a ringside seat": *DMN*, November 8, 1967.
151 "Reviving a charge": Bloom, *NFTU*, December 1, 1967.
151 "Offered a deal": Baker, *Icon*, December 6, 1974.
152 "God knows we've": Burns, *NFTU*, December 1, 1967.
152 "NOTES is a year old": Burns, *DNotes*, March 17, 1968.
153 He did not pay himself: Burns, interview.
153 "opened by mistake": Baker, *Icon*, December 6, 1974.
153–154 "Recalls Stoney Burns": Bailey, *DalObs*, December 8, 1988.
154 "Dallas as a whole": *DNotes*, April 16, 1968.
154 "The niggers": Burns, *DNotes*, June 16, 1968.
155 "personally, I'd rather": Burns, *DNotes*, March 3, 1968.
155 "Dallas' favorite": *DNotes*, May 1, 1968.
155 "We published a story": Bailey, *DalObs*, December 8, 1988.
155–156 "Detectives from the Vice": *DNotes*, November 6, 1968.
156 "can't trust anyone": *DMN*, November 1, 1968.
156 "broke down the back": Baker, *Icon*, December 6, 1974.
156 "Two men and three": Burns, *DNotes*, January 8, 1969.
157 "Members of the Dallas": *DNotes*, January 22, 1969.
157 "so why not freak": Burns, *DNotes*, January 8, 1969.
157 "The Dallas Pig Department": *DNotes*, February 5, 1969.
158 "NOTES editor Stoney Burns'": *DNotes*, February 19, 1969.
158 "When editor Stoney Burns": *DNotes*, March 5, 1969.
158 "not used to being treated": Burns, interview.
158 "Who Controls Dallas?": *DNotes*, May 7, 1969.
158–159 A *Notes* story quoted: *DNotes*, April 16, 1969.
159 Stoney Burns was arrested: *DNotes*, May 21, June 4, 1969.
159 "admitted that parts": *DNotes*, May 7, 1969.
159–160 "Granny Hate": Burns, *DNotes*, May 21, 1969.
160 "There is a definite pattern": *DNotes*, June 4, 1969.
160 "By July 1969": Todd Gitlin, *The Sixties*, p. 343.

160   But hundreds of other: James P. Danky, *Undergrounds*.

160   "on or near military": Peck, *Uncovering*, p. 80.

160–161   On July 5, 1968: Geoffrey Rips, *Unamerican Activities*, pp. 59–63.

161   Chroniclers of this: Rips, *Unamerican*, pp. 102, 107–108; Peck, *Uncovering*, pp. 135–136; Lawrence Leamer, *The Paper Revolutionaries*, pp. 139–141.

161   "Criminal charges": *DNotes*, July 2, 1969.

161–162   "Stopping the Presses": *Wall Street Journal*, July 7, 1969.

162   "Some one hired": Baker, *Icon*, December 13, 1974.

162–163   "Today, the people": "Brief for the Appellants, In The Supreme Court of the United States," October Term, 1969, #565.

163   "Those guys that want": Burns, *DNotes*, December 31, 1969.

163   In January 1970: *DNotes*, February 4, 1970; Baker, *Icon*, December 13, 1974; Burns interview.

163   "But words are not obscene": *DNotes*, March 18, 1970.

164   "While the police": Baker, *Icon*, December 13, 1974.

164   "when the cops busted in": Burns, interview.

164   "first really fine day": Baker, *Icon*, December 13, 1974.

164   "Bottle-Throwing Melee": *DMN*, April 13, 1970.

164   "Police said Stein": *DMN*, April 14, 1970.

164–165   "Stoney Burns and I": *DNotes*, April 15, 1970.

165   Stoney discussed the charge: Burns, *DNotes*, April 15, 1970.

165   "Editor Stoney Burns decided": *DNotes*, June 17, 1970.

165   "They've got me": *DTH*, September 24, 1970.

166   "sold their 998 shares": J. R. Compton, *Hooka*, January 22, 1971.

166   "It is the responsibility": *Lone Star Dispatch*, November 20, 1970.

166   "I was just trying": Burns, interview.

166–167   "Stoney Burns, controversial": *Hooka*, January 22, 1971.

167   *Notes* was "pretty tame": *DMN*, November 17, 1970.

167   "in the first hearing": *DNotes*, November 20, 1970.

167   Court ruled eight to one: *DTH*, February 24 and 25, 1971.

167   "Cessna testified": Baker, *DNews*, March 10, 1971.

167   "It's too bad": *DTH*, February 25, 1971.

167–168   Stauffer offered: Baker, *DNews*, March 10, 1971.

168   He called Stoney a "guru": *DNews*, May 28, 1971.

168   "He had a long beard": *DNews*, June 4, 1971.

168   Roy Stein "wrestled": *DMN*, June 12, 1971.

168   Stoney had been estranged: Burns, interview.

169   "Stoney's Greatest Hit": Michael Grant, undated flyer.

169   "Are you hip": Gilbert Shelton, *Icon*, July 23, 1971.

169   "he voluntarily left": *DMN*, August 24, 1971.

170   "why Newsroom doesn't give": *Icon*, December 25, 1971.

170   But another "Newsroom" veteran: Billy Porterfield, interview, April 15, 1989.

170   Some *Iconoclast* stories: *Icon*, December 25, 1971; January 14 and 21, 1972.

170   "One of the jurors": Burns, *Icon*, February 4, 1972.

170   "The not-for-profit": Burns, *Icon*, February 11, 1972.

171   "Patsi Aucoin": Baker, *Icon*, December 20, 1974.

171   Sergeant Wayne Fowler: *Icon*, March 17, 1972.

171   The *Morning News* quoted police: *DMN*, March 5, 1972.

171   "Brent 'Stoney Burns' Stein": Burns, *Icon*, March 17, 1972.

172   On April 6: *Icon*, April 7 and 21, 1972.

172   "but that is how narcs": Burns, *Icon*, September 1, 1972.

172   "Dallas and Harris counties": *Icon*, September 19, 1972.

172   "Stoney Burns Tells": Burns, *Icon*, September 29, 1972.

173   "Judge R. T. Scales": *Icon*, October 6, 1972.

173   "how many would be reluctant": *DMN*, November 22, 1972.

173   "Not only am I not guilty": *DTH*, October 4, 1972.

173   "I beg you": *DTH*, October 7, 1972.

173   "That ten year sentence": Burns, *Icon*, October 13, 1972.

174   Bullfeather said such: Burns, *Icon*, December 22, 1972.

174   "Some people have": Burns, *Icon*, October 27, 1972.

174   "DPS narc Bob Hardin": Burns, *Icon*, February 9, 1973.

174   On April 11: Baker, *Icon*, April 27; *DMN*, April 12, 1973.

175   "Snip, snip": *TxObs*, June 13, 1973; *HC*, March 25, 1989.

175   "lifelong desire to retire": Burns, interview.

175   "*Buddy* (the magazine)": *Icon*, June 22, 1973.

175   The court voted three to two: *Icon*, January 18, 1974.

176   "The average sentence": *HC*, November 15, 1987.

176   "My charge was possession": *DT*, October 22, 1974.

176–177   "Burns is the last": *DT*, December 4, 1974.

177   "A t-shirt and petition": *DT*, December 6, 1974.

177   "which he says is run": *Icon*, December 27, 1974.

177   "Stoney is now": *Dallas Life*, January 2, 1983.

177   "Personally, I hope they never": *Dallas Life*, January 2, 1983; *DalObs*, December 8, 1988; interview, March 4, 1987.

178   "many of the 'facts'": Compton, *DalObs*, December 15, 1988.

178   "operator of a tour bus": Bailey, *DalObs*, December 8, 1988.

178–179   "Freedom of the press": Burns, *Buddy*, December, 1986.

6. Writing Wrongs

180   "Issues seem to reappear": Norman D. Brown, *Hood, Bonnet, and Little Brown Jug*, p. 437.

180   "If Jimmy Allred says": Hubert Mewhinney, in Sam Kinch and Stuart Long, *Allan Shivers*, pp. 211–212.

180   "the first law of all": Alexander Cockburn, *Corruptions of Empire*, p. 188.

181   "Issue of evolution": Andrea D. Greene, *HC*, February 11, 1989.

181   A 1987 poll: T. Stutz, *DMN*, February 11, 1989.

182   "Texas Time Machine": Richard Woodbury, *Time*, August 14, 1989.

182   In June 1950: G. R. Farrell, *DT*, February 16, 1989.

183   "failed to carry out": *HC,* June 6, 1989.
183   "paranoid style": Richard Hofstadter, *The Paranoid Style in American Politics and Other Essays,* pp. 4–10.
184   Alexander Cockburn: Cockburn, *Corruptions,* pp. 181–186.
187   Morris, who confronted: Willie Morris, *North toward Home,* p. 185.
187   Molly Ivins: After the demise of the *DTH* in 1992, Ivins began writing for the *Fort Worth Star-Telegram.*
188   "After covering them": Molly Ivins, *HP,* July 9, 1989.
188   "a report on the corporate": Ray Reece, *The Sun Betrayed.*
188   Reece became active: Reece, interviews, 1989.
189   "We are committed": Reece, *West Austin News,* April 27, 1989.
189   "does not cover local": Slusher, interview, August 17, 1989.
189   "the city council": Slusher, *Austin Chronicle,* June 8, 1990.
190   A former press officer: Joe Nick Patoski, *TxMon,* March 1990.
190   "all the time": Jack D. McNamara, interview, December 11, 1990.
190   "We gave ourselves": McNamara, *Nimby News,* June 1990.
190   Diana was already: Samuel and Diana Jackson, interview, August 29, 1989.
191   a "czar" who favors: Samuel Jackson, *Gazette Express,* March 3, 1989.
191   "As the officer": *Pasadena Citizen,* May 3, 1988.
191   "dreaming up": Jackson, *Gazette Express,* May 6, 1988.
191   "I found that if": Jackson, *Gazette Express,* August 25, 1989.
191   "Some of you may": Webb Branen, *Hays County Guardian,* February 23, 1989.
192   They made use: Vicki Hartin, Zeal Stefanoff, Joe Gaddy, and Webb Branen, interview, December 14, 1990.
192   "worst road": *Hays County Guardian,* May 18, 1989.
192   less than two hundred yards: *Hays County Guardian,* July 27, 1989.
192   "is obviously upsetting": Vicki Hartin, *Hays County Guardian,* June 1, 1989.
192   "Drug War Over": *Hays County Guardian,* November 9, 1989.
192   In October and November: "Plaintiffs' Second Amended Original Petition, Cause No. 477,753, Court of 201st Judicial District," March 6, 1990.
192   The Society: Voinis and Borges, letter, September 15, 1990.
192   Supple replied: Jerome Supple, letter, October 2, 1990.
193   As of October 1991: J. Patrick Wiseman, telephone call, October 17, 1991.
193   Daryl Slusher: interview, August 17, 1989.
193   "a vehicle": Susanna MacKenzie, *Texas Environment,* August 1990.
193   Frank Morrow: *Utne Reader,* July/August 1990.
193   "We expect": McNamara, *Nimby News,* June 1990.
193   "senior White House official": *New York Times,* September 10, 1989.

References

Books and Articles

Abernethy, Francis E., ed. *Tales from the Big Thicket.* Austin: University of Texas Press, 1967.

Alexander, Charles C. *The Ku Klux Klan in the Southwest.* Lexington: University of Kentucky Press, 1955.

Bagdikian, Ben. *The Media Monopoly.* 2d ed. Boston: Beacon, 1988.

Bailey, Brad. "The Pen and the Sword." *Dallas Observer,* December 8, 1988, 22–27.

Ballard, Lee. "Barefeet in the Park." *Dallas,* April 1986, 133–135.

Barr, Alwyn. *Reconstruction to Reform: Texas Politics, 1876–1906.* Austin: University of Texas Press, 1971.

Biggers, Don Hampton. *From Cattle Range to Cotton Patch.* Abilene, Tex., 1905; Bandera, Tex., 1944.

———. *German Pioneers in Texas.* Fredericksburg, Tex.: Fredericksburg Publishing, 1925.

———. *A Handbook of Reference Containing Directory and Description and a Summary of the Various Advantages of Eastland County, Texas.* N.p., n.d.

———. "History That Will Never Be Repeated." In *A Biggers Chronicle,* edited by Seymour V. Connor. Lubbock: Texas Tech, 1961.

———. "J. Frank Norris—Salvation Specialist." *Haldeman-Julius Monthly* (Girard, Kan.), March 1926, 417–425. Courtesy of Kansas Collection, The University of Kansas Library, Lawrence, Kansas.

———. *Our Sacred Monkeys or 20 Years of Jim and Other Jams (Mostly Jim) the Outstanding Goat Gland Specialist of Texas Politics.* N.p., 1933.

———. *Shackleford County Sketches.* Albany, Tex., 1908, reprinted and annotated by Joan Farmer, Albany, Tex.: Clear Fork Press, 1974.

Branch, Taylor. *Parting the Waters: America in the King Years, 1954–1963.* New York: Simon and Schuster, 1988.

Brann, William Cowper. *Brann the Iconoclast: A Collection of the Writings of W. C. Brann.* 2 vols. Edited with notes by J. D. Shaw. Waco: Herz Brothers, 1911.

————. *Complete Works of Brann, the Iconoclast.* 12 vols. New York: Brann Publishers, 1919.

Brown, Norman D. *Hood, Bonnet, and Little Brown Jug: Texas Politics, 1921–1928.* College Station: Texas A&M University Press, 1984.

Burd, Gene. "Jacob Fontaine Rallied for UT and Black Higher Education." *Daily Texan,* February 16, 1989, 7.

Carleton, Don E. *Red Scare: Right-wing Hysteria, Fifties Fanaticism, and Their Legacy in Texas.* Austin: Texas Monthly Press, 1985.

Carver, Charles. *Brann and the Iconoclast.* Austin: University of Texas Press, 1957.

Chalmers, David M. *Hooded Americanism: The First Century of the Ku Klux Klan, 1865–1965.* Garden City: Doubleday, 1965.

Cockburn, Alexander. *Corruptions of Empire.* New York: Verso, 1988.

Connally, Tom. *My Name Is Tom Connally.* As told to Alfred Steinberg. New York: Thomas Crowell, New York, 1954.

Connor, Seymour V., ed. *A Biggers Chronicle.* With biographical sketch. Lubbock: Texas Tech, 1961.

Cranfill, J. B. *Dr. J. B. Cranfill's Chronicle: A Story of Life in Texas, Written by Himself about Himself.* New York: Revell, 1916.

————. *From Memory.* Nashville: Broadman, 1937.

Danky, James P. *Undergrounds: A Union List of Alternative Periodicals.* Madison: State Historical Society of Wisconsin, 1974.

Dawson, Joseph Martin. "Image-Breaker Brann, Six Decades After." *Southwest Review,* Spring 1958, 148–154.

Demac, Donna. *Liberty Denied: The Current Rise of Censorship in America.* New York: PEN American Center, 1988.

Dickstein, Morris. *Gates of Eden: American Culture in the Sixties.* New York: Basic Books, 1977.

Dies, Martin. *The Trojan Horse in America.* New York: Dodd, Mead, 1940.

Dillon, Merton L. "Religion in Lubbock." In *A History of Lubbock,* edited by Lawrence L. Graves. Lubbock: West Texas Museum Association, 1962.

Dobson, Joan L. "Literature for All Tastes: Magazines Published in Dallas." *Heritage News* (Dallas County Heritage Society), Winter 1987–1988, 4–8.

Douglas, William O. *Farewell to Texas, a Vanishing Wilderness.* New York: McGraw-Hill, 1967.

Downie, Leonard, Jr. *The New Muckrackers.* Washington, D.C.: New Republic Books, 1976.

Dugger, Ronnie. *Our Invaded Universities.* New York: W. W. Norton, 1974.

Duty, Tony E. "Waco at the Turn of the Century." *Waco Heritage,* Summer 1972.

Elkind, Peter. "The Legacy of Citizen Robert." *Texas Monthly,* July 1986, 160–168.

Farrer, Traci. "J. Frank Norris, Crusader." *Texas History,* September 1980.

Fullingim, Archer. *Archer Fullingim: A County Editor's View of Life.* Edited by Roy Hamric. Austin: Heidelberg, 1975.

Gellerman, William. *Martin Dies.* New York: John Day, 1944.

Gitlin, Todd. *The Sixties: Years of Hope, Days of Rage.* New York: Bantam, 1987.

————. *The Whole World Is Watching.* Berkeley: University of California Press, 1980.

Gould, Lewis L. *Progressives and Prohibitionists: Texas Democrats in the Wilson Era.* Austin: University of Texas Press, 1973.

Granbery, John C., W. C. Holden, and H. B. Carson. *Introduction to the History of Civilization.* 2 vols. Mimeographed. Lubbock: Texas Tech, 1930.

Grant, Donald. *The Anti-Lynching Movement: 1883–1932.* San Francisco: R&E Research, 1975.

Green, George Norris. *The Establishment in Texas Politics: The Primitive Years, 1938–1957.* Westport: Greenwood Press, 1979.

Green, James R. *Grass-Roots Socialism: Radical Movements in the Southwest, 1895–1943.* Baton Rouge: Louisiana State University Press, 1978.

Griffith, Robert. *The Politics of Fear.* Amherst: University of Massachusetts Press, 1987.

Gunn, John W. *Brann, Smasher of Shams.* Girard, Kan.: Haldeman-Julius, 1924.

Gunter, Pete. *Big Thicket, a Challenge for Conservation.* Austin: Jenkins, 1971.

Haldeman-Julius, Emmanuel. *Brann, Who Cracked Dull Heads.* Girard, Kan.: Haldeman-Julius, 1928.

————. *The Outline of Bunk.* Boston: Stratford, 1929.

————. *The World of Haldeman-Julius.* Compiled by Albert Mordell. New York: Twayne, 1960.

Hayden, Tom. *Reunion.* New York: Random House, 1988.

Hodgson, Godfrey. *America in Our Time.* New York: Doubleday, 1976.

Hofstadter, Richard. *The Paranoid Style in American Politics and Other Essays.* New York: Vintage, 1967.

Hurt, Walter. "The Texas Tragedy." *The Gatling Gun: A Periodical of the Period* (Cleveland, Ohio), 1, no. 1 (June 1898): 1.

Karnow, Stanley. *Vietnam, a History.* New York: Viking, 1983.

Kessler, Lauren. *The Dissident Press, Alternative Journalism in American History.* Beverly Hills: Sage, 1984.

Kinch, Sam, and Stuart Long. *Allan Shivers: The Pied Piper of Texas Politics.* Austin: Shoal Creek, 1973.

Leamer, Lawrence. *The Paper Revolutionaries.* New York: Simon and Schuster, 1972.

MacPherson, Myra. *Long Time Passing: Vietnam and the Haunted Generation.* New York: New American Library, 1984.

Martin, Roscoe C. *The People's Party in Texas: A Study in Third-Party Politics.* Austin: University of Texas Press, 1970.

Matusow, Allen J. *The Unraveling of America: A History of Liberalism in the 1960s.* New York: Harper and Row, 1984.

Meyer, Adolph. "Advocatus Diaboli." *American Mercury,* September 1927, 46–50.

Morgan, Richard E. *Domestic Intelligence: Monitoring Dissent in America.* Austin: University of Texas, 1980.

Morgenthaler, Eric. "Stopping the Presses: Underground Papers Hit by Official Curbs." *Wall Street Journal*, July 7, 1969, 1.

Morris, Willie. *North toward Home*. Boston: Houghton, Mifflin, 1967.

Moser, Don. "Big Thicket of Texas." *National Geographic*, October 1974, 504–529.

———. "The Last Ivory Bill." *Life*, April 7, 1972, 52–62.

Mott, Frank Luther. *History of American Magazines*. Vol. 4, *1885–1905*. Cambridge, Mass.: Harvard University Press, 1957.

Ogden, August Raymond. *The Dies Committee: A Study of the Special House Committee for the Investigation of Un-American Activities 1938–1944*. Washington, D.C.: Catholic University of America Press, 1945.

Patner, Andrew. *I. F. Stone, a Portrait*. New York: Pantheon, 1988.

Peck, Abe. *Uncovering The Sixties: The Life and Times of the Underground Press*. New York: Pantheon, 1985.

Richards, David. "Brief for the Appellants, in the Supreme Court of the United States." October Term, 1969, #565.

Richardson, Rupert Norval, Ernest Wallace, and Adrian N. Anderson. *Texas, the Lone Star State*. 4th ed. Englewood Cliffs, N.J.: Prentice-Hall, 1981.

Rips, Geoffrey. *Unamerican Activities: The Campaign against the Underground Press*. San Francisco: City Lights, 1981.

Russell, C. Allyn. "J. Frank Norris: Violent Fundamentalist." *Southwestern Historical Quarterly*, January 1972, 271–302.

Sale, Kirkpatrick. *Power Shift: The Rise of the Southern Rim and Its Challenge to the Eastern Establishment*. New York: Random House, 1975.

Seal, Mark. "Stoney Burns, Alive and Living Well in Dallas." *Dallas Life, Dallas Morning News*, January 2, 1983, 8–16.

Sibley, Marilyn McAdams. *Lone Stars and State Gazettes: Texas Newspapers before the Civil War*. College Station: Texas A&M University Press, 1983.

Stevens, Jay. *Storming Heaven: LSD and the American Dream*. New York: Atlantic Monthly Press, 1987.

White, Theodore H. *In Search of History*. New York: Warner, 1978.

White, Walter. *Rope and Faggot*. New York: Arno Press, 1969.

Wright, Lawrence. *In the New World: Growing Up with America from the Sixties to the Eighties*. New York: Vintage, 1989.

Theses and Dissertations

Gregg, Susan Nelle. "Waco's Apostle." Master's thesis, University of Texas at Austin, 1986.

Morris, Clovis Gwinn. "He Changed Things: The Life and Thought of J. Frank Norris." Ph.D. dissertation, Texas Tech Institute, 1973.

Randolph, John W. "The Apostle of the Devil." Thesis summary, Vanderbilt University, 1939.

Sudo-Shimamura, Takako. "John C. Granbery: Three Academic Freedom Controversies in the Life of a Social Gospeler in Texas (1920–1938)." Master's thesis, University of Texas at Austin, 1971.
Whitaker, John R. "W. C. Brann: His Life and Influence in Texas." Master's thesis, University of Texas at Austin, 1938.

Index

Galveston Evening Tribune, 6–7
Galveston News, 7
Gerald, G. B., 31
Goat Bleats, 49
Granbery, Bishop John C., 67,
    69–70, 74
Granbery, John Cowper, Jr., 181,
    183, 186; as army chaplain, 74; in
    Brazil, 77; childhood of, 69–
    70; death of, 69, 100; doctoral
    dissertation of, 71; education of,
    69–71; and *Emancipator*, 65–69,
    79–100; against Ku Klux Klan,
    74–75; marriage of, 70; as minis-
    ter, 72; at Southwestern Univer-
    sity, 72–74, 77–79; at Texas
    Tech, 76–77
Granbery, Mary Ann (May) Catt,
    70, 72, 75, 77, 81, 89, 96, 98, 100
Green, George Norris, 79–80
Greene, A. C., 146–147

Hayden, Tom, 143
Hays County Guardian, 189–191
Hobby, Will, xiii
Hogg, James, xiii, 8, 103, 120
Holcomb, Paul, 92, 187
Hoover, J. Edgar, 88, 184
Horn, Paul W., 75–77
House Committee on UnAmerican
    Activities (HUAC), 83–84, 87, 93,
    95, 149–151, 183
Houston Chronicle, 53, 58
Houston Post, 3, 7, 9, 10, 18, 24, 74,
    115, 120

Ivins, Molly, 104, 187–188

Jackson, Diana and Samuel,
    188–189
John Birch Society, 103, 121–123
Johnson, Lyndon Baines, 90, 103,
    119, 149, 152, 154
Johnson City Record-Courier,
    51–52
Jones, Jesse, 53

Kemp, Louis Wiltz, 50–52
Kennedy, John F., 100, 101, 104,
    118, 122–123, 129–130, 141
Kennedy, Robert, 119, 154
King, Martin Luther, Jr., 88,
    132–133, 150, 154
Ku Klux Klan, 35, 48–51, 54–55,
    60, 74–75, 119, 159, 183

Los Angeles Free Press, 143, 160
Lubbock Morning Avalanche,
    76–77

McCarthy, Joseph, 69, 88, 93, 95,
    99–100, 114–116, 148
McKie, B. G., 31
McKnight, Felix, 158, 162–163
McNamara, Jack, 188, 193
Maverick, Maury, 79–80
Mayfield, Earle B., 54–55, 57–58,
    60, 74
Mewhinney, Hubert, 180
Moody, Dan, 51, 53, 56–58, 61
Morris, Willie, 108, 111, 187

Nixon, Richard M., 95, 99, 103,
    116, 119–120, 130, 135–136, 177
Norris, J. Frank, 54, 60, 77, 83, 181

O'Daniel, W. Lee, 61–62, 79, 81, 83,
    86, 131, 180

Pool, Joe, 140, 148–152, 155, 183
Porter, William Sydney, 15

Rainey, Homer, 84–86, 109
Rankin, George Clark, 73–74
Reece, Ray, 186–187

St. Louis Globe-Democrat, 6, 13
San Antonio Express, 3, 13–15, 58,
    73, 120
Seldes, George, 61, 92
Shaw, J. D., 30
Shivers, Allan, 103, 115–117
Slusher, Daryl, 187, 193